W9-AZT-611

ST PETERSBURG

COLIN AMERY
& BRIAN CURRAN

PHOTOGRAPHS BY
YURY MOLODKOVETS

ST PETERSBURG

FRANCES LINCOLN LIMITED
PUBLISHERS

Frances Lincoln Ltd
4 Torriano Mews
Torriano Avenue
London NW5 2RZ
www.franceslincoln.com

St Petersburg
Copyright © Frances Lincoln Ltd 2006
Text copyright © Colin Amery and
Brian Curran 2006
Photographs copyright © Yury Molodkovets
Illustrations copyright as listed on page 240

First Frances Lincoln edition 2006

The right of Colin Amery and Brian Curran to be
identified as the authors of this work has been
asserted by them in accordance with the Copyright,
Designs and Patents Act 1988 (UK).

All rights reserved. No part of this publication
may be reproduced, stored in a retrieval system
or transmitted, in any form, or by any means,
without either prior permission in writing from
the publisher, or a licence permitting restricted
copying. In the United Kingdom such licences
are issued by the Copyright Licensing Agency,
Saffron House, 6–10 Kirby Street, London
EC1N 8TS.

A catalogue record for this book is available
from the British Library

ISBN 10: 0-7112-2492-7
ISBN 13: 978-0-7112-2492-6

Designed by Caroline de Souza
Index by Judith Menes

Printed and bound in Singapore by Tien Wah Press

9 8 7 6 5 4 3 2 1

CONTENTS

Introduction

St Petersburg is an epic city. The story of its foundation, growth and survival is so remarkable that it sometimes seems scarcely credible. Even today, in the early years of the twenty-first century, the city is going through another transformation as Russia's windows are thrown open to let in a new climate of democracy and commerce. It is a good moment to examine how Peter the Great's vision became a reality and how years of siege and oppression under war and Communism affected the spirit of its citizens and the nature of their physical surroundings. It is a city named after the apostle St Peter, who was given the burden of founding and creating the universal church. In many ways the burdens laid upon the founders of the city of St Petersburg were almost as great – to transform Russia and be a setting for an enlightened autocracy open to the ideas of the rest of the world.

The megalomaniac methods necessary to achieve this meant that the city has been one built on imposed order and often the suppression of freedom itself. Even today a visitor feels, as he contemplates the infinite vistas of the great streets or plunges into the totalitarian depths of the subway system, that this is a city built with a sublime indifference to ordinary people. The ordered beauty and majestic palaces suggest a realm for powerful gods who will seldom appear but are a presence in their marble halls. Petersburgers feel this – the Tsars have long gone but their palaces are magnets of nationalist and artistic splendour. In this book we attempt to look at the spiritual, literary, artistic and political values that lie behind this extraordinary creation of a city. We also look hard at the architecture and its patrons – the men and women who brought Russia in touch with the cultural climate of the rest of Europe.

One thing cannot be ignored about St Petersburg and that is its climate. It has brutal and long winters and a short summer period when the sun is shining at midnight. In June you can read Pushkin sitting by his statue almost throughout the whole night. 'White nights' and frozen winters must have helped to form the character of the Petersburgers. It is true they don't like to go to bed early in the summer – if at all – and it takes a lot of vodka to keep things warm in the long winter nights. They have even been saved by the climate, when the Road of Life was the only way food could reach the city across the frozen Lake Lagoda during the Nazi siege. Sledges, troikas and the comfort of furs makes the St Petersburg winter romantic and when spring arrives it is made more dramatic by the sound of the ice cracking on the Neva and the sudden flowering of the lilacs. It is also the low northern summer light that illuminates the painted palaces so well and catches the gleam of the gilded spires and domes of the city. There is something about the water, too, that holds the city together by canal or river and there is the ever-present sense of the sea and ships. And the great ring of royal residences in their parks and gardens encircles the city like a separate realm of green beauty; somehow another world from the chill formality of the planned city. It is easy to understand how a dynasty could become remote in surroundings of such secluded and secret elegance.

But there is something even tougher than climate and environment that underlies the city and that is strength of will combined with a knowledge that the creation of cities as dynastic and imperial as this one cannot be achieved or defended without the spilling of blood. Peter's creation cost countless lives. Without serfdom the city could not have happened. The canals were dug by hand; mud, flood, ice and marsh had to be overcome. In the early years there had to be expensive experiment and there was hesitation about continuing such a grandiose plan. There was a tentative search for direction and purpose as the city grew and even when Moscow had become subsidiary to the gilded newcomer there was often uncertainty about how to fill the time in a courtly capital miles from anywhere. It was a city where Nikolai Gogol felt that emptiness was taken to the highest degree. But the will of the city to flourish and survive against the odds is a persistent theme of its history. When the Winter Palace burned, Nicholas I made sure that it was rebuilt perfectly in a year. When President Putin decided to restore the Constantine Palace at Strelna it was done in eighteen months to meet the deadline of the city's tercentenary.

The true grit of the city amazed the world when it survived 900 days of the German siege in the Second World War. Over a million civilians and over half a million soldiers died blockaded into their own city. And that terrible siege came to a city that had already seen revolution, terror and upheaval almost continually throughout the first half of the twentieth century. A city ruled under the Romanov trinity of values – autocracy, orthodoxy and nationality – was not a place where the protection of freedom and individuality flourished.

It was a trinity that would nurture and provoke bloody struggle and change. Throughout this book there is the undercurrent of revolution both political and cultural that is utterly a key part of the story of the city.

A major part of the fascination of the city today is to see how it is changing in a rapidly evolving new Russia. The casting off of Communism is only part of the story. The rehabilitation of the past century is also relevant, as it always has been in St Petersburg. In 1918, only a year after the revolution, committees were set up to protect the cultural treasures and the imperial palaces were open to the public. It was Stalin who agreed to start funding the restoration of the Tsarist legacy after the Nazis had torched the palaces and their restoration continues today. It will be interesting to see how the State handles the great weight of historic properties it has inherited. St Petersburg is a city of palaces and many of them are looking for new uses. It is also a city for tourists who are visiting for culture and comfort – sometimes the balance is more towards culture at the moment. To provide modern facilities means new buildings and it is important that they are of the quality the past of the city should inspire. The economic growth of the city must help the whole population. There is too much poverty in the city and too many older people who have suffered too much from the political changes. Often one step away from Nevsky Prospekt you will find an old babushka selling her shoes for food and families still living in over-crowded flats with poor water. There is a huge amount of real work that needs to be done in this dream city and its heritage and cultural status must be the major engine for economic recovery.

Poets and artists have always loved this city and its beauty continues to inspire and no one can quite explain the potency of its atmosphere. Spend a long hot summer there and you will be seduced by its intense beauty. Walk from your boat through the long grass of Yelagin Island and have a picnic by its enchanting Flag Pavilion. Take a look out of the windows of The Cottage Palace and you will see the Baltic as the Tsars saw it. Walk into the untouched eighteenth-century rooms of Catherine the Great's Chinese Palace at Oranienbaum and you understand delicate Arcadian seduction. Move on to the Cameron Gallery at Tsarskoe Selo and you will feel the clarity of the Enlightenment and the pleasures of philosophy.

Stand at the foot of the Peter the Great statue and enjoy the swaggering riverside and then walk down to his modest house lined with Delft tiles, where he planned it all and worked with his own lathe and tools. Take in the curved sweep of Palace Square and move into the new entrance to the Hermitage and hope Quarenghi's theatre is open – one of the great rooms of the city. Always look out of the windows of the Hermitage to see views that haven't changed, except that the revolutionaries have gone and the Tsars are no more. Wander along the smaller canals and admire the glorious bridges and the sudden appearance of churches, gryphons and sphinxes. If you time it right you may see the flames roaring from the tops of the Rostral Columns on the island in the Neva and imagine celebrating the defeat of Napoleon, the end of the siege, the collapse of inhuman Communism and through it all the triumph of the people who made and continue to make St Petersburg such an extraordinary city. This book is dedicated to them.

Colin Amery
Brian Curran

CHAPTER 1:
THE FOUNDING OF A CITY

There, by the billows desolate,
He stood, with mighty thoughts elate,
And gazed, but in the distance only
A sorry skiff on the broad spate
Of Neva drifted seaward, lonely.
The moss-grown miry bank with rare
Hovels were dotted here and there
Where wretched Finns for shelter crowded;
The murmuring woodlands had no share
Of sunshine, all in mist beshrouded.

And thus he mused: 'From here, indeed
Shall we strike terror in the Swede?
And here a city by our labour
Founded, shall gall our haughty neighbour;
'Here cut' – so Nature gives command –
Your window through on Europe; stand
Firm-footed by the sea, unchanging!
Ay, ships of every flag shall come
By waters they had never swum,
And we shall revel, freely ranging.

Alexander Pushkin, *The Bronze Horseman*[1]

Peter stood transfixed as the great black slab of the river Neva slid silently by. Across its breadth a solid line of nature stood at attention broken only by the occasion of a wisp of smoke, the only evidence that humanity existed in such wastes. Here on the northern bank where the saturated ground formed little lakes with each passing step, here, shrouded in the mists and surrounded by the enemy, a new Russia would be born. Here his destiny lay. Peter turned suddenly, startling his shivering companions. He quickly approached a soldier, wrenched a halberd from his grasp and returned to the spot of his contemplation. With the force and purpose of a man possessed, he slashed a mark into the sodden earth. Here it would begin. There was still much to accomplish – a war to be fought and an enemy defeated – but here, Peter declared: 'Here will be a city!'

Over a century following the founding of St Petersburg, Tsar Nicholas I would say to that interminable critic and observer of the Russian Empire the Marquis de Custine: 'St Petersburg is Russian, but St Petersburg is not Russia.' Built by Russian hands, populated with Russian subjects, ruled by a Russian court, St Petersburg was most certainly a Russian creation. However, it was built with the idea of being anything but Russian. The city was conceived and designed as Peter the Great's version of a European paradise forged from the swamps and set in the icy wastes of northern Russia. Rejecting the forms and character of Russia's ancient capitals of Kiev, Novgorod, and Moscow, Peter envisioned his city as a new Amsterdam, a window on the West, free from the shackles of tradition and orthodoxy. St Petersburg was the palimpsest upon which he would transcribe his vision upon the reality of Russia.

But how did Peter come to stand upon the misty shores of the Neva and why did he choose this place, of all places, to build what would become one of the most celebrated and legendary cities in all of Europe? The story of how St Petersburg came to be is actually the conclusion of the tale of the city's illustrious founder. This is a necessary story that contains the answers to these questions and the soul of the city. It seems as if Peter's life, driven by the dual passions to bring political and social change to Russia and for Russia to become a great seafaring nation in the tradition of Great Britain and the Netherlands, guided him to this point. He knew instinctively that Russia, set deeply within the fold of Orthodoxy and Old Muscovy, would take generations to change. However, rather than seek to transform Moscow through fire and knout, he sought to build a new world, a backdrop for his grand experiment. Peter was determined that Russia would find its true potential and claim its place among nations here on the sea rather than on the steppe. St Petersburg was Peter's dream and Russia's destiny.

Following Peter's death in 1725, St Petersburg would be briefly abandoned by the court. Construction halted, houses were left vacant and the city reverted to its embryonic state as a haunt for military personnel and merchants. But the call of Peter's creation would remain strong. After the return of the court to St Petersburg by Peter's niece, the Empress Anna, no tsar or empress would dare leave the capital and sever ties with Peter the Great's legacy. For, with the founding of St Petersburg, the power of Old Muscovy was broken and Russia had begun its inevitable shift westwards towards the future.

LEFT In a modern day tableau to celebrate the city's tercentenary a contemporary Peter the Great sails in the shadow of the Fortress of St Peter and St Paul.
NEXT PAGE Valentin Serov's romantic 1907 depiction of *Peter I at the Building of St Petersburg* (Tretyakov Gallery, Moscow) held the Tsar up as a determined monarch unbending before the forces of nature and history.

PETER'S EARLY LIFE

Peter the Great was born into the dark world of Old Muscovy. Sixteenth-century Russia was a civilization that had developed out of resistance to the invading Mongol hordes in the thirteenth century and an allegiance to strict Orthodoxy. As a consequence, an insular and suspicious society evolved, Christian in nature but Asiatic in practice. At its centre stood Moscow, the Third Rome, heir of Byzantium and capital of all of the Russias, which was home to over 200,000 Muscovites. Moscow was a teeming world of politics, religion and commerce, on whose streets the noble boyar, the priest, the merchant and peasant commingled. It was also a city of wood and log structures whose rustic character was tempered by the Russians' skill at decorating them with rich and intricate carvings. Fire was the bane of most Muscovites' existences as a kitchen fire could grow to consume entire quarters, as it did four times from 1571 to 1671.[2] To the Westerner, Moscow was a strange and exotic spectacle considered at first glance to be 'rude and without order',[3] resembling a warren of winding and filthy lanes, where houses and outbuildings spilled over into the streets haphazardly. Upon closer examination, foreigners found that Moscow revealed a vibrant landscape of onion-domed churches filled with glittering icons and a fur-clad populace enjoying a multitude of street entertainments and thriving markets, where all of the goods of the East could be found for a price.

This great hive of activity reached its climax at the foot of the Great Kremlin in Red Square. Here dense crowds gathered in the shadow of the kaleidoscope domes of St Basil's Cathedral, commissioned by Ivan the Terrible, who put out the eyes of the great church's architect rather than allow him to create anything as magnificent ever again. Hemmed in by walls of lean-to shacks and wooden chapels, a sea of stalls emerged, row after row connected by a veritable wooden highway of logs floating above the mud. This was the beating heart of Muscovy, where the goods flowed in and out through trade or theft, deals were bartered and marriages arranged, all to the musical shouts of vendors and prostitutes

ABOVE The beating heart of Old Muscovy: Until Peter's maturity Red Square and the adjacent Kremlin served as the commercial, political and spiritual centre of the ancient Russian state. Painting by Apolinari Vasnetov, 1920s (National Museums, Moscow).

hawking their wares. Behind St Basil's the flow of commerce descended to the riverbank and the animal markets, where livestock and fish were sold, barges picked up and delivered goods and women washed clothing. All this din ceased at dusk as the city locked up for the night, giving the streets over to wild dogs, drunkards, thieves and murderers.

If Red Square was Moscow's heart, the Great Kremlin was its crown. Glittering on a hill at the centre of the city, its palaces, golden domes and spires were secured behind walls 75 feet high and surrounded by moats and two rivers. The historic *kreml*, or fortress, was seat of the tsars of Russia. From here they ruled the largest nation on earth. It was also the spiritual and administrative centre of Russian Orthodoxy and site of its principal churches and cathedrals. Here beneath the watchful eyes of mournful saints, whose sacred images were depicted everywhere on icons and frescoes, tsars were crowned, patriarchs and bishops invested, governments wrought and then brought down. The Kremlin was not unlike Beijing's Forbidden City, the great within, where the Tsar anointed by God dwelled but was rarely seen, except on great ceremonial occasions. During these times he would appear crowned and in full robes encrusted with jewels so that his subjects could see the 'light of his eyes'.[4] Onlookers would fall prostrate to the ground rather than gaze too long upon his divine countenance.

Peter Alexeievitch Romanov was born on 9 June 1672 in the Terem Palace of the Moscow Kremlin. Its incense-scented halls and small, darkened rooms were the private domain of the Tsar and his immediate family. It was an environment dominated by the women of the imperial family who were cloistered together and shielded from the outside world, as it was not permitted for a woman of high birth to be seen in public, except on the rarest of occasions. Even at Church and State banquets women participated only from behind a screen. Untouched by education or exposure to the outside world, such a life was typified by boredom, gossip and self-indulgence, an atmosphere ripe for intrigue.

Peter's father, Tsar Alexis, administered his empire from these gloomy chambers. The Tsar's heavily regimented life was spent mostly within the confines of his palace and in church, with brief visits to summer estates or pilgrimage sites. While a strong proponent of tradition, Alexis was also attracted to many of the influences that had begun to filter in from the West through merchants and diplomats. These Western ideas and influences were deemed heretical and unclean to the Church, which viewed them as a threat not both to its own power and to that of the Tsar. Nevertheless Alexis tolerated the existence of a 'foreign quarter' in the suburbs of Moscow and allowed trade to flourish there.

Also in contrast to his upbringing, Alexis chose Natalia Naryshkina to be his second wife. Although from an old and powerful Russian family, Natalia had been raised in the home of Artemon Matveev, Alexis' chief minister, and his Scottish wife Mary Hamilton, whose Western ways and dress scandalized Moscow. Mary had seen to it that Natalia was well educated and that she learned to hold her own in the world of men. Natalia would help open Alexis' world to new experiences. Soon after their marriage Natalia began to appear in public and introduced orchestral music and theatre to the court, two of her favourite pastimes, although technically both were outlawed by the Tsar's own edicts.[5] Natalia's greatest gift to her husband, however, was the birth of Peter, Alexis' third son and his greatest hope

Alexis' death in 1676 led to the outbreak of open hostilities between the court's most prominent families, the Miloslavskys and the Naryshkins. This power struggle would have a profound effect on Peter's life, as he witnessed the deceit, the intrigue and massacre of those close to him as his enemies jockeyed for power. He would forever associate this with the dark halls and sinister chambers of the Kremlin, which symbolized the world of Old Muscovy. At the centre of the whirlwind stood his half-sister Sophia, a Miloslavsky. Sophia, along with her brother Feodor, was classically educated and studied Latin, Polish and history. Her tutors were in awe of her 'marvellous understanding and judgment' and 'masculine mind'.[6] On her brother Feodor's ascension she began to fully participate in the governance of Russia, attending councils of state and advising senior officials. This period was short-lived, however. With the death of the sickly Tsar Feodor in 1682, the ten-year-old Peter was

ABOVE Tsar Alexis I; Although Peter's father was a conservative and deeply religious man his toleration of the foreign settlement and marriage to Natalya Naryshkina showed an interest in Western ways.

proclaimed Tsar with his mother Natalia as regent. Once again the Naryshkins were in the ascendant.

Sophia was furious at this turn of events, as she believed that her half-brother Ivan, who was lame and partially blind, would assume the throne with her as regent. Sophia immediately began plotting the downfall of Peter, Natalia and the Naryshkins, spreading rumours among the Streltsy (the Imperial Guard) that the Naryshkins and their boyar supporters had murdered Feodor and intended to massacre Ivan and those members of the imperial family connected to the Miloslavsky clan. What transpired was a horror well beyond the expectations of Sophia and her supporters. The Streltsy stormed the Kremlin and, although Natalia was able to prove to them that Ivan and Peter were very much alive, their thirst for vengeance could not be quenched. The soldiers seized Natalia's venerable protector and surrogate father Matveev and threw him from the Red Staircase on to the waiting pikes of the soldiers below. For three days an orgy of pillage and murder ensued. Naryshkin family members were hunted down and murdered indiscriminately along with their supporters or anyone else who got in the way. The young Tsar witnessed his uncles and cousins being hacked to pieces and tossed in a bloody pile before the palace. He would never forget the horrific events of that day or his sense of powerlessness before the Streltsy and the powers of the Kremlin. Peter was later crowned as co-Tsar with his brother Ivan. Natalia was removed as regent with Sophia in her place. Sophia, threatened by Peter and his mother's presence, banished the two from the Kremlin and sent them to the Romanov estate at Preobrazhenskoe in the suburbs of Moscow. Thus, Peter left his old life and childhood behind along with the ways of Old Muscovy.

PETER BECOMES A MAN

Although Peter received some formal education during his years in the Kremlin, this ceased following his removal to Preobrazhenskoe. In this small, suburban village he began his real education, that of becoming a man and a leader. Peter had always been fascinated by military history and begged tutors to tell him the stories of Russia's great victories. At the age of fourteen Peter began to organize a play militia to aid him in his education of military organization. As he matured so did the militia, growing so large that it split into two regiments, the Preobrazhensky and the Semyonovsky, made up of the sons of all classes from boyar to serf. Little did Peter know that these two regiments would serve his successors as the Tsar's personal bodyguard until the Revolution in 1917.

Peter's lack of knowledge of military technique and strategy required him to search for experienced commanders. Peter himself held only a low rank, as he wished to experience fully every aspect of military action. His search led him to the so-called German Quarter. Referred to by the Russians as the Nemetsky Sobor or 'mute district', as its residents could not speak Russian, the village was founded in 1652 after Tsar Alexis ordered all foreigners to move to the settlement so that they could conduct business but not contaminate the local populace with their heathen ways.[7] When Peter first entered the quarter he must have believed he had entered another world. Broad tree-lined streets filled with carriages and people in Western-style dress led to grand squares, which displayed an order beyond the comprehension of Russians used to the chaos of Moscow. Neat rows of two- and three-storey brick houses and stately homes, whose façades were embellished with columns and stone decoration, also had ornamental pleasure gardens complete with follies, pavilions and fountains. Peter would not forget this years later when planning his dream city of St Petersburg.

Peter's experience in the German Quarter transformed him. Its cosmopolitan atmosphere inflamed his curiosity for all things Western, be they military, naval or mechanical. Here he found craftsmen to help teach him basic trades, such as carpentry and metalworking, as well as to build fortifications for his war games. One of his most auspicious contacts was a Dutchman, Karsten Brandt, who introduced Peter to sailing and shipbuilding. Brandt restored a boat that Peter had found in an old shed on the royal estate of Ismailovo. It was in this humble vessel, referred to as the *Standart* and later as the 'Grandfather of the Russian Navy', that Peter first learned to sail. This produced in him a love for the sea that would later hasten his desire for a Russian outlet to the sea and the building of a new port city.

THE ROAD TO ST PETERSBURG

Following the overthrow of his sister Sophia in 1689, Peter was free to rule as Tsar but, at seventeen, he refused, choosing instead to leave the duties of state up to his mother, again regent, and his family. Displeased with Peter's lifestyle, Natalia tried to limit his contact with foreigners and required him to marry Eudoxia Lopukhina, the scion of a conservative Moscow family. Regardless of their efforts Peter began to spend even more time in the German Quarter, shirking his royal and husbandly duties. In the taverns and brothels of the quarter Peter made many new friends. Among them were

Francis Lefort and Patrick Gordon – who were to become his most trusted advisors and mentors during this significant point in his life – and Alexander Menshikov, his most loyal and closest friend. Originally a pie seller on the streets of Moscow, Menshikov was discovered by Lefort and enlisted in Peter's play militia, quickly distinguishing himself and becoming one of the Tsar's personal aides, forging a deep friendship which would last until Peter's death.

Peter assumed his full role as ruler of Russia following the death of his mother in 1694. After a brief war, in which he seized the port of Azov near the Black Sea with the help of a small fleet of hastily built galleys, Peter realized that Russia's destiny and future strength lay in its possession of a navy. He therefore decided to send fifty Russians, the cream of Russian nobility, many of whom had never seen the ocean, to Europe to learn the arts of shipbuilding, navigation and seamanship. Peter himself decided to take a European tour as well, to oversee their education as well as to recruit foreign shipbuilders and sailors to help him build Russia's fleet. In 1697 he, along with a retinue of more than 250, embarked upon an eighteen-month journey to Poland, Germany, Holland, England and Vienna. It would be known as the Great Embassy and always be fondly recalled by Peter.

Voltaire later described the Great Embassy as Peter resolving 'to absent himself from his dominions in order to learn better how to govern them'.[8] This was partially true, as Peter sought to learn the ways of Europe in order to transform Russia, but first and foremost he sought the knowledge of shipbuilding in order build his navy. Peter was fascinated by everything he saw on his tour, from the clothes to the architecture. Nothing was too inconsequential to garner his attention, including whalebone corsets, which he originally mistook for actual ribs, describing German women as having 'devilish hard bones'.[9] At each stop Peter studied and indulged in scientific pursuits from botany to dentistry, taking the time to observe and experiment. He even visited the dissecting theatre of the famous surgeon Dr Frederick Ruysch. During the visit one member of his entourage expressed horror at seeing a dismembered human body, enraging Peter so much that he forced the poor man to sink his teeth into the corpse.[10] In Holland, however, Peter found his paradise. He explored the enormous Dutch shipbuilding enterprises in the shipyards of Amsterdam and Zaandam. He spent several weeks as a shipwright's apprentice, learning the trade and earning calluses, which he proudly displayed to the bemused rulers of Europe.

Peter's European tour came to a sudden and violent end when news reached him that the Streltsy, incited by his deposed sister Sophia and her supporters, had gone into open revolt against him. Peter left Vienna immediately for Moscow, where he found the revolt had been suppressed by his friend and military commander Patrick Gordon. En route to Moscow, Peter decided that the time had come to begin to dismantle the state of his forefathers. He would make Old Muscovy undergo a series of reforms and use the fruits of his education to transform Russia into a modern power and society. Immediately on his return Peter ordered his court to shave their beards and adopt Western forms of dress. The move blasphemed the Church and the nobles but the symbolism was clear. For Russia's transformation to work it would have to be seen as well as felt. His next move was to dispatch his wife Eudoxia to a convent, thereby setting himself free and severing his marital ties to Old Russia. Other early reforms instituted by Peter included the adoption of the Julian calendar, a new monetary system and stamp taxes on all official documents.

For Peter, the Streltsy remained the last piece of unfinished business that stood in his way before he could impose his vision upon Russia. Following the suppression of the revolt the majority of the Streltsy were imprisoned, tortured and interrogated. Nevertheless, Peter's thirst for revenge against the Streltsy and their leaders would not be sated. These were the soldiers who had murdered members of his family in front him and had then dared to rise again humiliating him before the eyes of Europe. He would show no mercy. The Streltsy were systematically rounded up out of their prisons and brought to Preobrazhenskoe to be greeted by fourteen torture chambers. For nearly two months they were again tortured and interrogated, often by Peter himself. His sister Sophia, implicated in the revolt, was sent into permanent seclusion in a remote convent. The majority of the Streltsy were then executed over a six-month period; their bodies hung from scaffolds in Red Square, dangled off the walls of the Kremlin and grimly adorned all the gates of Moscow. Many were also beheaded by other condemned Streltsy or by obliged members of Peter's court. There were even rumours that Peter himself acted as executioner.[11] The remaining ineffective and potentially rebellious Streltsy regiments were then disbanded, finally ending the last vestige of armed opposition to Peter's rule. From Peter's play militias Russia's new military emerged and was soon put to the test.

PETER REACHES THE SEA

Peter's first attempts at the creation of a navy had been centred on the River Don in the town of Voronezh, near the Black Sea. While he had been successful in creating a sizeable naval force, he was still barred from the Black Sea after cessation of hostilities with the Ottoman Empire in 1700. For Peter, however, when opportunity withdrew one prize it uncannily always presented another. The Great Northern War erupted in July 1700 as Poland and Denmark sought to break the Swedish chokehold over the Baltic Sea. They invited Russia to join them, promising Peter the provinces of Ingria and Karelia. Having failed in his attempts to gain access to the Black Sea in the south, Peter finally saw his chance to fulfil his dream of a Russian outlet to the sea and Europe beyond. With the greatest alacrity, Peter ordered his adolescent army into action and declared war on Sweden. Peter chose to test his metal on the coastal fortress town of Narva in Estonia. The Russians laid siege to the city but failed to reduce it in time before the young warrior-king Charles XII arrived. The Swedish infantry attacked, scattering the much

larger Russian forces, who were forced to flee across the River Narva. Peter, his army routed and disgraced in the eyes of Europe, did not lose hope, but immediately set about completely modernizing the training and outfitting of his military force to again confront the Swedish enemy.

In the mythology of St Petersburg, the region that Peter sought to conquer and later to found his new capital on was a bleak and inhospitable landscape of overgrown woodlands, soggy marshes and inaccessible islands. In reality this image, later enshrined in the collective memory of Russia through the works of numerous writers, was far from true. The estuary of the River Neva, sandwiched between Lake Ladoga and the Gulf of Finland, was a highly strategic region teaming with wildlife and home to more than forty villages and hamlets.[12] Historically the region had changed hands several times from Finn, to Russian, from Russian to Swedish. From the tenth century, the estuary was held by the Russian city state of Novgorod and served as northern point of the trade route that ran from the Baltic to the Black Sea. Novgorod

ABOVE Vasily Surikov's 1881 painting of the *Morning of the Streltsy Execution* (Tretyakov Gallery, Moscow) portrays the demise of old Russia before the gaze of the indomitable Peter, who surrounded by his Westernized courtiers has clearly chosen a new direction for Russia.

endured almost constant attacks from the Swedes and from Teutonic Knights. The defeat of the Teutonic invaders on the banks of the Neva led Prince Alexander Yaroslavovich to be forever known as Prince Alexander Nevsky. Although Sweden was ceded the territory in 1617 following Russia's defeat in the Livonian War, the population remained a mélange of Swedes, Finns and Russians. To Peter, as with most Russians, this territory remained part of the Russian state whose duty under God was to reclaim it for the future of Holy Mother Russia.

Two years after the disaster at Narva Peter was again ready to take the offensive. Charles, thinking he had eliminated the Russian threat, had moved south and invaded Poland. Peter seized his chance in January 1702 and attacked the remaining Swedes in Livonia, driving them from their winter quarters. The following spring Peter's armies again defeated the Swedes, eradicating the Swedish threat to the west. Peter, overjoyed with the knowledge that he could indeed defeat the Swedes, then turned his attention to the weakly defended settlements along the Neva itself – the very prize he yearned for. Appropriately, he began his campaign to gain access to the sea with a naval engagement. Between June and September 1702 Peter's flotillas on Lake Ladoga harassed and then drove the Swedish squadron from the lake. The Swedes, however, still had one more hand to play.

The fortress of Nöteborg ('nut city'), originally named Oreshka by its Novgorodian founders, was so named because of the hazelnut-shaped island upon which it sat and was the final obstacle delaying the Russian conquest of the Neva estuary. With its six mighty towers armed with 142 guns, the fortress controlled the flow of trade from the lake to the Baltic and had been used by the Swedes to shield the region from Russian encroachment.[13] This was the 'nut' that Peter would need to crack before he could finally reach the sea. In October Peter surrounded the fortress with a flotilla and lined the shore with heavy siege mortars. After the failure of the initial seaward assault, Peter ordered the bombardment of the fortress and, for ten days, shells fell upon Nöteborg until finally the Swedish garrison, battered and with no

escape, surrendered. Elated at his victory, Peter renamed the fortress Schlüsselburg, Dutch for 'key city', as the fortress had been the 'key' to the Neva and the campaign.

Peter's armies camped for the winter and waited until the ice had melted the following spring before they began their approach to the sea. In April 1703 Peter began sailing down river accompanied by 20,000 men, who marched down the north bank. Their destination was the fortified town of Nyenskanz, the last significant Swedish settlement on the Neva. Nyenskanz, whose site now lies in Okhta district of St Petersburg, was a well-developed town with cobblestone streets laid in a grid pattern with a central square. A Lutheran church stood in a commanding position at the town's centre while an Orthodox church near by served the town's Russian community.[14] Peter's forces soon surrounded the town and set up siege works. Bombardment began on 30 April 1703 and continued throughout the night. The next morning the town surrendered. This victory, however, was almost cut short with the unexpected arrival of a Swedish squadron of nine vessels at the mouth of the Neva. Two of the ships sailed up the river towards Nyenskanz not realizing it had been occupied. The Russians fired a false signal and the two ships weighed anchor downstream for the night. Under the cover of darkness Peter sent thirty ships down river past the moored ships to block any escape, while his remaining force fell upon the enemy and captured both vessels. This was the first naval battle in which Peter had participated and he was ecstatic. Not only had he defeated the Swedes on land and on water, but with this victory he now controlled the length of the Neva from Lake Ladoga to the sea, restoring to Russia its historic inheritance and giving it the key to its future.

THE FOUNDING OF ST PETERSBURG

Although Peter rejoiced at Russia's military success and her newly acquired territories, he also realized that they were far from secure. A Swedish fleet still hovered beyond the mouth of the Neva and Swedish detachments still roamed to the north and west. Peter was now faced with the challenge of how best to fortify the Neva

ABOVE Like his city, a bust of Peter the Great has stood resolute by his first city residence, surviving the challenges of nature and history.

estuary to ensure the protection of the passage to Lake Ladoga and his precious new shipyards there. At first it was thought that the fortress of Nyenskanz, renamed Sloteburg or 'lock city', could be used, but Peter took the council of his commanders and determined that the fortress was too small, too far up river and too vulnerable from an attack by land to truly serve as the key defence for Russia's embryonic navy.[15] A new location would have to be found. Peter began taking boats down the Neva, examining various points and determining their suitability and appropriateness for the task ahead. It is unclear whether from the outset of the campaign Peter intended to found a new city, but as he glided down the Neva and took stock of its marshy shores he must have grasped the potential for greatness in this wilderness as it began to burst into life at the first signs of spring.

With the help of a French military engineer by the name of Joseph-Gaspard Lambert de Guerin, who had formerly been in the employ of Louis XIV, Peter decided to build a new fortress on an islet referred to by the local Finns as Yannisarri, or 'hare island'. Its location was ideal. The island lay strategically at the centre of the Neva delta closer to the sea and overlooking the only navigable section of the lower Neva. The island was small enough for engineers to design a fortress, which would cover its area entirely, and, once armed with cannon, it would hold within firing range any warship able to enter the delta. Yannisarri would also be protected from land by a small channel and a treacherous swampland to the north, making siege operations all the more difficult.

On 16 May 1703, the day of the Holy Trinity, construction on a new fortress began. This is about all that known about this fateful day, considered to be the date of the founding of St Petersburg. There is a conspicuous lack of first-hand accounts of the events of the day and the whereabouts of Peter and his lieutenants, and there is even debate about whether Peter was there at all.[16] Whatever the truth of the matter, a wealth of stories and legends has developed in the vacuum left in the absence of evidence. One claimed that Peter was led to the site by an eagle, the imperial mascot, and that later a trench was dug on the spot that Peter had indicated. In the trench a box was placed containing relics of St Andrew, Russia's patron saint, upon which was inscribed: 'In the name of Jesus Christ on 16 May 1703, His Tsarist Majesty and Grand Prince, Peter Alexeievich, Autocrat of All the Russias, founded the Tsarist city of St Petersburg.' At that moment the story says that the eagle miraculously appeared again and landed on two birch trees bent to

A modern aerial view of the Fortress of St Peter and St Paul. St Petersburg's first major monument, the fortress was never tested in combat, but served as a reminder of the city's origins and a symbol of its strength.

form an arch. This arch was later claimed to be the site of the Peter Gateway to the Peter and Paul Fortress.

The stories of Peter planting the halberd into the virgin soil of the Neva delta and the visitation by the eagle recalled the legend of St Andrew planting his staff on the shores of the Neva and of the eagle guiding Constantine to Byzantium.[17] Both tales, which were encouraged by Peter's loyalists and embellished over time, reflected the deeply held belief that Russia was the inheritor of Byzantium and defender of the Holy Orthodox Church and that the actions of Peter, Tsar and autocrat, were ordained by God. Peter was the master of symbolic gestures and understood the power of myth. By adopting the fables of Old Russia he was using them to create the character of the new.

Construction of the new fortress began in earnest. Russian labourers without proper tools dug into the earth with their hands, carrying dirt in their shirts or rough sacks to the slowly rising ramparts. Thousands of wooden piles were driven into the saturated soil to serve as a foundation for the fortress. During this period Peter ordered the construction of a Spartan cabin where he could live while the construction progressed. St Petersburg's first imperial residence, preserved to this day as the city's oldest building, consisted of only three rooms – a bedroom, a dining room and a study. Although the house was made of hand-hewn logs, the Tsar had it built in the fashion of Holland with large mica windows and even instructed that its exterior be painted to resemble brick and its shingle roof to imitate clay tile.[18]

Within six weeks the fortress had begun to rise. Built to the design of de Guerin, the earth ramparts had started to take shape, complete with a makeshift battery. New buildings also began to be built within the grounds of the fortress. On 29 June 1703 Peter

ABOVE The double-headed eagle of the Romanovs adorns the Peter Gateway to the Peter and Paul Fortress.

oversaw the laying of the foundation of the fortress's Orthodox church. As it was the Feast of St Peter and St Paul, and also the name day and baptismal anniversary of the Tsar, Peter named the church after the two saints. While the names of Peter and Paul would later be extended to include the fortress as well as the church, Peter also made a historic decision that day to begin referring to his new port town and its environs by the Dutch name, Sankt Piter Burkh.

At first, Sankt Piter Burkh, which was gradually Germanized to St Petersburg, was just a ramshackle collection of tents, huts and earth ramparts set with marshy woodland, but soon the construction effort began to take on a completely new rhythm as the project was imbued with new purpose. During the summer of 1703, more than 20,000 men, soldiers and peasants went to work on the building of the fortress. Peter himself often personally supervised the construction of the fortress's six earth and timber bastions to ensure that work would be conducted as fast as possible. He still feared that the Swedes would return before he was prepared to meet them. That July Peter had led six regiments against an approaching Swedish force of 4,000, driving them into retreat from the banks of the Neva. However, a remaining Swedish fleet continued blockading the Neva and served as a reminder to Peter of his grand project's vulnerability.[19]

The pace of the construction of the fortress was also hastened by the need to protect the shipyards of Lake Ladoga, which had just begun to build warships. Following his July victory over the Swedes Peter left for the lake to oversee the creation of his new fleet. Weeks later Peter sailed down the Neva in the first frigate. The *Standart*, accompanied by several smaller vessels, weighed anchor before the Peter and Paul Fortress, which had been largely completed that September. The next month Peter took command of the ship and ordered full sail towards the Gulf of Finland. The Swedish fleet had retreated into winter harbour in Vyborg, leaving the entrance to the Gulf unblocked. The *Standart*, skimming over the thin ice that had already begun to form, sailed out into the Gulf of Finland with its flags fully unfurled. Peter had breached a barrier unthinkable a generation ago. A Russian Tsar, commanding a Russian-made warship, was sailing on the waters of the Baltic.

With the capture and construction of the fortresses of Schlüsselburg, St Petersburg and, soon afterwards, Kronschlot in the Gulf of Finland, Peter's task of securing his access to the sea was finally complete. Although the Swedes would continue to harass Peter's new port until 1708 they could never dislodge the Russian forces nor capture their forts. The Russian victories of 1703 and the founding of St Petersburg caused little concern across Europe, who cared little about who controlled the icy swamps of northeast Europe. Swedish King Charles XII would exclaim upon hearing of the founding of St Petersburg, 'Let the Tsar tire himself with the founding of new towns. We will keep for ourselves the honour of taking them.'[20] The historic shift was almost imperceptible, yet it had sown the seeds of the decline of Sweden as a regional power and foreshadowed the rise of Russia. St Petersburg and the Neva were secure; now it was time to build.

THE CITY RISES

> A giant built it; lacking stones
> He paved the swamps with human bones.
>
> Mikhail Dmitriev

At the beginning of 1704 St Petersburg was little more than a rough frontier town. The town itself was situated largely to the north of the fortress on Birch Island, today known as Petrograd Island. The monuments of St Petersburg in its first year consisted largely of the fortress, the Lutheran and Orthodox churches and the tavern, the Four Frigates, which also served as the Town Hall and later the central meeting place of the diplomatic community.[21] These principal buildings were built around the city's earliest public piazza, known as Trinity Square. Due to the concentration on military construction, there had been few efforts expended on housing but, with the influx of builders, labourers and soldiers, this began to change. In 1703 there had been only fifteen houses in the vicinity of the Peter and Paul Fortress, but a year later the number had grown to 150. Life for these first residents was far from comfortable. The cold, the damp and the mud, made worse by periodic flooding, meant for a miserable life. Not long after the first permanent structures were erected in August 1703, the new inhabitants got their first taste of the raging floods for which St Petersburg would be known.

Peter was undaunted. On 1 March 1704, with the Swedes temporarily held at bay, the Tsar decreed that the building of St Petersburg would require at least 40,000 labourers to work in shifts of two and later three months from April to October.[22] These conscripts were to come from all over Russia, each locality providing a share of able-bodied men. Much to Peter's dismay barely half that number arrived, so he ordered the use of convict labour and Swedish prisoners of war to drain the marshes and drive in piles. Peasants arriving from deep in the Russian hinterland were confronted by a quagmire on the shore of the Neva, where houses seemingly floated on a sea of mud amid the chaos of construction. Taken from their homes at the peak planting and harvesting times, these miserable men and boys were crowded into low rows of small birch huts lacking floors or anything resembling basic sanitation. Disease was rampant and scores of labourers died. Although today it is still debated how many actually met their deaths in the effort to build St Petersburg, rumours at the time were spread that the construction had claimed 100,000, giving rise to the myth that St Petersburg was 'a city built on bones'. Such rumours, added to the reality of the backbreaking work, compounded the terror of the conscripts, who then deserted in droves. At first captured deserters were treated harshly; their families threatened, they faced being led back to St Petersburg in chains or even execution.[23] Such unfortunate scenes were later avoided by the use of strictly hired workers.

While many of the conscript labourers were employed in the building of the city proper, others were sent to the shipyards on Lake Ladoga. From the beginning, the placement of such an enterprise on the shores of the lake proved problematic. The stormy waters of the lake were the bane of the navy's existence as newly built ships capsized, ran aground or sank before they could be put to use. After a particularly disastrous storm in October 1704 Peter ordered the shipyards of Lake Ladoga to be closed and their operations moved to the site of a fishermen's hamlet on the south bank of the Neva across from Hare Island. Here the yards could be protected by the guns of the fortress and were located conveniently to receive supplies and materials from the Russian heartland. The new shipyards were re-christened the Admiralty House. The Admiralty also provided another layer of protection for St Petersburg, as Peter ordered its walls fortified to protect the southern approach the city. The relocation of the Admiralty also led to the establishment of a new settlement for the shipwrights and craftsmen employed by the navy. More than a hundred houses were built for their use as well as for sailors and naval officers.

Materials also posed a major problem for Peter and his builders. Most of the earliest structures were wattle and daub or simple wooden shacks. Stone was virtually unobtainable locally and had to be brought in. Wood became so precious that Peter ordered that no trees on the islands could be cut down for fuel and that bath houses were only allowed to be heated once a week.[24] The old Swedish fortress and town of Nyenskanz was almost completely dismantled,

its materials hauled down river to St Petersburg to be used in the building of the fortress and embankments.[25] With scarce access to materials from Europe due to the blockade, entire industries had to be built from scratch to produce bricks, lumber, tiles, glass, lime and cement. As the population increased, demand for these products soared. The new factories and mills were unable to keep up, so customers were required to import materials from the Russian interior at with delay and and expense. Later, in 1714, the demand for stone grew so great that Peter would order that, to gain admittance, all carriages entering the city were required to bring a number of stones with them.

THE NEW CAPITAL

When, in 1710, St Petersburg became the official residence of Peter, the city remained a garrison town of 8,000 souls, the majority of whom were soldiers, sailors, shipwrights, craftsmen and labourers.[26] The presence of such a population lent the city a sense of coarseness and impermance; St Petersburg's inhabitants had little reason to improve their surroundings or the city's cultural life, which revolved around the various taverns and markets. Although Peter himself had been referring to St Petersburg as the capital as early as 1704,[27] he knew that to make this a reality he required the removal of his court from Moscow to his 'paradise' on the Baltic. He understood that this would be no easy task, as few would be willing to transfer their households to the icy wastes of the Neva delta. The process took place slowly beginning with the 'invitation' to his sister Natalya and several other members of the imperial family to move to St Petersburg. They were followed by selected noblemen, government officials and ministerial departments, which by necessity were required to assist in the day-to-day administration of the empire. By 1712, although there was no formal declaration, St Petersburg had become Russia's capital.[28]

With his family and government firmly housed in his new capital, Peter now desired that the Russian nobility join him to help populate his city and learn the ways of his new court. Because he knew that the nobles would refuse his invitation, a *ukase* was put into effect in 1714 ordering 350 nobleman, 300 merchants and 300 craftsmen, including their families and servants, to move to St Petersburg.[29] The English Ambassador Charles Whitworth would be the first major foreign diplomat to relocate to St Petersburg, but after 1714 the other embassies followed suit. This new influx of the elite classes and their retinues, as well as merchants and more labourers, tripled the city's population by 1717.

For the new arrivals, used to the easy and affordable Moscow, life in St Petersburg was abysmal. The new arrivals were required to build their own houses according to their class and means. Nobles were instructed to construct wood-beam houses of plaster and lathe at their own expense on the south bank of the Neva. Those with more than 500 serfs were required to build a stone house of two storeys. For merchants and craftsmen, land was reserved for the construction of wooden housing. These early wooden houses were often inadequate to deal with the cold, and stone and brick would only become widely available much later. Because new residents were forced to find accommodation while permanent homes were being built, many wooden houses were constructed hastily. During the first winter, their walls cracked, their floors sagged and their roofs leaked. And their miserable occupants cursed the Tsar and his new city.[30]

They had reason to curse. The cost of living in St Petersburg was so high – everything had to be imported and paid for in cash – that it reduced the income of these families by two thirds.[31] Persistent damp, periodic flooding and dark freezing winters were all endured in the new Western dress of frock coats, breeches, silk stockings and waistcoats, instead of the traditional furs and caftans of Moscow. Even the streets were unsafe. The Hanoverian Resident (the ambassador from the Kingdom of Hanover) wrote: 'The godless rabble breaks into houses both day and night and perpetrates all sorts of insolent deeds. . . . People scarcely consider themselves safe in their houses, and at night have to use all imaginable precautions.'[32] In the still-untamed forests of the Neva estuary there were not only bears roaming, but wolves. During the winter these animals invaded the city in search of food in packs of thirty or forty. It was not uncommon for them to attack citizens. In one highly publicized case in 1715 a woman was devoured in the street in broad daylight on Vasilievsky Island.[33]

Such hardships led to opposition of Peter's rule and his city. His own sister, the Tsarevna Maria, prophesized that 'St Petersburg will not endure after our time. May it remain a desert.'[34] When, in 1716, Peter's son and heir Alexis was implicated in a plot to overthrow his rule, it was discovered that he had sworn to abandon St Petersburg

The Kikin Mansion (1714) is among the best surviving examples of Petrine palace architecture. The mansion's large windows and classical proportions delineated a clear break from traditional Russian house design.

and his father's precious navy and move the capital back to Moscow to resume the old ways.[35] Religious opponents saw the floods, which caused incredible chaos and death, as evidence that Peter was truly the Antichrist and that God himself was trying to destroy the city with another Biblical deluge. All of these curses, oaths and prophecies were the part of the widespread reaction to the changes Peter was carrying out as he moved Russia into the future. They served as the death rattle of the old ways and of Old Muscovy. By relocating the nobility of Moscow to St Petersburg Peter had deprived them of their traditional base and made them dependent on him. Never again would they hold the power they had in Moscow. Russia had moved on.

THE BIRTH OF THE PETRINE STYLE

Following the Battle of Poltava in 1709 and the capture of the port of Vyborg in 1710, St Petersburg, with its formidable defences, was finally secured from attack. Up until that time Peter had largely been concerned with the fortifications of the city and the prosecution of the war against Sweden. He now turned his energies to the

development of his beloved city. In its first few years St Petersburg had had no discernible pattern. One observer even remarked that the city was a set of interconnected villages more resembling a West Indian plantation than a capital. Houses sprang up everywhere and anywhere as there was no official city plan. The need for greater civic organization and administration became apparent. As early as 1706 the Chancellery of Urban Affairs had been formally established to provide standards for construction and the power to enforce them, although it rarely did. In his imagination Peter saw St Petersburg in the image of Amsterdam or London, well-ordered cities of brick and stone punctuated by soaring spires. In Domenico Trezzini and Jean-Baptiste Alexandre Le Blond, he found the men he needed to transform this vision into reality. They would become St Petersburg's most influential architects of the Petrine Age.

Domenico Trezzini was a native of Switzerland, who had been in the employ of the Danish King Frederick IV working on military fortifications.[36] Trained in Lugano, Trezzini found work in Scandinavia and northern Europe before being recruited by the Russian envoy to the Danish court. In 1704 he arrived in St Petersburg with a team of

ABOVE The sombre portrayal of the interrogation of the Tsarevitch Alexis by Peter I at Peterhof (Tretyakov Gallery, Moscow) by Nikolai Ge (1831–94), captured the final act of a troubled relationship which would end in the torture and death of Alexis in 1718.
RIGHT The pinnacle of the Petrine baroque, Domenco Trezzini's Cathedral of St Peter and St Paul (1712–32) broke new ground by eschewing any reference to traditional Orthodox architecture.

engineers, master builders and artisans and set to work on the construction of the fortress of Kronschlot off Kotlin Island and the restoration of the fortress at Narva.[37] Peter had lost his chief military engineer in charge of the rebuilding of the Peter and Paul Fortress in masonry, so he hired Trezzini in 1706. He was so impressed with Trezzini that within a year he made him Chief Architect of the newly established Chancellery of Urban Affairs.

Peter and Trezzini's collaboration in the early architecture of St Petersburg launched the Petrine revolution in Russian architecture. Trezzini, having worked in the cities of northern Europe and Scandanavia, understood perfectly the Dutch architectural idiom that Peter desired for St Petersburg and added to it the flourish of northern Italian baroque. Beginning with the Peter and Paul Fortress, Trezzini helped Peter use architecture to project the monumentality and greatness of Peter and the Russian Empire. For the centrepiece of his triumphal Peter Gates at the fortress, Trezzini designed a bas-relief depicting the casting down of Simon Magnus by the Apostle Peter: a clear allusion to Peter's defeat of Charles XII.[38] At his master's behest Trezzini also rejected the architecture of Old

Russia in the construction of churches. His Cathedral of St Peter and St Paul, with its basilica form and towering spire, was considered austere and almost Protestant in comparison to St Basil's in Moscow. For Peter himself Trezzini also built a small Summer Palace within the confines of the Tsar's beloved Summer Garden on the banks of the Neva at the junction of the Fontanka Canal. Here Trezzini, using a combination of simplicity and perfect proportion, produced the ideal home for Peter, modest in size with unpretentious interiors in the Dutch manner. The last of Trezzini's monuments was the Twelve Colleges. It was built to house the various ministries of Peter's government under one roof and, with its repetitious plan and uniform façade stretching for 420 yards, displayed Peter's desire to impose upon his government modern principles of organization.[39]

Working through the Chancellery of Urban Affairs, Trezzini was able to guide the development of the early city and helped to start the tradition of uniformity that has endured throughout its history. Not only did he control the design and construction of major projects, he was also largely responsible for the training of architects, the recruitment and management of the labour force and

ABOVE Inspired by the austere architecture of Holland and Northern Europe, Peter the Great's Summer Palace (1711–14) was modest and largely unadorned except for a series of plaster panels attribted to master sculptor Andreas Schlüter.

the procurement of materials and funding for building projects.[40] Although Trezzini was replaced as Chief Architect by Andreas Schlüter, former architect to the Prussian Court, in 1713, he continued his work on the Peter and Paul Fortress, as well as his other St Petersburg monuments, until his death in 1734.

In 1714 Peter took stock of his rising city. His naval victory at Hangö had given Russia free rein over the Baltic, enabling him to dedicate ever more resources to the enhancement of St Petersburg. Realizing the great expense and indignation he would incur were he to attempt the razing and redevelopment of the existing portions of the city, he chose to reorient the city centre and to found his new Amsterdam, complete with neat brick row houses and canals, on the low-lying marshes of Vasilievsky Island. He had bestowed the task of reclaiming the island upon his most trusted and loyal servant, Prince Alexander Menshikov, whose palace was located there. Before leaving on his second European tour, Peter ordered Trezzini to draw up a comprehensive urban plan for the new centre. Peter hoped that Vasilievsky Island would consist of a grid network of straight avenues and canals intersecting at right angles, which would serve as the city's main thoroughfares for travel and commercial activities while assisting in the abatement of the chronic flooding which plagued the low-lying terrain.[41]

A TEST OF WILLS: THE ARCHITECT AND THE PRINCE

Throughout his journeys Peter was always on the lookout to recruit talented architects, engineers and craftsmen to serve him in St Petersburg. While taking the cure in Bad Pymont, Peter was introduced to an architect of renown: Jean-Baptiste Alexandre Le Blond, who offered his services to the Tsar. Le Blond's pedigree was impeccable; a pupil of the André Le Nôtre, the great designer of the gardens of Versailles, he was also author of *The Theory of the Art of the Garden*, with which Peter was familiar.[42] The Tsar was so enthusiastic that he retained Le Blond as 'Architect General' of the city and charged him with the task of designing a new master plan for the entire city of St Petersburg with Vasilievsky Island at its centre. Le Blond arrived in St Petersburg with his family and a army of

ABOVE Stretching 420 yards long, the building of the Twelve Colleges (1722–41) was designed to house the various departments of Peter's government under one roof in a rational and organized manner.

architects, masons and craftsmen in August 1716 and quickly set about his work.

Le Blond's plan for St Petersburg is perhaps one of the most inspired works of eighteenth-century urban planning. Encapsulating the all of the major civic ideals of the era, he produced a magnificent city in the French manner of broad avenues, massive squares and intersecting canals flanking grand monuments, surrounded by a colossal network of fortifications in the spirit of Vauban.[43] Peter was amazed by the scale and beauty of the project but recognized its impracticality. The plan did not take into account the existing parts of the city, which could not be dismantled. The fortifications alone, whose massive proportions were wholly unnecessary for the protection of St Petersburg, were simply too costly to execute. Yet Peter was not discouraged; Trezzini's plan still existed and he ordered work to begin.

Unknowingly Peter set Le Blond on a collision course, which would yet again change the course of the development of the city.

Until 1715 Vasilievsky Island had been Menshikov's personal domain. Peter had named him governor of the city soon after its founding in 1703. He had been Peter's companion since he was a boy and had introduced him to Peter's second wife and future empress, Martha Skavronskaya, later Empress Catherine I. Menshikov was a field marshal, the first senator, a 'Serene Highness' and a Prince of Russia and the Holy Roman Empire.[44] Simultaneously charming, haughty, bold and ambitious, he had used his position as the second most powerful man in Russia and Peter's confidant to amass untold wealth. Menshikov's arrogance often put him at odds with Peter and it was not uncommon for Peter to beat him publicly for stepping over the line. Yet Menshikov's loyalty to Peter was unwavering and for that Peter always forgave him.

Taken from the memoirs of Hanoverian Ambassador Friedrich Christian Weber, this urban plan of around 1716 by Jean-Baptiste Alexandre Le Blond and Domenico Trezzini shows Peter's intention of creating St Petersburg as a 'New Amsterdam' on Vasilievsky Island with a grid of streets and canals.

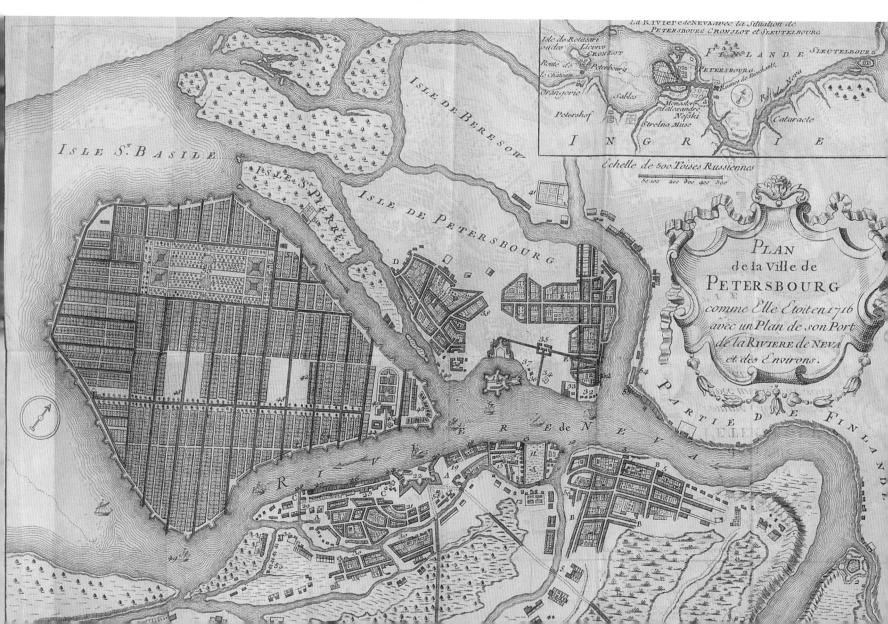

Menshikov was far from pleased at the news that his property had been reclaimed. His lavish new palace and gardens on the south-east corner of the island on the Neva designed by his own architect Giovanni Maria Fontana was nearing completion. His pride was most likely further piqued by the instruction he received from Peter: 'Welcome Le Blond in a friendly manner and respect his contact, for he is better than the best, and a real wonder, as I could see in no time.'[45] Menshikov was jealous at the favour that Peter bestowed upon his architects. As governor, with control over all matters, including construction, he was already known to have locked horns with Trezzini and was not about to let any architect get his way at his expense. When Peter ordered that work begin and that the first residents were to be relocated to the island, Menshikov took over the management of the construction. With the Tsar gone again on yet another European tour Le Blond had little leverage to question the progress of the excavation of the canals or the construction of houses.

What transpired upon Peter's return became legend, as recorded by J.V. Stählin-Storckburg in his *Original Anecdotes of Peter the Great* in 1788:

On his return to Petersburg in 1718, he postponed every other care to pay [Vasilievsky Island] a visit. He saw in most of the streets, with much satisfaction, complete rows of houses, built either of wood or stone, and was particularly pleased with the beautiful palace of Prince Menshikov, situated fronting the principal avenue; but his joy was soon overcast when he perceived the pitiful dimensions of both streets and canals. He was struck dumb with astonishment; but his gestures plainly showed how

A portrait of Catherine I hangs in a Delft-tiled study in the Menshikov Palace (1710–20s) on Vasilievsky Island. As a favourite of Peter, Prince Alexander Menshikov amassed great wealth and built the largest palace in St Petersburg.

much his contempt and indignation were excited by so egregious a blunder.

Fearing, however that he had been deceived in the dimensions of those of Amsterdam, which he was given as a model, he went immediately to the house of Mr Wilde, the Dutch Resident, and asked him if he knew the breadth of the canals of that city. Mr Wilde presented a plan of it to the Tsar, who took out his compasses, and having measured the length and breadth of the canals, wrote down their dimensions on his tablets. He then begged the Resident to go with him and see the works that had been finished in his absence. On measuring the first canals he met with, he found that their breadth, and that of the street added together, were not equal to the the width of one of the canals of Amsterdam. In a transport of rage he cried out, 'The Devil take the undertaking – all is spoiled!'[46]

Menshikov had instructed that the canals be dug too narrow, which would not allow two boats to pass by one another, making the canals impractical for the purposes Peter intended. Peter then turned to Le Blond who had remained silent during the inspection and asked, 'What can be done to salvage my plan?' Le Blond responded, 'Raze, sire, raze. There is no other remedy than to demolish all that has been done and dig the canals anew.'[47] Peter seeing his plans and dreams dashed turned to Menshikov, he ordered the works to cease and then proceeded to beat him with his stick.[48] Peter, it is said, would later return to Vasilievsky Island to gaze at the canals, mourning in silence.[49] Although Peter would repeatedly pass edicts requiring the settlement of Vasilievsky Island, few would obey and it would be nearly a century before the island was populated and developed along the street patterns set in the time of Peter. His beloved canals and his dream of a Russian Amsterdam however, vanished into history.

ABOVE The magnificent Menshikov Palace at Oranienbaum (1711–25), the Prince's country retreat. Designed by Giovanni Maria Fontana and Gottfried Schädel, the palace rivalled neighbouring Peterhof in size and grandeur.

Le Blond turned his efforts to new projects in the city, such the expansion and embellishment of the Summer Gardens as well as the planning of St Petersburg's great thoroughfare, the Nevsky Prospect. At the Summer Gardens, Le Blond produced a layout for Peter's gardens in a formal French style, importing hundreds of varieties of flowers, trees and shrubbery. He also introduced fifty fountains, complete with sculptures of classical figures, animals and monsters, and even finshed the grotto originally designed by Schlüter.[50] The pleasure at Le Blond's work further enraged Menshikov, who wrote to the Tsar while he was travelling, alleging that Le Blond was disobeying the Tsar's orders and cutting down many of Peter's favourite trees. Upon his return Peter confronted Le Blond before investigating for himself. Infuriated by Le Blond's denials and confusion, he beat him as he had beaten Menshikov on Vasilievsky Island. Le Blond, battered and horrified, took to his bed sick with shock. Peter later realized his mistake and, seeing that his tress were merely trimmed, apologized profusely and caught up with Menshikov shouting, 'You alone, you rascal are the cause of Le Blond's illness!'[51] Although Le Blond eventually recovered, the following year he contracted smallpox and died in February 1719.

PETERHOF

Before his death Le Blond worked most earnestly on what can be considered his greatest contribution to St Petersburg and its environs, the palace and gardens at Peterhof. Peter had discovered the site 13 miles to the west of the city as the quickest and least troublesome spot to cross the water to examine the progress of the fortress of Kronschlot and later the naval community of Kronstadt.[52] He ordered two modest wooden houses to be built there and soon was enchanted by the coastal environment, where he spent time relaxing and gazing at the sea. Peter had awarded many parcels of land along the coast to his loyalists, where they had built mansions

ABOVE At Strelna, Peter abandoned his vision of a second Versailles in favour of Peterhof, but retained his first humble cottage (1719–20) for use while hunting and fishing.

overlooking the sea. The grandest of these was of course Menshikov's elliptical palace of Oranienbaum, designed by the Prince's court architects Giovanni Fontana and Gottfried Schädel. Peter's first country estate was at Strelna, at which Peter had yet another modest two-storey cottage with views of the bay. At Peterhof, however, Peter began to envision something altogether grander, where he could not only enjoy his preferred level of comfort but also have a showplace where he could entertain on a level expected of an emperor.

At first Peter commissioned Johann Friedrich Braunstein, an assistant of Andreas Schlüter, to build two palaces – the first, 'Mon Plaisir', on a bluff directly on the water, and the great palace 550 yards to the south with commanding views of the gulf. Beginning in 1714 and labouring for two years, Braunstein had laid the foundations of the two buildings and begun the outlines of the upper and lower

parks. In 1716, Le Blond, newly arrived from France, took command of the works at Peterhof. He brought to bear the full magnitude of his talent, not only as a student of Le Nôtre but as an extraordinary landscape architect. He understood that Peter required a *Versailles au bord de la mer*[53] and produced for him a magnificent baroque landscape of palaces, terraces, fountains and avenues, which rivalled the grandeur of many of the finest parks and palaces in eighteenth-century Europe.

Le Blond's fountains and cascades were the wonder of St Petersburg. He had designed a system of wooden pipes, which carried fresh water down to the site, forcing it into the air, over marble steps and through the mouths of monsters. At Peterhof water was everywhere, in fountains, pools, canals, moats, and basins overseen by a legion of statues of gods and goddesses, mythological creatures, and a panoply of animals and fish. These aquatic features were linked by tree-lined paths, formal gardens, baroque terraces and

Peter's Versailles, the palace at Peterhof (1714–52). LeBlond, taking over from Johann Braunstein, drew on French sources for Peter's show palace and its famous fountains.

were overlooked by Le Blond's elegant great palace, lavishly decorated yet entirely ceremonial. Set within this celebration of water, stone and flora, three smaller palaces, which better suited Peter's tastes, were designed by Le Blond and Braunstein. The first, known as the Hermitage, is a delicate miniature palace surrounded by a moat. Here Peter gave private dinners assisted by a mechanical table that would rise up from the floor to prevent any disturbance from servants. The second minor palace was called Marly, named after Louis XIV's favoured refuge, although it looked nothing like its namesake. It was an elegant house in the Dutch manner, which sat in peaceful repose on the shores of a reflecting lake. Peter's favourite was undoubtedly the third of these palaces, Mon Plaisir. When at Peterhof, Peter lived within its oak-panelled chambers decorated with delicate Dutch tiles, paintings of ships and French arabesques on the ceilings. Light spilled into these rooms through enormous French doors, which led to either long galleries or terraces overlooking the sea. Peter took great delight in Mon Plaisir and returned to it constantly during the last years of his life. There at peace with himself and his people he could lay down the burden of empire and enjoy all he had accomplished.

THE TWILIGHT OF THE GIANT

In the late summer of 1720, Peter Alexievich, Tsar of all the Russias, ascended the new tower of the incomplete Cathedral of St Peter and St Paul, whose construction would continue until 1732. From such great heights Peter witnessed for the first time the breadth of his creation. He could see from his estate at Peterhof and the tiny island fortress of Kronschlot to the west, to the ruins of Nyenskanz in the east. In between lay a vast new city taking shape. St Petersburg's population was reaching 40,000 souls, who were beginning to be quartered in well-built houses of brick and stone. Intersected by canals, boulevards

While Peter delighted in the French grandeur of his 'Versailles', he perferred the seclusion and intimacy of his Dutch 'Mon Plaisir', where he could relax and gaze out over the gulf of Finland.

traversed the city's various quarters on both sides of the Neva, stretching outwards toward the horizon. Although the development followed no set plan, the order that was to characterize the city's future was becoming apparent. All across St Petersburg Peter saw monuments rising. Trezzini was at work on the cathedral in which he stood. Also under construction was the Kunstkammer, which would hold his legendary museum of curiosities, and the second Winter Palace, this time in stone. Both of these were designed by the Swiss-German architect Georg Johann Mattarnovy. St Petersburg still hummed with the din of building, music to Peter's ears.

One year later the Peace of Nystad would be signed, ending the over two decades of war with Sweden. The Baltic states were awarded formally to Russia, ending Swedish hegemony over these lands for ever. Having secured his capital politically he now wished to enrich it financially. In 1722 Peter ordered that all but a few goods were to be imported through St Petersburg rather than through Arkangelsk, formerly Russia's chief port. The city, which had formerly survived merely on government subsistence, began to thrive. The new wealth enlivened St Petersburg. Its wealthy elite now enjoyed a style of living that had been out of reach of their ancestors. They also enjoyed a level of freedom unhindered by the superstitions of the Church or the shackles of Muscovite tradition. Women began to play a full role in the city's social life, unheard of in the cloistered world of Moscow. Chief among them was Catherine, crowned as Peter's empress in 1724 to the horror of the conservative establishment.

Before his death a year later, in 1724 Peter ordered the relics of St Alexander Nevsky brought to St Petersburg from the city of Vladimir deep in the Russian heartland. Fourteen years earlier he had ordered Trezzini to design and build the capital's first great monastery as a signal to his people that he had not forgotten his faith. In an occasion of great ceremony and solemnity he deposited the sacred remains in the Cathedral of the Trinity in the Alexander Nevsky Monastery. Peter, the emperor who had defeated the mighty Swedes, had brought home the warrior saint responsible for driving the same hordes from the sacred land of Mother Russia in 1240.[54] Ever the master of symbolism, he had completed the historic mission to return to his nation the land of their fathers. Yet upon it he had set his seal – a gleaming new capital, which would forever stand as a symbol of his reign and his dream.

LEFT The palace of Marly (1720–3) in the Lower Garden of Peterhof combined French planning and design with Peter's taste for intimacy.
FOLLOWING PAGES The Alexander Nevsky Monastery (c.1720–40), St Petersburg's first monastery, followed Peter's insistence on European design principles.

Chapter 2:
August Ambition:
The Rise of Imperial
St Petersburg

Peter's Dream Deferred

Peter the Great died in the Winter Palace on 27 January 1725. His embalmed body lay in state in the palace until 10 March, when it was carried across the Neva on a specially built wooden bridge for a funeral in the Cathedral of St Peter and St Paul. The whole event was rich in symbolism to mark the end of the life of the creator of the city. It all began early in the morning darkness with the entire route from the palace to the cathedral lined by soldiers carrying flaming torches. Ten thousand guards escorted the coffin and the procession took two hours to cross the river in a snowstorm. Peter's coffin was not interred in a grave for six years. It was as though the city that he had forced upon the Russian people could not, in the end, bear to give him up.

His chosen heir, his second wife Catherine, was wise enough to try to carry on with Peter's policies and reforms, keeping the army happy and allowing Prince Menshikov plenty of scope to serve her and his own ambitions. It was by no means a certainty that Catherine would be made Empress – she was, after all, a Lithuanian peasant girl who was Peter's mistress before she became his wife. Her reign as Empress was short – only two years and three months – and during that time she made little impact on St Petersburg. In fact she appeared to favour Moscow and had no great projects in her late husband's dream city beyond building a Winter Palace by Domenico Trezzini. Catherine did inaugurate the new Academy of Sciences in 1725 and let the building of the great city continue without any spectacular additions. Her particular political concern was not to impose any additional tax burdens to finance construction and so the pace slowed down. There was, after the death of Peter, a gradual withdrawal from St Petersburg by many noble families, especially those who had been coerced to stay and now wanted to escape to their estates and return to their lives in Moscow. The city suffered and, for the first time, its future began to look uncertain.

Catherine's health declined rapidly and she died in 1727 after excessive exposure to the intense cold of the city, having had to flee from her flooded palace as the Neva rose knee-deep in icy water.

Peter's treasure house of curiosities, the Kunstkammer (1718–34) became symbolic of his interest in science and learning. The building contained a library, a museum, an anatomy theatre and an observatory.

Her successor was the grandson of Peter the Great, the Grand Duke Peter Alexevich, who became Peter II. Catherine decreed that the entire Supreme Privy Council should act as regents to the eleven-year-old boy. Prince Menshikov's influence continued for a while but he soon fell from grace and was dramatically banished by order of Peter II, first to the Ukraine and then to Siberia, where he died aged fifty-six in November 1729. Soon after, Menshikov's daughter Maria, who had once been betrothed to the young Emperor, also died. The glorious career of Menshikov really depended on Peter the Great and so, it seemed, did the fate of the city of St Petersburg.

Under Peter II Moscow grew increasingly important as a centre of Russian life. He went there after the fall of Menshikov and his elaborate coronation took place there in January 1728. The entire court followed the Tsar to Moscow and the palaces of St Petersburg began to empty. The Tsar never formally transferred the capital but from 1729 he began moving several government department from their premises beside the Neva to Moscow. He had refused to return to St Petersburg after his coronation, saying 'What am I to do in a city where there is nothing but salt water? I do not intend to sail the sea like my grandfather.' He preferred to hunt around Moscow and leave much of the government to the Council, now dominated by the Dolgoruky family. St Petersburg's industries and trade began to decline and the academies found it hard to attract students. The Naval School's numbers almost halved and the Academy of Sciences lost its state subsidy. Houses and palaces wee left half-built and almost all construction stopped. Mrs Ward, who was the wife of the British Resident, wrote in 1729:

> On Vasilievsky Island the merchants had designed to live; but though the houses and the streets are very handsome, they are uninhabited . . . a mile from the town is the monastery of St Alexander Nevsky . . . which will be fine if ever it is finished. There are many fine houses in the town belonging to the nobility, but now, in the absence of the court, quite empty.[1]

The city's population declined at this time to about half what it had been when Peter the Great died. Peter II appointed a new governor – a German, Burkhard Münnich, from an Oldenburg family of engineers – who saw the potential of the city's position as a Baltic port. He had also worked under Peter the Great on the building of the Ladoga Canal from 1721 to 1732 – a vital link that ran from St Petersburg for some 65 miles into the interior of Russia. The canal helped the city enormously in the long term, lowering the costs of the movement of goods and easing its development. During his governorship Münnich also built the stone bastions around the Peter and Paul Fortress and tried to complete the work on the Twelve Colleges on Vasilievsky Island designed by Trezzini. Merchants, sailors and traders now dominated the city, but without a court there was no mistaking the city's steady decline. The Tsar himself, from his fastness in Moscow, realized things had gone too far and issued a decree in July 1729. This called for the mandatory return to the city of merchants, craftsmen and coachmen, with their wives and children, and the remaining inhabitants were forbidden to leave. There were stiff penalties for disobeying, exile to hard labour camps and confiscation of property. None of these worked effectively – instead of obeying people began to set fire to many of the wooden buildings and the decline continued until the Empress Anna succeeded and returned to St Petersburg determined to rescue and complete it.

In January 1730 the fourteen-year-old Peter II became ill and was diagnosed with smallpox, which rapidly worsened and he died in the same month on the day fixed for his wedding to the Princess Dolgoruka.

ABOVE Eugene Lanceray's 1906 portrayal of St Petersburg at the beginning of the eighteenth century (State Russian Museum, St Petersburg) shows windblown ministers about to embark on a perilous trip across the Neva.

REVIVAL: ANNA IN ST PETERSBURG

Peter II's speedy demise came before he had followed the procedure laid down by his grandfather to nominate his successor. The Supreme Privy Council deliberated and selected Anna Ioannovna, the second daughter of Ivan V, Peter the Great's older half-brother and his wife, Praskovya Fedorovna. Anne had married Frederick William the Duke of Courland in 1710 (Courland was a small state in part of what today is Lithuania) but her marital happiness was brief as Frederick William died a few months after the wedding celebrations when they were travelling from St Petersburg. Poor Anna was seventeen, a widow and not the most beautiful woman in Russia. Her life was sad; she spent nineteen years living on her late husband's Teutonic estate in Mitau and her contacts with her relations in St Petersburg were usually limited to unanswered appeals for money.

The Council thought that Anna was a neutral choice and imposed strict conditions that would have made Russia almost a constitutional monarchy. The 'conditions' also insisted that Moscow should be the capital to suit the oligarchy of Muscovites who selected Anna hoping to reverse many of Peter the Great's radical changes. Anna had little choice but to sign the document but on arrival in Moscow gathered the support of the guards regiments and the service gentry, tore up the conditions and re-established the autocracy. Her coronation was held in Moscow on 28 April 1730 in a ceremony of extreme magnificence held in a special wooden palace in the Kremlin designed for her by Bartolomeo Rastrelli. This was matched by a firework display in St Petersburg organized by Münnich, reputed to be the largest ever seen in Russia. Anna had lived in Courland for nearly twenty years and was thoroughly Westernized, so she enthusiastically moved the court back St Petersburg. Once there, her trio of German ministers, Biron, Ostermann and Münnich, helped her with the revival of the city in the next ten years of her reign, with Biron becoming a powerful First Minister.

St Petersburg has to be grateful to Empress Anna. She rescued the city from its decline and put it firmly on the road to imperial greatness. She set about repairing the damaged infrastructure and collapsing buildings to make the city an appropriate setting for the first real royal court – an imperial court on the European model – in Russia. She also saw the city as a cultural centre for ballet, music and opera. Once welcomed into the city in 1732 with grand processions and balls, she and Münnich began to complete many of Peter the Great's unfinished projects, including his Kunstkammer, containing all of Peter's curious collections, the Cathedral of St Peter and St Paul and the Twelve Colleges.

Anna needed a court architect to design suitably enhanced setting for the Empress of all the Russias and the choice of Bartolomeo Rastrelli (1700–71) was an inspired one. He was a Papal Count and the son of the Italian sculptor (Bartolomeo Carlo Rastrelli) who went to St Petersburg with the French architect Jean-Baptiste Le Blond (1679–1719). He had trained in Paris under Robert de Cotte (1656–1735), a leading French exponent of the rococo. His work was to flourish in the reigns of both Anna and her successor, Elizabeth. Rastrelli's first project for Anna was a Summer Palace by the Neva (now destroyed) by Peter the Great's Summer Garden. He also built, for the horse-loving Biron, the magnificent Manège, an indoor riding school that became a stylish gathering place for first-class riders and horses. Anna had initially taken up residence in the palace that had once belonged to Count Apraxin but it was inadequate and she summoned Rastrelli, who had designed the triumphal arches that welcomed her to St Petersburg, and commanded him to build a great stone Winter Palace. It was four storeys high with a great hall, a gallery, a chapel, a theatre and a very grand formal staircase. It was a great commission and Rastrelli made good practical suggestions that both added new elements and reconstructed some older ones combining the existing Winter Palace, the Apraxin and the old Kikin Palace and many minor buildings. The result was probably more harmonious within than without and indeed it was the interior decoration that was regarded as exceptionally fine, especially the 180-foot-long Grand Hall, with its painted ceiling.

Because many of the city's buildings were still built of wood, there was a permanent danger of fire. In 1736 and 1737 two very serious fires broke out on the Admiralty side of the Neva. Many noble families and foreign ambassadors lost their houses, causing the government to act effectively to plan the rebuilding. A Commission on the Construction of St Petersburg was established under the direction of Peter Eropkin, an architect who had been sent to Italy by Peter the Great. He returned to the city after ten years in 1725 and was well qualified to direct the Commission, which assumed powers to replan the city and continued through several reigns. The members of the Commission were all Russians who had benefited from Peter the Great's inspired scheme of sending talented people abroad to be thoroughly trained.

The Commission ordered that the centre of the city be developed in a planned manner and built in stone. Trades and factories were to be moved to the outskirts and three main prospects focussing on the Admiralty were to form the spines of the capital. These are present today, the Nevsky Prospect being the central one. The width of these three streets and their well-built bridges over the canals was not determined by purely aesthetic reasons – it was strategically important to allow the movement of large numbers of troops to defend the monarchy and keep public order at a moment's notice. The guards were carefully and comfortably housed on a neat grid plan of streets with their families – all part of the plan to ensure their loyalty.

On Nevsky Prospect Anna decreed the building of many churches for the foreign communities and the result was a remarkable series of churches for the Evangelicals, French, Swedish, Dutch and Roman Catholic communities.

Alexandre Dumas, who visited the city in the 1860s, called the Nevsky Prospect 'the street of religious toleration'.[2] Today, many of these churches are enjoying a second revival after the official atheist years under Communism, when many were closed or converted to other uses. Anna also moved the sacred icon of Our Lady of Kazan into a new church on Nevsky Prospect, which lasted until Alexander I built the Kazan Cathedral. She was also determined to complete the building of the Twelve Colleges on Vasilievsky Island. Also on the waterfront of the island a special illumination theatre was erected for the immense firework displays to be seen from the Winter Palace across the river. Gradually the population rose again, growing by the time of Anna's death to over 70,000 – having been well below 40,000 at the time of Peter I.

Anna's court was at the core of the reviving city. It was elaborate but, with its dwarves and buffoons, it had strong elements of crudity about it. Anna's continued to debase the families of the Moscow boyars who had tried to impose conditions on the way she was to conduct her reign by making the princes of these families

Set back along the Nevsky Prospect, St Catherine Armenian Apostolic Church (1770–72), by Yury Velten, is a reminder of the religious tolerance included in city planning.

perform ludicrous and humiliating duties, while she pursued her favourite pastimes of hunting and shooting and exhibiting exotic animals and birds for the court's pleasure. She was not an educated woman but she did save the city of St Petersburg from potential collapse with her efficient German staff and made it possible for her successors to elevate the city once again to international status open to the influences of the West.

GILDING THE LILY: ST PETERSBURG DURING THE ELIZABETHAN ERA

Anna died in 1740, leaving the throne to the son of her niece Catherine of Mecklenburg, who became Ivan VI at the age of two months with his mother to act as regent. This was predictably a disaster and, after some months of intrigue, Peter the Great's daughter Elizabeth seized the throne to reign from 1741 to 1762. Elizabeth was intensely Russian and soon dispatched her predecessor's foreign advisers. Her court reflected her popularity with the Russian people. She was devoted to the memory of Peter the Great and shared his vision for the growth of the city. She also commissioned Voltaire to write his history of the reign of Peter the Great – thus securing an intelligent and sympathetic version of his epoch.

The Empress Elizabeth came to power at a moment of relative peace and prosperity and she was able to initiate a period of serious building and the creation of the sort of architectural magnificence that Peter could only have imagined. Elizabeth was not anti-Moscow; she saw the point of both the old and new cities but was determined to build substantially in St Petersburg and to encourage the nobility to do the same. The result was a baroque building boom unprecedented in Europe. Her reign saw the building of palaces at Peterhof, Tsarskoe Selo, Strelna, churches and convents in the city and houses for the noble families – the Stroganovs, the Vorontsovs, the Sheremetevs and many others.

To continue the urban development of the city Elizabeth maintained the Commission for the Construction of St Petersburg to build the major streets, strengthen the embankments and reconstruct the fire-damaged districts. Buildings on Nevsky Prospect had to be made of stone and trees planted along the avenue to ensure a green view in the short summer period. More ground was properly drained to allow for good paving and canals were improved. Fire regulations and public order measures were imposed, including the siting of taverns away from the main streets and the removal of visible laundry and obtrusive signs.

Elizabeth's reign also saw the great triumph of Rastrelli – who had become an adopted Russian mainly because he was such a good teacher to his many Russian students and assistants. His first project for Elizabeth was to complete a Summer Palace in his individual Russian baroque style. It was demolished in 1797 so that Paul could build his Mikhailovsky Castle, but many views and engravings of Rastrelli's palace survive. It was built of wood and looked like a relaxed version of a Parisian *hôtel*, with its large central block being a two-storey ballroom. It was a taste of what was to come for the new Winter Palace, especially its skyline of balustrades, urns and statuary. Elizabeth decided that the Winter Palace Rastrelli had put together for the Empress Anna was simply not up to European standards and in June 1754 she issued the order for the old palace to be demolished and a completely new one to be built on the site as speedily as possible. A temporary wooden palace was built within a year for the Empress on a site on Nevsky Prospect. The immense new palace – over 400,000 square feet with more than a thousand rooms – was finished in 1762. Elizabeth saw it almost completed but died before she could move in. It is the palace we see today (although rebuilt after a fire) and it is unlike any other baroque building in Europe. It is a special Russian baroque, which Rastrelli invented, mixing rococo and baroque in a style inclusive of traditional Russian elements. The painted façade

ABOVE RIGHT The Summer Palace of Elizabeth Petrovna (1741–3) was the first of Bartolomeo Rastrelli's ebullient baroque structures in St Petersburg to make an indelible mark upon the capital. Painting by M. Makhaev, 1749 (State Russian Museum, St Petersburg).

may have inspired the Russian term, *fasadnost*, which suggests reliance on external appearances. Peter the Great's first wooden house had been painted to resemble brick. Despite all the talk of rebuilding the city in stone many wooden buildings (in St Petersburg and Moscow) were replaced by stuccoed brick painted in bright colours. This fact was amusingly observed much later in the 1830s by the perceptive Marquis de Custine: 'If you judge the reality of this appearance you will find yourself strangely deceived.'[3] The façades of Rastrelli's Winter Palace continue to amaze us today. Its immense length is broken up by his use of the classical orders, Ionic and Doric, marking a series of bays and projections with varying window designs. Most remarkable are the troops of bronze statues on the roof – many of them larger than life size – looking out over the Neva and Palace Square. Rastrelli introduced the colour we associate with St Petersburg today. Originally, the Winter Palace was painted yellow and white; it turned blood-red in the early post-Revolution days of the early twentieth century and today it is sea-green and white. Colour was important because it was not possible to bring to the city the quantities of coloured marbles that would have been needed, and the city's grey and cold winter climate needed the relief of brightly coloured buildings. Often very bright colours were used. Turquoise, pink and orange were not unusual and there seemed to have been a particular taste for pistachio and even emerald green.

Rastrelli was inevitably asked by the Empress Elizabeth to design a palace for her lifelong favourite Alexei Razumovsky. The result was the Anichkov Palace on the corner of Nevsky Prospect and the Fontanka Canal. It is so much altered today, it is hard to imagine except from old engravings, but it was dominant with its domed cupolas and rooftop trophies. Royal patronage and the big success of the giant Winter Palace made Rastrelli everyone's favourite architect. The Stroganov and Vorontsov families used Rastrelli for their town residences and other families had summer residences built by him on the outskirts near the river.

After the royal palaces Rastrelli is best remembered today for the remarkable Smolny Convent and Cathedral, which he designed in 1746. The Empress politely interfered to ask him to make it feel more Russian, pointing to the Kremlin in Moscow and the plan and arrangement of the Dormition Cathedral. She instructed Rastrelli to include a bell tower in the likeness of 'the Ivan bell tower to be found in Moscow . . . and a large bell'.[4] She was referring to the famous bell tower of Ivan the Great and its giant Tsar bell. Rastrelli's

With more than a thousand rooms, Rastrelli's monumental Winter Palace (1754–64) was a feat of extravagance both architecturally and financially, one which the Empress Elizabeth herself would not live to see complete.

design for Smolny with the tower is the most grandiose scheme of eighteenth-century Russia. We can see how it would have been if it had been built by looking at the remarkable contemporary model that survives in the collections of the Academy of Fine Arts in St Petersburg. The model was exhibited at *The Triumph of the Baroque* exhibition in Turin in 1999 as the climax to the show. It is the combination of the convent buildings, the cathedral and the bell tower that represents the triumph of Rastrelli's Russian baroque style. He followed the Empress's wishes and looked at the Ivan the Great elongated tower and the lower Kremlin belfry alongside it and decided, as only Rastrelli could do, to place one on top of the

other to produce the tallest six-tiered structure in St Petersburg. The lower part of his tower conveys, by the piling up of triumphal arches, the imperial and baroque magnificence of the new St Petersburg crowned with a bell tower that is reminiscent of Russia's ancient glories. Rastrelli is one of the first architects ever to include 'quotations' from the past in his style, and to allow a much freer treatment of classical forms in his architecture. His Smolny Cathedral, with its five domes, its strong palette and profusion of gilding, is magnificent. In fact it is at Smolny, especially if the whole scheme including the tower had been built, that we see all the important features of the Russian baroque. Here is the regular plan

LEFT Among the only surviving Rastrelli interiors in the Winter Palace today is the magnificent Jordan Staircase, which the tsars would descend every year for the blessing of the Neva.
ABOVE Rastrelli accomplished Elizabeth's grandiose nod to the Orthodox Church through the construction of the Smolny Convent (1748–64), a religious community and school for noblewomen.

It would have been the most famous structure in St Petersburg and expressed to the very highest degree the pathos of the creation of Russia's new capital that was started by Peter the Great and taken to a brilliant state in the era of the Russian baroque under his daughter Elizabeth I.[5]

One particular church in the city is resonant of Rastrelli's influence. This is the Church of St Nicholas of the Sea, designed by Rastrelli's pupil Savva Chevakinsky for a site on the Kryukov Canal. It is one of the few churches that were used for services during the Soviet era and it is a remarkably intact survival of a well-preserved church of the 1760s.

During Empress Elizabeth's time a great deal of work was started on the suburban palaces. It was Elizabeth who inherited the small palace in the village of Saaskaya Myza that her mother Catherine I had given to Peter the Great as a surprise retreat. But it was not until she herself became Empress that she decided to rename the village Tsarskoe Selo ('Tsar's Village') and make it the site of the chief summer residence for the imperial family. Several architects worked on enlarging the palace for her but she wasn't satisfied until she commissioned Rastrelli in 1751 to completely redesign it. He finished it in 1756 having extended each side of the original palace to an overall length of 1,000 feet. Architect and Empress both thought on the grand scale and the shadow of Versailles irresistibly lurked in their minds. Rastrelli placed the church at one end of the palace and the grand staircase at the other, cleverly making visitors experience the huge scale of the place, both on their arrival from the outside and when they entered and gazed awe-struck along the entire gilded enfilade.

There were two great experiences to be had at the palace that Elizabeth re-named the Catherine Palace after her mother. A visit to the grand gallery and to the amber room is still impressive today, as both have now been miraculously restored. The gallery, mirrored on both sides between each of the eleven windows, still gives an impression of a gilded court setting hovering on the brink of vulgarity. The walls positively bristle with carved and gilded sconces and girandoles while restless putti flit above every looking glass. The amber room was originally a gift to Peter the Great from Frederick William I of Prussia in exchange for fifty-five selected tall and fit grenadiers. It was stolen or destroyed by the Nazis in the Second World War but has now been replaced with new amber panels based on old photographs. The initial impact of this famous room can be a

and a hierarchy of spaces, a sense of glorious opulence and monumentality, combined with a luxurious abundance of infinite decorative details. It sums up the vision and intentions of Empress Elizabeth, who built to astound the world on Peter's drained marshes. After all, she was the empress who, when she died, left behind more than five thousand dresses embroidered with gold and precious stones. The brilliant Russian architectural historian Dmitri Shvidkovsky has said of Rastrelli's unbuilt tower:

ABOVE Although never completed, Rastrelli's design for the bell tower at Smolny remains one of the greatest fantasies of the Russian baroque.
RIGHT The influence of Rastrelli continued under Russian architect Savva Chevakinsky, whose Church of St Nicholas of the Sea (1753–62) served as the last glorious gasp of the baroque era.

disappointment, despite the incredible workmanship – there is something almost plastic about the finishes of so much amber. The way to see it is to wait for the low northern light to fill the room, and then it is true as Sacheverell Sitwell wrote: that the very air in the room turns pure gold.[6] It is a wonder. The vast main courtyard of Rastrelli's great Catherine Palace exemplifies at a glance Elizabeth's penchant for excess. The blue, white and gold façades set in the enormous park, with Rastrelli's Hermitage and Grotto, still express a world of baroque magnificence today that is almost exhausting.

At Peterhof, Elizabeth and Rastrelli performed a similar feat to their work at Tsarskoe Selo. In the late 1740s she asked her favourite architect to redesign the palace and Rastrelli added a storey to Le

Blond's original building begun in 1716 and added galleries and side pavilions with cupolas to his extended wings. He painted the palace pink and white and, legend has it, was ordered by the Empress to gild as much as possible to make the interiors much more lavish. He also enhanced the park and fountains, installing iron pipes instead of wooden ones to make the fountains 'play high'. Elizabeth also had her simple moments and a small Dutch kitchen was installed for her next to Mon Plaisir so that she could cook herself the occasional meal. It seems unlikely, however, that she did the washing up. Her real preference was for grandeur and glittering balls, masquerades, metamorphoses (when men dressed a women and women as men) and the settings devised for here by

ABOVE Over a thousand feet long, the grand façade of Rastrelli's Catherine Palace (1748–56), once completed, left visitors either awestruck or appalled.

A regiment of Atlases wrestle with the weight of Elizabethan opulence at the Catherine Palace in Tsarskoe Selo.

Rastrelli were never modest. It was the marriage of Grand Duke Peter to Catherine in August 1745 that the Empress Elizabeth planned to be the greatest social event St Petersburg had ever seen. She had received full accounts of the recent wedding of the Dauphin of France at Versailles and determined to make this Russian royal wedding more impressive. Her newly built city of palaces was ready for a great occasion.

At three o'clock on 21 August 1745, a procession of 120 carriages rode down Nevsky Prospect towards the Church of Our Lady of Kazan; the Empress and the young couple were conveyed in a gilded and carved carriage dawn by eight white horses. After hours of religious ceremony there was a ball and a dinner at the Winter Palace while fountains in the city flowed with wine. Peter's vision had indeed been embellished by his daughter, who had in so many ways enhanced the cultural, educational and social life of the city. The future of St Petersburg would in due time lie in the hands of the young and highly intelligent young woman who had been weighed down with the Empress's jewels for her wedding to the strange and difficult grand duke, heir to the Russian throne.

The Empress Elizabeth died on 25 December 1761 and was succeeded by her thirty-three-year-old nephew Peter – the son of Peter the Great's daughter Anna and the Duke of Holstein-Gottorp. She had arranged the marriage of Peter to a cousin, Sophia Augusta Fredrike – a princess of Anhalt-Zerbst – who became Orthodox and

LEFT Gilded gods and goddesses frolic in the fountains of Peterhof.
ABOVE 'Gild as much as possible,' was the order given by Elizabeth to Rastrelli as he undertook the expansion and redecoration of Peterhof (1745–55). His Midas touch is in evidence in the Small Ballroom.

took the name Catherine Alexeevna. Catherine had endured sixteen years of a marriage to Peter, who was mentally unstable and scorned his wife, preferring his own infantile activities – tormenting animals and playing and drinking with his servants and drilling his soldiery. He was thrilled by the death of Elizabeth, smiling and joking at her funeral and alienating everyone by his offensive behaviour. He upset the army with unwise manoeuvres in Schleswig preparing for war with Denmark and by abruptly ending the war with Prussia with a peace that was disadvantageous to Russia. He upset the Church with his enthusiasm for Lutheranism. And he upset the Senate with his attempts to rule through a coterie of unrepresentative favourites.

Peter's reputation has been demolished by history (and by Catherine) despite some of the enlightened things he did, such as abolishing the secret police. While Peter was offending so many constituencies Catherine was busy courting them and preparing to take the reins of power. In June 1762 the plotters were forced to act quickly as one of their number had been arrested, and within hours Catherine was declared Empress. Peter was arrested and exiled to the palace at Ropsha, where he was found dead a few days later. No one accused the Empress of murder but many people saw the government of Russia at the time as 'despotism tempered by assassination'.

THE AGE OF CLASSICISM:
THE EMPRESS AND THE ARCHITECTS

Catherine was ready for her powerful role and lost no time in making use of her long education in the ways of the European Enlightenment. She was extremely well read and full of energy and determined to improve the lives of her people and to civilize the court. Her days were full – she rose at five in the morning, often making her own strong coffee and working hard on the affairs of state until ten o'clock. She would then take breakfast and attend prayers and work until she dined at two. Retiring to her own rooms she would take tea at five and see company or have some entertainment until supper and always in bed by ten.

She had no enthusiasm for Moscow. In her memoirs called it 'the city of sloth'.[7] But she wanted to improve standards of construction throughout the country and set up a special Commission on Masonry Construction of St Petersburg and Moscow and extended its brief to all Russian cities following the terrible fire that levelled the city of Tver in 1763. By the end of her reign the Commission had prepared and approved plans for over three hundred cities. She reformed the government of the provinces and the cities and in St Petersburg the government of the city was reorganized on the basis of democratic home rule. There was an elected City Duma and City Governor and many of the rights of the Empress and the Senate were transferred to the municipality. The city could own land and, for the first time ever, had its own budget and could found schools, markets, taverns and regulate local trade.

Catherine continued to play a major role in the city's development and took a special interest in the architecture and planning so that her capital should be the showcase to the world of her ideas and the people's prosperity. To help realize her vision of a grand capital she announced in December 1762 an international competition for the planning of the city. Entrants were to make two sets of proposals. One was to leave existing buildings as they were but attempt to find a plan to harmonize and improve them; the other was a *carte blanche* approach to propose idealized plans. Sadly, the results of this competition do not survive but the exercise clearly fed the Commission with some new ideas. Certainly the Neva played a more prominent role in planning and new embankments were built in the centre of the city from 1764 to 1788, designed elegantly by a German architect, Yury Velten, and executed in a beautiful pink granite from Finland. Graceful granite staircases led down to landing stages and some new bridges were added over several of the canals. The Commission, seeing the excellent nature of the setting for the river and the city that the new embankments provided, suggested to Catherine that there should be an unbroken line of palaces on the mile-long Palace Embankment between the Admiralty and the Summer Palace. The Winter Palace was already complete and there were some other important residences but there were substantial gaps and the need for uniformity in an architectural style that would be recognisably the style of Catherine's rule.

LEFT Peter's dream of Versailles exceeded: the staircase at Peterhof Palace.
ABOVE Portrait of Catherine the Great in Travelling Costume (1787), painting by Mikhail Shibanov (State Russian Museum, St Petersburg).

Catherine's architectural taste had to match her intellectual enthusiasms and her desire for intelligent originality. She naturally wanted to distance herself from the almost barbaric glamour of the baroque of her predecessor the Empress Elizabeth, whose buildings represented the colourful masquerade of her court life. As a child of the Enlightenment, Catherine was aware of and interested in the discoveries being made at Pompeii and Herculaneum and their effect on the Western architects who were travelling the classical world of Greece and Italy on the Grand Tour. She sought the purity of classicism and the Palladian style and fulfilled her wishes for her private world in the country at Tsarskoe Selo. In the city the design of the French architect Jean-Baptiste Michel Vallin de la Mothe (1729–1800), commissioned by Count Ivan Ivanovich Shuvalov, for the Academy of Fine Arts on the Vasilievsky Embankment, marked the end of the Russian baroque style. He worked with the young Russian architect Alexander Filippovich Kokorinov, who became rector of the Academy, to produce a large square sober building around a central circular courtyard. The interior is grand, with a great double staircase and fine exhibition rooms. (Today it has to be visited to see the fine collection of architectural models that are contemporary with the building of the city.) Catherine must have been impressed by the Academy because she commissioned Vallin de la Mothe to build her the first (the Small) Hermitage next to the Winter Palace as her private retreat from the acres of splendour of the Winter Palace. This small building, with its fine portico and

delicate detail, is important because it shows how Catherine was able and wanted to separate her private and her public life. Throughout her reign she made the distinction – she was an enlightened European citizen and an autocratic empress – thus remaining always something of an intriguing, contradictory and powerful enigma. This meant that there were private and public architectural worlds. In her private world, when she was married to Peter, she used the talented Antonio Rinaldi (1709–94) to work at Oranienbaum. Rinaldi was an Italian who had worked with the Neapolitan architect Luigi Vanvitelli (1700–1773), the architect of Caserta – the last baroque palace to be built in Italy. He started by enlarging the pleasure pavilions around the old Menshikov Palace but his triumph there was to build for Catherine in 1762–8 the exquisite Chinese Palace. Rinaldi's taste was perfect and this little pavilion, miraculously undamaged by the Nazis and left alone by the Communists, still has the atmosphere of an exotic discovery of the eighteenth century. The Chinese taste is limited to the interior but some drawings survive that show that Rinaldi wanted it to be surrounded by Chinese bridges and little Chinese wooden lacquer pavilions in the gardens.

Catherine would have shared the enthusiasm of other European rulers for the exoticism of the East and especially China. Her Chinese Palace is in date and style close to the Tea House at Potsdam, built for Frederick the Great by Johann Gottfried Büring, and the Chinese Pavilion at Drottninghom, built for Frederick the Great's sister Queen Louisa Ulrika of Sweden by the architect Karl

ABOVE LEFT *The Senate Embankment (The English Quay)* (1801), painting by Benjamin Patterson (State Hermitage Museum, St Petersburg).
ABOVE RIGHT Catherine's civic improvements included the reconstruction of quays, the lining the rivers and construction of bridges in red granite.

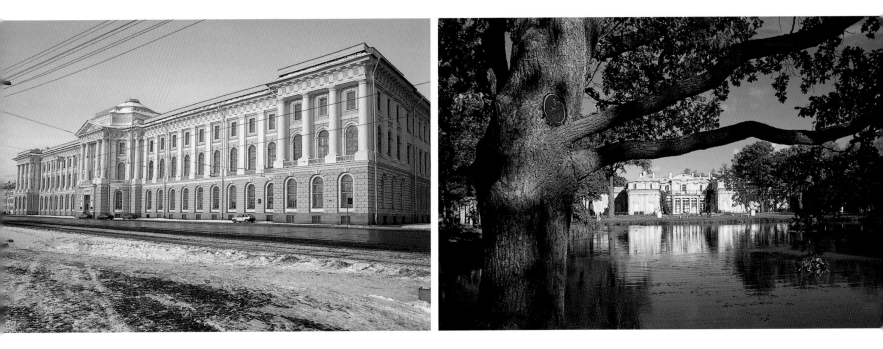

Frederick Adelcrantz in the 1760s. She would also have known the published works of Sir William Chambers, who travelled in China recording buildings and was later to design the pagoda at Kew. His book *Designs of Chinese Buildings, Furniture, Dresses, Machines, and Utensils, Engraved by the Best Hands, From the Originals drawn in China by Mr Chambers. . . . to which is annexed A Description of their Temples, Houses, Gardens, etc.* was published in 1757 for the author in both English and French and enjoyed a wide circulation.

The Chinese Palace was barely finished before Catherine went on to embrace other architectural styles, which luckily Rinaldi was able to produce with designs for two palaces for Grigory Orlov: the austere Marble Palace (1768–85) on the Palace Embankment in the heart of St Petersburg and Gatchina (1766–81), which was some thirty miles to the south-west of the city in a beautiful park.

One question that occupied Catherine for some years was how to commemorate the founder of the city of St Petersburg and where to place his memorial. It was decided to place some sort of sculptural memorial to Peter the Great on the new square below the Admiralty and Catherine sought advice. Lomonosov and Diderot proposed a great allegorical panorama, but this did not appeal to her. Instead she wanted a something straightforward and not allegorical: a personal portrayal. It was her ambassador in Paris, Prince Dmitri Golitsyn, who found her the perfect sculptor in Etienne-Maurice Falconet. The sculptor was to be in St Petersburg for twelve years working on the great equestrian bronze, the result

being the most famous statue in Russia: an equestrian sculpture that can legitimately be compared to Marcus Aurelius in Rome and Frederick II in Berlin. Peter is not depicted simply as another warrior. As Falconet explained:

> It is necessary to show mankind a more splendid sight, that of a creator lawgiver, and benefactor of his country. . . . My Tsar does not hold a baton in his hand: He extends his beneficent hand over the country over which he soars, and climbs on to the cliff which serves as his support – an emblem of the difficulties he overcame.[8]

The horse that Peter rides is wild and unruly representing Russia about to gallop into the void. His clothes are neither Roman nor Russian but vaguely heroic and the horse tramples on a snake – the one allegorical element, representing evil and envy. The huge granite rock was transported from the Gulf of Finland in one piece to Senate Square and the whole ensemble was unveiled by Catherine in August 1782 to mark the hundredth anniversary of Peter the Great's accession to the throne. The Empress linked herself forever to her great predecessor in the inscription she chose: 'To Peter the First, Catherine the Second'. The sculptor had been exhausted by Russian red tape and had left the country two years earlier, so never saw his completed masterpiece. It immediately became known as *The Bronze Horseman* and was immortalized as a symbol of the city and Russia's destiny in Pushkin's poem:

ABOVE LEFT The Academy of Fine Arts (1765–89) on Vasilievsky Island.
ABOVE RIGHT Catherine's rococo retreat, the Chinese Palace (1762–8) at Oranienbaum by Antonio Rinaldi.

Proud charger, whither art thou ridden,
Where leapest thou? And where, and on whom,
Wilt plant thy hoof?[9]

Catherine's life in the city had a focus in the Winter Palace and in her own Small Hermitage, where she held her private social activities in as orderly a fashion as she could. But even she found it difficult, as her letters reveal, even to find her lovers in the Palace, which she describes as 'full of human cattle'. She had social rules for her guests:

On entering, the title and rank must be put off, as well as the hat and the sword.

One shall speak with moderation and quietly so that others do not get a headache.

Eat slowly and with appetite; drink with moderation, that each may walk steadily as he goes out.[10]

All these and other regulations of manners were designed to encourage good conversation and a sense of being in an enlightened court. But the great balls also still went on with immense jewelled retinues and elaborate costumes for both sexes. It is not surprising that Catherine often longed for the 'return to

ABOVE It paid to be Catherine's favourite. The Marble Palace (1768–85) by Antonio Rinaldi was a gift to Catherine's one-time lover and co-conspirator, Prince Grigory Orlov.

Etienne-Maurice Falconet's masterpiece, *The Bronze Horseman*. A tribute to Peter the Great from Catherine II eulogized by Pushkin, the equestrian statue has since become a symbol of the city and of Russia.

paintings which had been intended for Frederick the Great, his financial difficulties after the Seven Years War making it impossible for him to afford them. Her agent and ambassador in Paris, Prince Dmitri Golitsyn, secured for her Rembrandt's *Return of the Prodigal Son* as well as some contemporary French artists' work including paintings by Chardin. The thousand pictures belonging to Pierre Crozat, including Raphael's *Holy Family*, were purchased for 500,000 francs; Catherine then snapped up the entire collection of the Duc de Choiseul, followed by the collection of Augustus III of Saxony's Chancellor, with its masterpieces by Rubens and Watteau. In 1779 she outbid everyone and bought the vast collection of Sir Robert Walpole – including works by Van Dyck, Raphael, Poussin, Titian and Rubens. She also collected sculpture and the decorative arts and furniture and assembled an amazing library of some 38,000 books.

Catherine revived the Imperial Porcelain Factory and commissioned tapestries from Gobelins and china from Sèvres. One of her most interesting English commissions was the 'Frog' service from Wedgwood for her little Chesme Palace, or 'palace on the frog marsh', which was also known as the Kekerekeksinensky Palace, designed by Yury Velten in 1774 in the Gothic style and used for informal entertaining. Wedgwood and Bentley had been trading with Russia since 1769, helped by the wife of the British Ambassador. The commission was a very special one; the order was a dinner service and dessert service for fifty people to be made in pottery (Queen's ware) and decorated in virtual monochrome with views of Britain. The Empress was very specific: the views were to be confined to the British Isles and to contain as many gothic remains as possible as well as 'Natural Views and Improved Scenes and Ornaments in Parks and Gardens.'[11] The gothic style implied to Catherine virtue and strength and the English landscape garden had become symbolic of liberty. As Catherine wrote to Voltaire from Peterhof in 25 June 1772,

antiquity' and the Arcadian world she was creating at Tsarskoe Selo with the help of a remarkable Scot, Charles Cameron.

But it was in the Hermitage that she exposed to the city and the world her determination to make St Petersburg a city of the fine arts. She supported the Academy of Fine Arts and sent Russian students abroad to study, and made her own mark with her intense, almost compulsive passion to collect Western art. She spared absolutely no expense and no one in Europe could compete with her buying power. In Berlin in 1764 she bought 225 Old Master

I love English gardens to the point of folly: serpentine lines, gentle slopes, marshes turned into lakes, islands of dry ground, and I deeply despise straight lines. I hate fountains which torture water to make it a course contrary to nature; in a word my plantomania is dominated by anglomania.[12]

Parts of the Wedgwood service are now on view in the British Galleries of the Hermitage, and its quality and simplicity reveals much about the tastes of the Empress.

Her true paradise is still to be discovered at Tsarskoe Selo, where she had the inspiration to employ Charles Cameron to realize her dream. In the 1770s Catherine decided to build a 'Graeco-Roman rhapsody' in the park of Tsarskoe Selo. She sought international help: 'We are seeking one or several artists to find in Greek or Roman antiquity a completely furnished house. It must summarize the era of Caesar, Augustus, Cicero and Maecenas and be a house in which all of them could be found in person.' Many architects were excited by this challenge and Charles de Wailly and Clérisseau were among the entries. The Empress decided to employ Charles Cameron, a somewhat mysterious Jacobite figure, educated in Rome but possibly only the son of a humble London builder. His fame rested on a book *The Baths of the Romans*, which he published in 1767 and 1772, basing it on his own measured drawings and recordings made in Rome, where he was friends with Clérisseau and is rumoured to have lived in the house of the exiled Jacobite Pretender. He was involved in the excavations of the Imperial Baths at the command of Pope Clement XIII. He must have charmed the Empress and the neo-classical style was just what she had been looking for. He moved to Russia and, aged thirty-six, was to become responsible for the two major imperial ensembles – firstly Tsarskoe Selo and then Pavlovsk. His two-storey bath pavilion at Tsarskoe had baths on the ground floor and rooms above. The ground floor was made of weather-beaten stone – succeeding in looking ancient and a 'pedestal of time' above the richly ornamented interiors gave the pavilion its name – the Agate Pavilion. The walls are agate, rock crystal, marble and bronze and jasper – all Russian stones that came from Russian sources. Next to this he built what is now called the Cameron Gallery, partially glazed for winter promenades. The whole gallery is lined with busts of great men and a gentle ramp glides into the park. In Rastrelli's Catherine Palace Cameron re-arranged several rooms to make a completely private apartment for Catherine. Many of these have rooms been restored and the Green Dining Room and the Empress's bedroom are more Pompeian than Pompeii itself, suggesting the imperial richness of ancient Rome. Cameron is far more original than his contemporaries the Adam brothers and it is doubtful that there is a more beautiful series of neo-classical spaces anywhere else in the world.

In the park he worked with Catherine to create an idealized world in the English-style landscape. For Grand Duke Paul and his wife Maria Feodorovna he worked for four years building their palace at Pavlovsk. He did not always get on with other architects and found it hard to work on Pavlovsk's interiors with V.F. Brenna. Cameron's Temple of Friendship (1780) in the park was the first use of the Greek Doric order in Russia. The palace at Pavlovsk does reveal Cameron's genius – especially in the Italian and Grecian halls – in his subtle palette of colours and the references to the Pantheon and other Roman sources. The house also relates directly with the gardens and the park in a completely English way that was new to Russia and suited the flower-loving Grand Duchess.

ABOVE RIGHT Yury Velten's Church of John the Baptist, better known as the Chesme Chapel (1777–80), was among the first 'Strawberry Hill gothic' structures built in Russia, reflecting Catherine's growing Anglophilia.

ABOVE The Marble or Palladian Bridge (1772–4) by Vasili Neelov signalled Catherine's move toward classicism as well as her enthusiasm for English gardens such as those at Stowe in Buckinghamshire, from which the bridge was copied.
RIGHT Charles Cameron's Cold Baths or Agate Pavilion (1780–5) were designed in the fashion of a Renaissance villa, and its sumptuous interiors recalled ancient Rome.

What is important to remember when visiting Pavlovsk and Tsarskoe Selo is that so much of what you see is the result of the most painstaking reconstruction and restoration carried out since the destruction of the palaces by the fleeing Nazis in World War II.[13]

One palace at Tsarskoe Selo that has not yet been fully restored was built by Giacomo Quarenghi in 1792–6 on Catherine's orders for her favourite grandson, Alexander, after whom it is named. Its colonnaded front and simple interiors were to make it almost the favourite residence for the imperial family right up to end of the Romanov dynasty. Quarenghi had already built the uncompromisingly Palladian English Palace at Peterhof (now destroyed) and his theatre at the Hermitage (1783–7) shows that he worked in such an assured and strong classical mode – temperamentally miles away from the originality of Cameron. But Quarenghi was important for the city and he served as an adviser on many projects in the last two decades of the eighteenth century, continuing to help the Emperor Paul after Catherine's death in 1796.

Catherine the Great died from a sudden stroke in the Winter Palace surrounded by her family. Despite her unofficial wishes that her favourite grandson Alexander should succeed her, she died without making any changes to the natural succession of her son Paul. From almost the moment of the death of his mother Paul I made it clear that he intended to return Russia to the way it was in the year his father had been assassinated in 1762. He insisted in bringing his father's body from its resting place in the Alexander Nevsky Monastery and putting the coffin next to Catherine's to lie in state under a banner which bore the words 'Divided in life – united in death'. The funeral was a joint one and onlookers described it as a wedding of ghosts.

LEFT Cameron's most ambitious project, the palace and park of Pavlovsk (1782–6) for Catherine's son Paul. It remains Russia's greatest Palladian monument.
ABOVE The heroic efforts of curators and conservators have preserved Pavlovsk's interiors and collections among the finest and most intact of all the suburban palaces.

'DON QUIXOTE WITH A CROWN'

Paul's one desire was to undo as much of Catherine's work as he could – he had never recovered from the conviction that he should have been proclaimed Emperor as a child and that his mother should only have been regent. He regarded his mother's court as immoral and admired the Prussian court for its militaristic discipline. Between 1781 and 1782 he travelled in France, Italy, Austria and the low countries as Count of the North; he learned a great deal and liked the style of the Old Regime. In the long wait to ascend the throne he had occupied himself with a miniature kingdom at Gatchina where he had a private army of some 2,000 enlisted men and 130 officers. He ran and improved his estate while his devoted and loyal wife ran and improved Pavlovsk, but his mental weakness was known. Alexander Herzen was to call him 'Don Quixote with a crown'.[14]

For St Petersburg the first visible change was the surge of soldiery all over the city and the British ambassador thought the city had become Potsdam overnight. Soldiers wore tight Prussian uniforms and a civilian dress code was imposed: breeches and stockings, powdered wigs and special clothes for servants. Endless regulations were imposed and discontent soon spread because of the unpredictable nature of Paul's petty tyranny. His son Alexander observed it all in a letter in September 1797 to his tutor:

Everything has been turned upside down all at once, and that has only increased the confusion of affairs, which was already too great. The military waste almost all their time on parades. In other areas, there is no coherent plan. An order given today will be countermanded a month hence. . . . There is only one absolute power which does everything without rhyme or reason. . . . My poor country is in an indescribable state: the farmer harassed, commerce obstructed, liberty and

ABOVE Ignored by Catherine, Paul entertained himself by drilling troops at his favorite residence, Gatchina (1766–81) by Antonio Rinaldi, originally built for Prince Grigory Orlov.

personal welfare reduced to nothing. That is the picture of Russia; imagine what I suffer in my heart.[15]

This perceptive picture of the state of the nation almost suggests that there could be only one answer; today that would be called regime change.

Paul's ludicrous adoption of the Knights of Malta – a Catholic chivalric order with theatrical ceremonies – made him a laughing stock and revealed the level of his mental disturbance. His other passion was for building himself a castle-like residence in the city. He wanted to live in the fortress of the new Mikhailovsky Castle, disassociating himself from his mother's regime at the Winter Palace. In 1797 he burned down the Summer Palace and commissioned Brenna to replace it with his castle. It was surrounded by moats and drawbridges and was full of secret passages. The exterior was painted a dark red. The very appearance of the castle and the strange regimes that went on in it seemed to presage disaster and on 11 March 1801, just over a month after Paul had moved in, the plotters moved in and murdered Paul in his nightshirt in his sleeping quarters. The reign of Alexander had begun and the sad fantasy of Paul's reactionary reign had come to an abrupt end.

Paul's ideas and his mania were antithetical to the founding ideas of the city of St Petersburg and the openness of the city to enlightened thinking. Paul's reign almost prophesied the way the Romanov regime would end in 1917 by its remoteness from reality and wish to put a straitjacket of military order on a free city.

EMPIRE EXALTED:
ALEXANDRINE ST PETERSBURG

Alexander I was hailed as a saviour from the beginning, but his reign from 1801 to 1825 was in fact to be a struggle of ideas that affected the whole of Russian life. His upbringing gives a clue – he always had divided loyalties. Catherine the Great ensured he had a liberal education and provided him with a Swiss republican tutor. His father imbued him with an enthusiasm for the military life and Prussian values. Somehow he managed to be loyal to both, only reluctantly supporting the coup against his father because of his dismay at the confused state of his mind and the visible slow ruin of the nation. At the same time as he was willing to tackle the state of his country, part of him wanted to

abandon it all and live on the Rhine observing nature with his family. He could act almost any role and it was hard to know what he was thinking. Even Napoleon called him the 'sphinx of the north'. He was to try throughout his reign to introduce constitutional reforms and to encourage the freedom of the serfs and the rights of citizens, but he never quite succeeded – he lacked the backbone of a real reformer. He realized he had failed the people and fell back on his determination to defeat Napoleon, even then wavering between compromise and defeat until the trauma of invasion and the ultimate victory of 1812 at a terrible price.

Alexander's troubled reign still left him time and inclination to continue to build in the city and to do all he could to beautify it. He loved architecture and thought about his capital even when he was away on military campaigns. Like his enemy Napoleon, Alexander was to leave behind a style of building that bore his

ABOVE RIGHT Increasingly paranoid and security conscious, Paul demolished Elizabeth's Summer Palace to build his personal fortress, the Mikhailovsky Castle (1797–1800), where he was assassinated in his own bedroom.

name and defined the city in its Alexandrine Empire period. He started by using a group of architects early on in his reign – Adrian Zakharov, Thomas de Thomon and Andrei Voronikhin; after the Napoleonic war he encouraged the neo-classical empire style carried out to perfection in the city by Carlo Rossi, Vasily Stasov and Auguste Montferrand.

The great Kazan Cathedral on Nevsky Prospect was commissioned by Paul I from Voronikhin but it was completed in Alexander's reign, becoming the burial place of Marshal Kutuzov and a memorial to the heroes of the Napoleonic wars. It is a strange building – more Catholic than Orthodox, with its embracing colonnade so clearly derived from Bernini's colonnade for St Peter's in Rome. In Communist times it became the official Museum of Religion and Atheism.

On Vasilievsky Island Alexander commissioned the Mining Institute from Voronikhin – its design being modelled on the Temple of Poseidon at Paestum, and on the end of the island that surveys the city the 'strelka' Thomon built the Stock Exchange in the form of a great Doric temple, which he framed with a remarkable pair of giant red rostral columns, which blaze with flames on festive occasions. Alexander also completed the Admiralty using the architect Zakharov and created more gardens on the south side to enhance the city.

The victory over Napoleon inspired the city and Alexander saw the need to unify the centre and bring the parade squares closer in to the centre than the Field of Mars. In 1816 Alexander established the Committee for Buildings and Hydraulic Works, which commissioned the architect Carlo Rossi (1775–1849) to evolve a

ABOVE Built to house the miraculous icon of Our Lady of Kazan, the Cathedral of the Kazan Mother of God (1801–11) by Andrei Voronikhin adopted Bernini's great colonnade of St Peter's in Rome.

triumphant but disciplined neo-classical style for the city. Rossi had been trained by the architect Vincenzo Brenna and he had worked with him at Pavlovsk, Gatchina and the Mikhailovsky Castle. Many of the set pieces we see today are his work: he unified he Senate, Synod and various ministries, his *tour de force* being the General Staff Building and Palace Square. This created a new setting for the Winter Palace, a grand semi-circle of office buildings for the General Staff and a grand arch into Bolshaya Morskaya Street topped by a massive bronze sculpture of Victory in her chariot. Rossi was brilliant at creating an urban ensemble that unified the city and highlighted important building and monuments. In Palace Square he built the grand sweep of four-storey buildings on an elegant curve and in the centre of the square he placed the giant granite column designed by Montferrand topped by the thoughtful angel holding a cross. Rossi

also reorganized what is now called the Square of the Arts, and his Theatre Street is now justly named after the architect. His palace for the Grand Duke Mikhail Pavlovich, which is now the Russian Museum, is one of Rossi's best buildings and is now beautifully restored.

Outside the city Alexander asked Rossi to create a home for the Dowager Empress Maria Feodorovna on Yelagin Island. Her small palace is at the centre of a picturesque landscaped park raised on a high terrace and the park is filled with small pavilions housing the kitchens, a music pavilion and the elegant Imperial Flag Pavilion that looks down the Neva to greet the imperial yacht. Everything at Yelagin is by Rossi and his cool neo-classical interiors are superbly decorated – every detail down to the door handles received his meticulous attention. He was undoubtedly the master of precisely

ABOVE The Mikhailovsky Palace (1819–25), now the Russian Museum, was designed by Carlo Rossi, whose mastery of Alexandrine classicism would leave the most discernible mark on St Petersburg than any other single architect.

the right style for the time and he worked well into the next reign of Nicholas I. Rossi was still planning urban ensembles for St Petersburg when he died in 1849. He left a vast inheritance of well-planned, logical and elegant civic spaces which shaped the city we see today.

Rossi's work stood alongside the palaces of the old regime and gave a new setting for a more enlightened aristocracy to operate outside the court. The last years of Alexander's reign were to see the reaction between his own and his government's uncertain but conservative nationalism and the rise of the aristocratic and internationally influenced intelligentsia keen on more reform for the Russian nation. Once again the evolving city of St Petersburg was to be a crucible of changes. Architecturally we see today the settings that the rulers left behind at the end of the Napoleonic wars. Would Nicholas I, who succeeded his brother, continue to be inspired by architecture derived from classical antiquity and the West or would he take the road of Muscovite nationalism and try to create a new Russian style?

ABOVE Rossi's genius across St Petersburg. Left: the General Staff Building (1819–29). Centre: home of the Imperial Ballet, Theatre Street, which terminated at Rossi's Alexandrinsky Theatre (1828–32). Right: Rossi's first major imperial commission, the Yelagin Palace (1818–24).

In 1815 Alexander decided to rebuild the cathedral of St Isaac and, after a competition, the Committee decided to award the work to Ricard de Montferrand (1786–1858), who then faced the challenge that seemed to be facing Russia – how to fit an Orthodox cathedral into a classical mould. He decided on a Greek cross with a central dome, four subsidiary domes and porticoes on the long sides, each with a double row of columns. Gradually his design was modified and became heavier, until the building we see today – commissioned by Alexander and completed under the authoritarian Nicholas – represented the confusion of scale and the rise of eclecticism at the expense of classical purity. St Isaac's cathedral somehow conveys exactly the heavy uncertainty of the end of the Alexandrine period. It echoes the confusion of the imperial ideas in St Petersburg and the complexities to come.

CHAPTER 3:
THE BABYLON OF THE SNOWS

THE DECEMBRIST REVOLT

Dawn arrived late in the imperial capital, bringing with it low clouds and ashen skies. The day's quiet entrance barely affected the climate of the Russian December, which stubbornly held the temperature at 8 degrees below zero. On the streets a bitter and icy wind whipped down the grand allées of Peter's city and through the bare trees of the Summer Gardens, its marble inhabitants boxed and sheltered awaiting the warm breath of spring. St Petersburg awoke in the grip of anticipation. For two weeks since the death of Emperor Alexander I, Russia had remained without a tsar. On the morning of 14 December 1825, rumours had quickly spread throughout the city that a revolt had broken out to prevent the ascension to the throne of Alexander's brother Nicholas in an effort to bring reform to Russia and establish a constitutional monarchy. Thousands of Petersburgers, men and women, young and old alike, hurriedly dressed and, bracing themselves against the cold, took to the streets to bear witness to the approaching battle between the forces of change and the powers of tradition.

Just after 9am the first units of the rebellious Moskovsky Regiment began slowly filtering on to Senate Square. Crossing over the bare snow-covered plain; they gathered around Falconet's bronze horseman, a deeply symbolic monument whose meaning was not lost on the gathering mutineers. Mounted on an enormous monolith of red granite, which had taken six months and hundreds of labourers to put in place, stood the likeness of Peter the Great. The city's illustrious founder pointed westwards toward the future while rearing defiantly on his steed, crushing beneath him a serpent which many saw as representing the backward ways of Old Muscovy. By noon there were 3,000 soldiers gathered at the foot of the monument to await the arrival of their leaders and prevent the swearing of the oath by Nicholas's government. The revolt had begun.

News that Nicholas had sworn in the commanders of the Imperial Guard as well as the Imperial Senate and Holy Synod in the early hours before dawn had thrown the leadership of the revolt into panic. The appointed commander of the rebel forces, Prince Sergei Trubetskoi, had already fled, taking refuge in the Austrian

Snow on Decembrist Square, formerly Senate Square, where on 14 December 1825 troops gathered in revolt around the Bronze Horseman to attempt to end autocracy and usher in enlightened constitutional rule.

Embassy while, of the original group of conspirators, only Prince Eugene Oblensky, Alexander and Nikolai Bestuzhev and the poet Kondraty F. Ryleev arrived. Ryleev, upon realizing the hopelessness of the cause the evening before, had proclaimed 'I am certain that we shall suffer ruin, but our example will remain. We shall sacrifice ourselves for the freedom of the motherland!'[1]

Meanwhile, the imperial reaction began to take shape. Although the new Tsar Nicholas had learned of the plot two days earlier, he had waited for developments, fearing that beginning his reign with a series of arrests would make a bad impression.[2] Finally, when the evidence was beyond question, he sprang into action, gathering the commanders of his Imperial Guard before him. Just before they began their oath of allegiance, he declared 'After this, you shall answer to me with your heads for the tranquillity of the capital. As far as I am concerned, even if I shall be emperor for only one hour, I shall show myself worthy of the honour.'[3] Later, after he had the

full confidence and allegiance of the government, Nicholas then ordered troops and artillery to surround the square in preparation to crush the rebellion if need be.

On the square the situation was becoming tense. Freezing and unsure of their fate, the rebels grew restless, even firing their weapons indiscriminately. Entreaties by the Russian Orthodox Metropolitan of St Petersburg, as well as the Tsar's brother Grand Duke Mikhail Pavlovich, were greeted with jeers and insults. Events took a turn for the worse when the Governor of St Petersburg, General Mikhail Miloraovich, approached the soldiers to negotiate and was fatally wounded for his efforts. By 3pm Nicholas had arrived on the scene to take command. Thousands of onlookers filled the surrounding streets and pushed in behind the troops. Even the builders engaged in the construction of the massive St Issac's Cathedral halted their work and began to pelt the loyal troops with firewood. Nicholas began to try to disperse the crowds himself.

ABOVE Nicholas confronts the mutineers. *14 December 1825, in Senate Square* (1825), painting by Karl Collmann (Pushkin Memorial Museum, St Petersburg).

J.H. Schnitzler, a French journalist who witnessed the scene, reported that Nicholas quietly approached some onlookers and said 'Do me a favour to return home. You have nothing to do here.' The crowd respectfully fell back but compelled by curiosity returned, with one old woman declaring with satisfaction, 'He comes to ask us himself! And how politely too!'⁴

As dusk approached the Tsar began to recognize the volatility of the crowd and knew that time was running out. He ordered his cavalry to charge and disperse the rebels. Unfortunately Nicholas' cavalry was not prepared to charge on ice, as the horses had not been properly shod. Pandemonium ensued as the horseguards, sabres drawn, slid wildly on the ice, unable to gallop towards their targets. The rebels fired into them, wounding several who also, as it turned out, had not bothered to carry sharpened swords. Onlookers were sniggering and even began to throw stones. Soon it was discovered that loyal soldiers had begun to defect to the rebels. Furious, Nicholas' commanders begged him to turn the artillery on the mutinous troops. General K.F. Toll pleaded 'Grapeshot is what they want! . . . The only way to put an end to this is to turn the cannon on this rabble.'⁵ The new Tsar demurred, unsure of what to do. Toll then said 'Your Majesty, either let us clear the square with gunfire or abdicate.'⁶ The Emperor's aide-de-camp, Prince Ilarion Vasilchikov, concurred, fearing that events were swiftly getting out of their control and that soon all would be lost. He said to Nicholas 'Sir, there is not a moment to lose. You must give the order to fire!' to which Nicholas asked 'Do you wish me to shed the blood of my subjects on the first day of my reign?'⁷ Vasilchikov replied, 'Yes sire, to save your empire.'⁸

After once more refusing to lay down their weapons, Nicholas acquiesced and ordered the cannons brought forward and filled with canister shot. The first volley was fired above the rebels' heads, its hot projectiles becoming embedded in the plaster of the senate buildings across the square and shattering its windows. The second blast was aimed directly into the centre of the rebel force. The thunderous fusillade exploded toward the mutineers, hurtling metal shot into the soldiers and the crowds beyond. A huge hole opened in their ranks as men and body parts fell to the ground, turning the white snow red with blood. All order collapsed as the mutineers fled in complete chaos towards the senate buildings and towards the iced-over Neva. Bystanders became swept up in the panic as hundreds fled down Galernaya Street. The cannons fired directly down the length of the street killing soldiers and civilians alike. Rebel officer Mikhail Bestizhev attempted to rally soldiers crossing the Neva to attack the Peter and Paul Fortress. However, artillery placed across the river began punching holes into the river's frozen surface throwing terrified soldiers into the freezing black water where they were sucked beneath the ice. Those that could escaped and retreated to the Academy of Fine Arts but soon it was every man for himself. The revolt was over. As the blood froze on Senate Square and twilight descended on the city a new era had begun. Nicholas I stood triumphant as Tsar and Autocrat of all the Russias, unbowed by the forces of change, his will was law.

'The poor soldiers seem to have been entirely misled by their officers,' wrote Charlotte Disbrowe, wife of the British Ambassador two days later:

> . . . soon [the soldiers] returned to duty. They have received a general pardon; but of course a similar clemency could not be extended those who conducted them and excited them to revolt, and a great many officers are arrested; I am told upwards of thirty.
>
> We are all in colours again during three days to cheer the accession of the Emperor Nicholas and his charming Empress Alexandrine . . . I grieve that he had such a sad inauguration on Monday . . . It put an end to all the rejoicings; no illuminations nor public ceremonies. However, I trust that all is at an end, and everything will go on quietly. I went out in a *traineau* for the first time today. The town presented a curious spectacle. The traces of the sad event on Monday were horrid; pools of blood on the snow, and spattered up against the houses; the Senate House is dreadfully battered.⁹

In the days and weeks following what history would remember as the Decembrist Revolt, Nicholas swiftly ordered the arrest of all suspected conspirators. He personally interrogated the leaders of the revolt and saw to the details of the specifics of the confinement of many others. The dungeons of the Peter and Paul Fortress overflowed with prisoners. Depending on their level of resistance prisoners were either treated to comfortable confinement or solitary imprisonment in the squalid cells of the dungeon.¹⁰ Peter's great fortress, the foundation of his Westward-looking ambitions, had become the cornerstone of the repressive autocratic state.

The five lead conspirators – Kondraty Ryleev, Peter Kakhovsky, Mikhail Bestuzhev-Rumin, Sergei Muraviev-Apostol and Pavel Pestel – were all condemned to death by hanging, a sentence reduced from decapitation due to the intervention of Nicholas.[11] The evening following the executions, Prince Kochubey gave a ball to lighten the mood of the brooding elite. As they celebrated the ascension of the new Tsar and toasted the success of his reign, an ominous spectacle passed beneath the windows of the palace. Over a hundred officers sentenced to exile were departing for their long and arduous journey to the icy wastes of Siberia. With them travelled their wives who, in defiance of the sentence, wore their ball gowns and jewels to compliment the chains and rags of their husbands.[12] As this procession of the condemned went slowly by, spectators above watched as their former friends, cousins and comrades passed into the night and, with them, Russia's first chance at liberty.

Although the door was shut for St Petersburg's elite to express themselves in the political arena, the St Petersburg ideal would remain alive. Upon founding the city and his new empire, Peter sought to take the best of Europe and put it to use to make Russia greater. While the reign of Nicholas I saw a reversal of this ideal with regards to politics and government, the continuing stream of ideas and influences coming from the West – carried by foreigners, Russian expatriates and tourists – sparked a new glittering age of cultural achievements that would once again establish St Petersburg as the focus for the aspirations of the nation. Alexander Pushkin, Nikolai Gogol, Mikhail Glinka and Karl Briullov set the tone of this cultural revolution and would pass the torch to heirs such as Fyodor Dostoyevsky, Peter Tchaikovsky, Modest Mussorgsky and Ilya Repin, who would honour and expand this legacy as St Petersburg and Russia entered the industrial age.

Onegin's Day: the St Petersburg of Alexander Pushkin

The news of the Decembrist Revolt and its subsequent failure reached the poet Alexander Pushkin at his parents' estate in Mikhailovskoe near Pskov, where he had been serving out a period of exile. Fearing that he might be implicated in the conspiracy Pushkin quickly burned all of his biographical notes pertaining to his knowledge of the condemned and their early activities. The words of Pushkin's 1817 sonnet 'Ode to Liberty' had been an anthem of the Decembrists, with its rebuke and warning to the monarchy:

And now know this, O Tsars:
Neither punishments nor rewards
Nor prison bars or altars
Will protect you any more.
Be the first to bow your heads
To the trustworthy force of the Law,
And then the eternal defender of your throne
Will be the peace and liberty of the people.

Pushkin was well acquainted and even close friends with several of the conspirators with whom he had attended school, as well as being a member of the Green Lamp, a theatrical-literary secret society whose members not only debated politics but also specialized in gambling, drinking and whoring.[13] As Pushkin awaited his imagined fate following the revolt, he longed to return once more to the capital. The St Petersburg of his youth had been an endless series of card parties, glittering balls, theatrical performances, dalliances and even duels. Peter's city had enchanted him, fashioned his character and still haunted his soul. In 1823, in exile on his estate, Pushkin began to distil his biographical reminiscences into an epic new work. A novel in verse, *Eugene Onegin*, when complete a decade later, would capture the essence of life in the early-nineteenth-century imperial capital. It was a city of parade, fashion and glamour. It was the St Petersburg of Pushkin.

Born in 1799, Pushkin was the scion of one of Russia's oldest and illustrious noble families. His father's ancestors had signed the petition electing the first Romanov, Mikhail I, Tsar in 1613, while on his mother's side he was a direct descendant of Abram Hannibal, the African servant of Tsar Peter I who was later immortalized by Pushkin in *The Blackamoor of Peter the Great*. Pushkin attended the renowned imperial lycée founded by Alexander I to educate the sons of the elite, but proved to be a mischievous and poor student in all subjects, with the exceptions of French and Russian literature and fencing.[14] Although he showed little aptitude for study, there were those that recognized his genius. At the final examination of his junior course, Gavriil Romanovich Derzhavin, poet extraordinaire of Catherine's reign, was so impressed by his *Recollections of Tsarskoe Selo* that he had wanted to embrace him. However, the young Pushkin, too overwhelmed by the honour, had already fled.[15] Pushkin's work also found its way into the hands of Vasily Zhukovsky, poet laureate of Alexandrine Russia. Zhukovsky took the young Pushkin under his wing, encouraging him in his

Pushkin's desk. The ultimate Russian dandy, Pushkin's decadence and domestic disarray belied the literary giant he was to become.

Some days he's still in bed, and drowses,
When little notes come on a tray
What? Invitations? Yes, three houses
Have each asked him to a soirée:
A ball here, there's a children's party;
Where shall he go, my rogue, my hearty?
Which comes first? It's just the same –
To do them all is easy game.
Meanwhile attired for morning strolling
Complete with broad brimmed Bolivar,
Eugene attends the boulevard,
And there at large he goes patrolling
Until Bréguet unsleeping chime
Advises him of dinner time.[17]

work and becoming his mentor. Although not blind to the youth's faults, Zhukovsky wholeheartedly believed in Pushkin's unequivocal promise. In a letter to his friend Prince Vyazemsky, Zhukovsky flattered the young poet while recognizing that he was all too human. Pushkin, he explained, 'is the hope of our literature. I fear only lest he, imagining himself mature, should prevent himself from becoming so. We should unite in order to help grow this future giant, who will outgrow us all.'[16]

Pushkin graduated from the lycée in 1817 with a commission in the Ministry of Foreign Affairs as a collegial secretary. Together with six other graduates, Pushkin made the journey to the capital to take his place in society and make a name for himself. St Petersburg seemed to the young Pushkin as a world of boundless freedom after his long years of adolescence in Tsarskoe Selo. He set himself up at his mother's spacious apartment in the unfashionable Kolomna district, where he lived in baroque squalor surrounded by antiques, books, filth and drunken servants. He existed not unlike many idle sons of the nineteenth-century Russian or even European aristocracy, living above his means and experiencing his first taste of independence. From the beginning, Pushkin was less than diligent about his official post. After his initial presentation to the Foreign Minister, Count Nesselrode, he showed little interest in his work and instead immersed himself in the intellectual, cultural and corporeal pleasures of the city, behaving in the manner befitting his ultimate and semi-autobiographical hero *Eugene Onegin*.

Pushkin rose late and would often begin the day with a stroll up and down 'the boulevard', a tree-lined section of the Nevsky Prospect between the Fontanka and Moika Canals, which was popular with the upper classes. He was easily identified by his distinctive style of dress, with his wide 'Bolivar' hat and long black cloak draped around him in 'the American style'. He supped at Talon's restaurant on the Nevsky Prospect in the afternoon, drinking cold champagne with friends and local courtesans. An arrant snob, he mixed with the elite of society in public yet often caroused in the lowest of establishments with whores and rakes. Pushkin's talent as a poet and man about town made him an instant celebrity, but his often boorish behaviour marked him as a target for gossip. Pushkin's neighbour Korff remarked:

It is astonishing how his health and his very talent could withstand such a way of life, with which were naturally associated frequent venereal sicknesses, bringing him at times to the brink of the grave . . . Eternally without a kopeck, eternally in debt, sometimes even without a decent frock coat, with endless scandals, frequent duels, closely acquainted with every tavern-keeper, whore and trollop, Pushkin represented a type of the filthiest depravity.[18]

While Pushkin revelled in the carnal delights of the St Petersburg he also enjoyed participating in the more sophisticated social pleasures that the capital had to offer. Pushkin was a frequent

ABOVE Pushkin's St Petersburg: *Admiralty and the Palace Square viewed from the Vasilievsky Island* (1817), painting by F.Y. Alexyev (State Russian Museum, St Petersburg).
RIGHT Pushkin's portrait still surveys the scene in his salon overlooking the Moika.

the curtain had risen and the spectacle began, Pushkin had little patience for poor staging or acting and gained a reputation for catcalling and talking loudly during the performance. Pushkin's boorish manner in public as well as his scathing wit often landed him in duels, a unfortunate habit which would eventually lead to his death in 1837.

> Up to the porch our hero's driven;
> In, past concierge, up marble stair
> Flown like an arrow, then he's given
> A deft arrangement to his hair,
> And entered. Ballroom overflowing . . .
> And band already tired of blowing,
> While mazurka holds the crowd;
> And everything is cramped and loud;
> Spurs of the Chevalier Guards are clinking,
> Dear ladies' feet fly past like hail,
> And on their captivating trail
> Incendiary looks are slinking,
> While roar of violins contrives
> To drown the hiss of modish wives.[19]

The social whirl of St Petersburg, with its endless succession of balls and parties, offered an infinite number of potential amorous infatuations and occupied a great deal of the young Pushkin's life, yet still he managed to find time to write. He frequented the 'garret' of Prince Shakhovsky, the repertoire director of several of the capital's theatres and *grand seigneur* of the cream of Bohemian St Petersburg, where Pushkin wooed several actresses and composed love poetry for them. He also gained entrance into the leading literary salons of the day where his poetry was widely celebrated. Yet it was through his association with the secret society known as the Green Lamp that he found true kindred spirits who shared his love of politics, women and especially gambling. Pushkin, a compulsive gambler throughout his life, was forever in debt, often forced to resort to borrowing from moneylenders or even wagering his manuscripts.[20]

In St Petersburg Pushkin's poetry was driven by his almost constant infatuations and love affairs with women as well as the growing political discourse which dominated the conversation of the circles in which he moved. While his love prose gained the attention of countless female admirers, his political verse earned him the attention of the authorities. Pushkin's antics and

attendant of many St Petersburg's theatres, which were among the best places to observe and be observed by the city's elite. The locus of this activity was the Bolshoi Theatre on Theatre Square, which held the distinction of being the largest theatre in Europe at the time and was the centre of Russian Opera and Ballet. Once he had arrived for the evening's entertainment, which included either a ballet and a comedy or an opera and a tragedy, Pushkin amused his noble friends by mixing in the orchestra with the cream of the Russian military before taking his proper place in the stalls. After

TOP *High Society Salon* (1830s), watercolour by an unknown artist (Pushkin Memorial Museum, St Petersburg).
ABOVE *Ball Given by Princess M.F. Baryatinsky* (1830s), watercolour by G.G. Gagarin (State Russian Museum, St Petersburg).

subversive work had even reached the ears of Tsar Alexander, who had at first wanted to send him to Siberia but, on the advice of several of Pushkin's allies, showed clemency and gave him a commission which sent the wayward poet to the south and away from St Petersburg. As he departed for Kishinev in 1820 his first novel in verse was published, *Ruslan and Ludmila*, which sold out instantly.

For four years Pushkin travelled through Moldova, the Caucasus and Crimea and lived for periods of time in Kishinev and Odessa. His commission ended in scandal after an affair with Countess Vorontsov, for which he was then exiled to his parents' estate Mikhailovskoe. These years of exile from St Petersburg were among his most productive. He wrote *The Gypsies*, *Boris Godunov* and began his masterpiece, *Eugene Onegin*. News of the Decembrist Revolt alarmed Pushkin, despite the fact that he was considered a political lightweight by his colleagues; although they enjoyed his political poetry, they would not have trusted him with conspiratorial knowledge.[21]

Ever the opportunist, he also saw the ascension of the new Tsar as a chance to end his long exile from St Petersburg. He dispatched a letter to his mentor Zhukovsky, along with a letter for Nicholas requesting a review of his circumstances.

Tsar Nicholas I, having read his letter, summoned Pushkin to Moscow in August 1827 in order finally to meet Russia's greatest poet. Through this meeting the Tsar wished to placate the fears of Russia's educated elite and mend some of the damage done after the repression of the Decembrists. Their meeting lasted over an hour, during which the story goes that Nicholas asked him if he would have stood with the rebels. Pushkin replied 'I certainly would have, Your Majesty. All of my friends were in on the conspiracy and I could not have stayed out of it. It was my absence that saved me, for which I thank God.'[22] Nicholas then told Pushkin 'You have been foolish long enough. I hope you will be more sensible after this and there will be no more quarrels between us. You will send everything you write to me. From now on I will be your censor.' After their long conversation was over Nicholas led Pushkin out and exclaimed to his attendants 'Gentlemen here is the new Pushkin for you. Let us forget about the old.'[23] Released from his exile, Pushkin spent two months in Moscow participating in the coronation celebrations and re-establishing himself in society. Soon afterwards he left for St Petersburg. After an absence of six years, Pushkin was finally home.

THE ASCENSION OF THE DRILLMASTER

The St Petersburg that Pushkin returned to was in the midst of transition. The Tsar had been alarmed and dismayed by the events of the Decembrist Revolt and had placed the blame squarely on the destructive Western influences favoured by his brother Alexander I and grandmother Catherine the Great. Nicholas sought to reinforce the system of autocracy, which he believed had fallen prey to his predecessors' desire to justify their power. There was no need for him to justify his rule: autocracy ordained by divine right was an absolute, requiring neither defence nor explanation.[24] His first moves as Tsar were aimed at ending the attempts of the educated elite to participate in the governing of the empire.[25] Within six months he had set up the soon infamous Third Section of His Majesty's Own Chancellery, which would act with his full confidence as his ideological and political secret police. The Section's powers were so vague and its purview so inchoate that a story arose claiming that Nicholas, upon setting up the section, handed its chief, Count Benkendorff, a handkerchief and said 'Here are your orders. Take this and wipe away the tears of my people.'[26]

Nicholas soon went on a campaign against the forces of sedition. He began by passing the 'cast-iron statutes' of 1826, strengthening censorship within Russia, even going so far as to edit the works of Pushkin, much to the poet's constant chagrin. Fearing infection of the masses by Western ideas, Nicholas began to restrict access to higher education both within Russia and in Europe. Students were refused visas to travel abroad for study as many returned 'with a spirit of criticism'.[27] The Tsar's advisors saw danger in private tutoring for Russia's gentry and suggested setting up a system of Cadet Academies to instil 'unswerving loyalty to the autocracy in the minds of Russia's younger generation'.[28] Western books were further restricted and immigration was heavily curtailed. At the universities, faculty autonomy was limited, liberal arts departments were reduced and subjects such as philosophy were banned. In 1833, the theory of the 'Nicholas System' of government was articulated in what became known as the 'trinity' of orthodoxy, autocracy and nationality.

As the capital of the Russian Empire, St Petersburg was inextricably linked to the power and personality of the tsars, who created and shaped its destiny as well as its physical appearance. Zhukovsky once exclaimed that Petersburgers were 'mummies surrounded by majestic pyramids, whose grandeur exists not for them'.[29] Under Nicholas there was no exception to this.

Architecture, as all else, was used to serve the state. Throughout his reign Nicholas continued the physical embellishment of the city with the construction of monumental classical structures, which proclaimed the primacy of the state and the might of the autocracy. The Customs House, the Moscow and Narva Gates, the Alexander Column, the Alexandrinsky Theatre and Rossi Street ensemble, the Senate and Holy Synod buildings, the Cathedrals of the Transfiguration and of the Trinity, the New Hermitage and the Mariinsky Palace, as well as completion of the General Staff Building and St Isaac's Cathedral, were built and finished for the most part during his reign. These structures served to be a considerable contribution to the modern appearance of the city.

The character of St Petersburg drastically changed with the ascension of Nicholas. He mobilized armies of civil servants, clerks and copyists to administer his domain. The city became a great hive of the bureaucracy of empire. Thousands entered the civil service, swelling the city's population to nearly half a million. These worker bees filled the lower end of the Table of Ranks, whose structure governed the imperial hierarchy, assigning duties and even dress codes. The city streets filled with uniformed government workers moving to and from the great edifices of state, beyond whose noble façades lay a dark warren of offices, canyons of files and mountains of paperwork. Soon this mass of administrative drones caused the channels of power to grow sclerotic, creating a bureaucratic logjam that caused interminable delays. Nicholas himself found that his commands and edicts became drowned in seas of red tape and often had to wait months for responses to his requests. His success was characterized by Pushkin's friend Prince Vyazemsky: 'Straight, correct, evened out, symmetrical, monotonous and complete, St Petersburg can serve as an emblem of our life. . . . In people you can't tell Ivan from Peter; in time, today from tomorrow: everything is the same.'[30]

THE BRONZE HORSEMAN

Pushkin's initial elation at returning to his beloved St Petersburg soon grew cool. Although he took up once again the distractions of his youth, he recognized that the capital no longer stood for the ideals espoused by the philosophers and salons of the eighteenth century, but that a new era had dawned. Peter's city, which had offered so much promise to Russia by bringing in Western ideas, was rapidly becoming the symbol of autocratic rule. Pushkin's own relations with Nicholas were becoming strained as the Tsar's pen

LEFT Imperial Eagles and iron spears stand guard beneath the Alexander Column in Palace Square; military pageantry and symbolism were a trademark of the reign of Nicholas I. OVERLEAF Aerial view of Palace Square, the heart of imperial St Petersburg.

often sought to take the heart out of his works. During the 1830s he became torn between his patriotic admiration of the monarchy and empire and his longing for freedom and the lost ideals of his youth. This internal conflict spread to his vision of St Petersburg, whose illustrious monuments began to cast dark shadows over his beloved city. This juxtaposition of reverence and defiance produced in 1833 what was considered Pushkin's greatest masterpiece and most celebrated work of homage to St Petersburg: *A Petersburg Tale*, better known as *The Bronze Horseman*.

The poem begins on the marshy shores of the Neva, with a description of the founding of the city by Peter the Great, who declares his ambition to 'strike terror in the Swede' by cutting a 'window through on Europe' and taking to the seas. From out of the 'gloomy wood and swamp' rises a great city 'in pride and splendour blazing' for the world to see. The tamed Neva becomes lined with palaces, its granite quays loaded with goods and its wide girth spanned by bridges. Peter's city has surpassed Holy Moscow, 'a dowager in purple', who bows before St Petersburg 'an empress newly crowned'. Pushkin declares his love for the city with its 'harmonies austere', its 'meditative gloom', its white nights and brutal winters, military spectacles and festive balls. He rounds out this ode with an exhortation: 'Now city of Peter stand thou fast, Foursquare like Russia; vaunt thy splendour! Let not nature, the waves or floods disturb Peter's sleep.' However this triumphant call is undercut by the introduction to Part Two, in which Pushkin gloomily laments 'Sad will be my tale.'

Part Two is the story of Evgeny, a lowly civil servant from the Kolomna district, who 'cared not of forebears dead and rotten, or antique matters long forgotten' but of his miserable poverty and his dreams of advancement. Outside a storm is ranging which has caused his separation from his beloved Parasha on the other side of the Neva. The next day the city awakens to a terrible flood. The city, half submerged, finds boats breaking through windows and wreckage everywhere, as the contents of homes and shops go floating down the streets. Coffins are lifted from their graves and sail past while the populace awaits its grim fate. Amid all this Evgeny sits upon a marble lion oblivious to the wind and rain and worries for Parasha across the Neva. From his perch he can see Falconet's statue of Peter the Great, *The Bronze Horseman*. When the waters subside Evgeny searches in vain for Parasha's house, which has been swept away by the raging waters. In despair and madness he wanders through the apocalyptic landscape of the post-flood city. Once again he encounters the bronze

TOP *Senate Square on a Winter Night* (1871), painting by Vasily Surikov (State Russian Museum, St Petersburg).
ABOVE *Bolshoi Theatre Square on 7 November 1824*, painting by Fyodor Alexeyev (Pushkin Memorial Museum, St Petersburg).

horseman, 'his arm flung wide', coldly sitting upon his steed. In his desperation Evgeny blames his pathetic state upon the Tsar founder, waving his fist and cursing it. The horseman suddenly comes alive and pursues Evgeny through the streets. Terrified, Evgeny is unable to escape the 'thunders that rattle in chorus, a gallop ponderous, sonorous, that shakes the pavement'. Later, Parasha's house is discovered floating in the Neva and Evgeny's body is found cold and lifeless upon its threshold.

This epic poem, romantic in style, inaugurated a literary tradition of works based on a new vision of St Petersburg. It would become among the most studied works of Russian literature and its meanings are still debated to this day. What made in unique was the fact that in Russia, before *The Bronze Horseman*, only praise was heaped upon Peter's creation and the monuments of his predecessors. Pushkin, however, while himself nodding to the adulatory literary tradition of the eighteenth century, boldly leapt into the future for

the first time, revealing the darker aspects of the city's character with its historical as well as human cost. Pushkin sensed an opportunity missed by Nicholas I to move the empire forward and witnessed instead an entrenchment of power and the growth of a bureaucracy which based its power on the beliefs of Old Russia and Moscow rather than the vision of Peter the Great. In *The Bronze Horseman* Pushkin had tapped into the growing sense of oppression and doom that would grip the culture of St Petersburg well into the next century.

Nicholas I was understandably alarmed by the poem's content and requested substantial cuts and revisions. Pushkin, although desperately short of money, refused. The consequences of this decision struck deeper as it meant he was unable to bring out another work in order to shore up his waning reputation, which was under scrutiny from the younger generation of writers and critics coming on to the literary scene.[31] Although during the last

Following his fateful duel, the mortally wounded Pushkin was returned to his appartment on the Moika, where he died two days later. Today the appartment houses the Pushkin Memorial Museum.

three years of his life Pushkin completed such works as *History of Pugachev*, *The Golden Cockerel* and *The Captain's Daughter*, he was clearly demoralized as the cycle of gambling, debt and scandal continued to hound him. Pushkin had married Natalia Goncharova, whose beauty and social status made her the object of several amorous advances, including those of Nicholas I himself. Pushkin, driven to distraction by one particular suitor, Baron Georges d'Anthés, demanded satisfaction. In January 1837 he met the Baron just outside the city near the Black River. Pushkin was mortally wounded in the duel and died at his flat at 12 Moika two days later.

Pushkin's death caused an unanticipated eruption of public grief, which overtook the city.

> All of St Petersburg is astir. There is an extraordinary commotion. At the Singer's Bridge on the Moika near his home, no one could walk or ride. Crowds and carriages besieged the house from morn to dusk. Cabdrivers all over the city were told simply, 'To Pushkin' and that was enough. It seemed that everyone, including those who could not read or write, considered it their duty to pay their last respects to the body of the poet.[32]

Thousands of Petersburgers filed through the poet's flat during the two days his body was available for viewing. There were so many that a wall had to be torn down to make way for them.[33] The spontaneous outpouring of public emotion alarmed the authorities, who attempted to limit the crowds by moving the services from St Isaac's to the small Konnyushennaya Church. Still the multitudes came, flooding the church after the official service and even taking souvenir clippings of Pushkin's hair and clothing.[34] Finally the poet bade his final farewell to St Petersburg; his remains were spirited out of the city in the middle of the night bound for his family estate, his final resting place.

Pushkin's death and the public's reaction sent shudders through the autocratic underpinnings of St Petersburg and fuelled the resentment of the capital's intelligentsia. Prince Odoevsky, in the literary supplement of the *Russian Invalid*, proclaimed the country's lament:

> The sun of our poetry has set. Pushkin has died, died in the flower of his years, in the middle of his career! . . . Every Russian heart knows the whole value of this irrevocable loss

and every Russian heart will be lacerated. Pushkin! Our poet, our joy, the glory of our people! Can it be that Pushkin is no longer with us?[35]

The young Mikhail Lermontov, in reaction to the poet's tragic end, penned the poem 'Death of a Poet', which became a smouldering indictment of the government's and the elite's complicity in the censuring of Pushkin's writings as well as his untimely death.

> Come be content, then – such a refinement
> Of pain was more then he could bear.
> The lamp of genius is no longer shining,
> The laurel wreath is fading now and sear.

Lermontov, having inspired the wrath of the nobility and the Tsar, was arrested and exiled to the Caucasus. He would be pardoned a year later and return to St Petersburg to pen his greatest work *A Hero for Our Time*. Lermontov, in a tragic coincidence, would meet the same fate as Pushkin in 1841 at the age of twenty-seven, when he was felled by a duellist's bullet during his second exile in the Caucusus.

SHADOWS FALL:
THE ST PETERSBURG OF NIKOLAI GOGOL

'All the joy of my life, all my highest joy is gone with him. . . . I never did anything without seeking his advice. I never wrote a line without imagining him in front of me.'[36] Nikolai Gogol wrote these lines upon hearing of the death of Pushkin, his mentor and friend. Pushkin had taken the young Gogol under his wing upon his arrival in St Petersburg in 1828 and they had maintained a close relationship until the end of the great poet's life. They were an odd couple: the witty, urbane romantic and the awkward, ambitious provincial. However, Pushkin saw something in Gogol and took care to encourage him in his endeavours. Perhaps he presaged a glimmer of the young man's potential, yet little did he know that Gogol's experience and writing would profoundly change the image of St Petersburg and influence a generation of writers in his wake.

Gogol was born and raised in Ukraine in the province of Poltava near the site of Peter the Great's decisive victory over Charles XII of Sweden. As a youth he dreamt of St Petersburg, convinced that he would make his name and fortune in the glamorous capital. He arrived in the city aged nineteen and wandered in awe down its

'The sun of our poetry has set!' cried the announcement of Pushkin's tragic death. This solemn obelisk marks the spot of the duel on the Black River.

МЕСТО ДУЭЛИ

А.С.ПУШКИНА

wide boulevards and through its vast squares. He was also amazed by the variety of life that surrounded him. It seemed to him an entire village lived in his apartment block, which he described in a letter home:

> The house in which I live contains two tailors, one *marchand de mode*, a shoemaker, a hosiery manufacturer, a repairer of broken dishes, a plasterer and house painter, a pastry shop, a notions shop, a cold storage for winter clothing, a tobacco shop, and finally, a midwife for the privileged. . . . I live on the fourth floor.[37]

Determined to begin his brilliant career he plunged into a succession of jobs. After being turned away from the imperial theatre, he switched to painting and, having little luck with that, he decided to join the government service and worked briefly as a low-level clerk. Finally he landed a position teaching history at the Patriotic Institute and supplemented his income with private tutoring until 1834, when Pushkin helped him secure a professorship of medieval history at the University of St Petersburg. At every one of these jobs Gogol was a failure. Highly strung, secretive, selfish and devious, he hardly endeared himself to many and soon became bitter and disillusioned with his life. He poured his vitriol into his writing which he practised throughout his various careers, yet he reserved his most searing hatred for one special target, the object of his desire which promised so much and delivered so little, St Petersburg.

'The idea of the city is emptiness taken to the highest degree,'[38] wrote Gogol, reflecting on urban life. Where once he saw a glittering city of opportunity, he now saw an oppressive maze of dark streets and barren wastes, which rewarded the callous and punished the pure. In Gogol's vision, St Petersburg, with all its apparent order and symmetry, obscured a seething underbelly of chaos and evil. He began to paint a portrait of a sinister world shrouded in mist and shadow, which hid a host of demonic and perverse characters. Gogol composed several short stories, often referred to as the *St Petersburg Tales*, that encapsulated his feelings about the capital he had grown to fear and loathe. These were *Nevsky Prospect* (1835), *The Diary of a Madman* (1835), *The Nose* (1836), *The Portrait* (1842) and his most revered work, *The Overcoat* (1842).

For the first of these stories Gogol chose St Petersburg's grand avenue, the Nevsky Prospect, as his venerable target. By the mid-nineteenth century the city's great thoroughfare was lined with churches and shops. Every major Christian denomination was represented and almost any desirable goods could be had behind the glass fronts of its numerous stores. The upper Nevsky contained such magnificent establishments as the English Magazine department store, Cabussue's gloves, Brocard's perfumerie and Gamb's furniture emporium,[39] while further down bookshops, patisseries and tearooms proliferated. Gogol begins his story cataloguing the various groups of people who paraded daily up and down the Nevsky, starting with peasants in the early morning and followed by civil servants and later nannies and tutors with their charges. By noon the Nevsky became the domain of the *beau monde*, with officers and government officials walking and riding alongside the *grande dames* of the aristocracy and the beauties of high society. After 3pm once again civil servants crammed the street returning from work.

By 4pm the Nevsky emptied, shops closed and twilight set in. The gas lamps were lit and the street became filled with 'an alluring, magic light'. The Nevsky was given over to unfortunates and groups of 'bachelors' young and old, vying for the attentions of the rouged ladies of the evening. This is where Gogol begins his story of a young and naïve artist who pursues a young lady only to find that she is a prostitute. In despair the artist refuses to see the reality of his obsession and retreats into madness and ultimately commits suicide. A parallel story follows the misadventure of Lieutenant Pirogov, who mistakenly pursues a married woman he believes is a prostitute. Undeterred by the discovery of the truth he continues his pursuit despite the protestations of the woman's husband. Finally Pirogov steals a kiss and is collared by the husband and his friends. The lieutenant, without recognizing his crime, threatens to report them but soon forgets about the whole episode and goes on carousing once again. Gogol as a final warning beseeches his readers:

> Oh do not trust that Nevsky Avenue! I always wrap myself up more closely in my cloak when I walk along it and do my best not to look at the things I pass . . . everything is full of deceit. It lies at all times, does Nevsky Avenue, but most of all when night hovers over it in a thick mass, picking out the white from the dun-coloured houses, and all the town thunders and blazes with lights, and thousands of carriages come driving from the bridges, the outriders shouting and

While Pushkin celebrated the majesty of St Petersburg, Gogol found its vast squares and boulevards sinister and alienating.

himself, discovers an unfinished portrait at the Shtchukinui Market and takes it home. That night the portrait comes alive and reveals a hidden cache of gold. The artist then goes about using the money to create a reputation and establishes himself as a fashionable portrait artist, abandoning his intention to be a serious painter in exchange for wealth and fame. Through this decision he is scorned by his fellow artists as a sell out. In the end Chartkov has an epiphany and tries to reclaim his lost abilities. However he finds that his talent is irrevocably lost due to his greed. Haunted by the mysterious portrait he is finally driven to madness and ultimately death.

In these first four of the *St Petersburg Tales*, the majority of Gogol's characters become psychologically deranged as a result of their exposure to the toxic and soul-crushing atmosphere of the city. It is in Gogol's final story, however, and arguably his masterpiece, *The Overcoat*, that St Petersburg itself becomes a force which seeks to harry its defenceless victim. It is the story of Akaky Akakievich, a middle aged copyist in an anonymous government department. Akaky, whose name translates into a vulgar word for excrement, is contented with his work, his tiny apartment and his life. It is not until he requires a new overcoat that his life suddenly takes a dark turn. After ordering a new coat from his neighbour, a tailor who acts as a metaphor for the devil, complete with cloven hoof, Akaky abandons himself to desire, fantasizing about the new overcoat as if it were a new wife, someone to depend upon for the rest of his life. Inevitably disaster strikes. Coming home from a party, an activity entirely out of character, Akaky is mugged in a vast empty St Petersburg square and his new overcoat is stolen. In desperation he seeks the help of the authorities where he encounters a self-important official who berates him for disturbing him with such a trivial matter. Devastated, Akaky is forced to walk home without a coat through the city streets, pelted by snow and barraged by winds, which blow from every direction and down every side street. He stumbles home, falls deathly ill and in a sputter of obscenities and delirium 'gives up the ghost'. Akaky's death occurs unnoticed by the city, until rumours begin to circulate of a ghost searching for a lost overcoat.

jogging up and down on their horses, and when the devil himself lights the street lamps top show everything in anything but its true colours.[40]

Gogol followed *Nevsky Prospect* with *The Diary of a Madman*, *The Nose* and *The Portrait*, which all showed him at his most fantastic when dealing with the subject of life in St Petersburg. In these short stories his characters reflected the disillusionment Gogol felt at not being accepted by the city's cultural elite, as well as his repeated failures to achieve the fame he so craved. In *The Diary of a Madman*, the main character Poprishchin, a government clerk, is subjected to humiliation and rejection at the hands of his employer, a government official, as well as the official's daughter, with whom he has fallen in love. Gradually Poprischin succumbs to insanity, experiencing delusions of grandeur eventually imagining himself to be the King of Spain. In *The Nose*, the hapless hero Kovalev awakes to find that his nose has disappeared and is parading around town. He discovers it praying in the Kazan Cathedral dressed as a state councillor in a uniform adorned with gold braid, a station high above its owner's rank! Kovalev, humiliated and without his nose, must report his loss to the unsympathetic police and press before he recovers his errant proboscis as well as his dignity.

While *The Diary of a Madman* and *The Nose* were rather light-hearted in their approach, the last story of the three, *The Portrait*, written later, reveals a rather baleful vision of St Petersburg. In this tale, Gogol tells of shallowness and avarice in the search of fame. A poor and promising young artist, Chartkov, who longs to make a name for

Gogol's *St Petersburg Tales* were not simply a personal condemnation of the imperial capital; through his writing he gave voice to those lost in the crowds, hallways and alleyways of the city, the faceless masses growing year by year to fuel the machinery of government. Gogol also voiced the growing unease with the St Petersburg ideal, further articulated by the nascent Slavophile

ABOVE *Nevsky Prospect near the Anichkov Palace* (1830s), lithograph by an unknown artist.
RIGHT Choked with cars, crowds and shops, the Nevsky Prospect remains the main thoroughfare of St Petersburg.

movement that advocated a rejection of Western ideas and a return to the values of Old Russia. This was a heresy, which challenged the very ideological foundations upon which the city had evolved. 'Russia needs Moscow; St Petersburg needs Russia', Gogol exclaimed. He contributed to the debate with his comparison of Russia's ancient and new capitals in *St Petersburg Notes of 1836* as well as his satirical play and masterwork *The Government Inspector*. Gogol left St Petersburg in 1836 for Europe after his play was coolly received and returned to the city only infrequently. Like his characters, Gogol could never quite shake St Petersburg from his soul as he wandered from city to city, becoming more reactionary and religious. Finally spending his last years between Moscow and Odessa, he succumbed

to insanity, burning his sequel to his last novel *Dead Souls* and starving himself to death in 1852. Gogol, however, would have enormous impact on the future of Russian literature as well as the myth of St Petersburg, so much so that one of his literary descendants, Fyodor Dostoyevsky, would exclaim that the whole of Russian literature 'came out from underneath Gogol's overcoat'.[41]

'BARBARISM BARELY DISGUISED'

While during the mid-nineteenth century Petersburgers began to look with scepticism on their city's traditional myths, to the foreign visitor St Petersburg continued to hold a reputation as an awe-inspiring spectacle on the edge of the civilized world. One principal

ABOVE In Gogol's *The Nose*, the Kazan Cathedral serves as the setting for Kovalev's ridiculous discovery that his errant proboscis is impersonating a state councillor.

foreign account of this period comes from the Marquis de Custine, a French aristocrat who visited St Petersburg in 1839. He wrote extensive journals of his experiences in the imperial capital, revealing the true nature of life in Nicolaevean Russia. His initial impressions were far from flattering, for he immediately condemned the choice of classical architecture as unsuitable for the monotonously flat landscape. However, even he could not fail to be impressed by the city's mere existence:

> . . . one cannot contemplate it without a sort of admiration for this city raised from the sea at the command of a man, which in order to survive must fight against periodic inundation by ice and permanent inundation by water. It is the result of an immense force of will, and, if one does not admire it, one fears it – which is almost to respect it.[42]

On the streets he observed first hand Tsar Nicholas's transformation of city life:

> The movements of the people I met seemed to me stiff and constrained; each gesture expresses a will which is not the will of the man who makes it. All those I saw passing were carrying orders. The morning is the time for commission. Not a person seemed to be working for himself . . . I observed few women in the streets – which were not enlivened by a single pretty face or the voice of a single young girl; everything was dismal, regulated as barracks or a camp; it was like war – but with less enthusiasm and less life.[43]

Originally, Custine had come to Russia in an effort to find an argument against representative government. His testimony, however displays that even he was unprepared for what he found. Custine observed St Petersburg through eyes tainted with the experience of the Enlightenment, revolution and war. Coming from France in the midst of industrialization and ruled by a representative monarchy under Louis Phillipe, Custine, a dyed-in-the-wool monarchist, was at once fascinated and appalled by what he found – Asiatic despotism clothed in European garb.

> It is only too easy in St Petersburg to let yourself be taken in by the appearance of civilization. When you see the court and the people who crowd it, you think you are in a country advanced in culture and political economy. But when you think about the relations that exist between the various classes of society; when you see how many classes are still insignificant in size; finally, when you study the basis of customs and events, you perceive a real barbarism barely disguised under a revolting magnificence.[44]

Being an aristocrat with respectable credentials, the scandal of his homosexuality having been forgotten or ignored, Custine was given entry to the highest levels of the court, even meeting the Tsar on more than one occasion. At one reception Nicholas encouraged him to go to Moscow and the provinces, explaining that the capital was not entirely representative of his empire. 'St Petersburg is Russian, but not Russia.'[45] Custine also had a chance to explore the Winter Palace, which had only just been rebuilt after a disastrous fire in December 1837. The fire raged for three days, gutting the sumptuous interiors of the building. Having saved his most prized possession – a stack of love letters from his wife – Nicholas I declared that in one year from the day of the fire he would 'again sleep in my room in the Winter Palace.'[46] Work began immediately and continued twenty-four hours a day, seven days a week. The pace at which the restoration was carried out caused multitudes of deaths and injuries among the craftsmen and workers. Conditions were nearly unbearable as well, with rooms being heated even in summer to well over 90°F to aid in the drying of plasterwork.

As he walked through the restored halls, Custine was mystified by the quality of work and troubled by its human cost.

> The fête which followed our presentation was one of the most magnificent I have ever seen. It was like a fairyland, and the admiration and astonishment that was inspired in all the court by each room of this palace, renovated in one year, added a dramatic interest to the rather cold pomp of the usual solemnities. Each room, each painting, was a subject of surprise for the Russians themselves, who had witnessed the catastrophe and had not seen the abode since, at the word of the god, the temple had arisen form its cinders. What an effort of will! . . . These wonders inspired a contagious admiration in the crowd; while seeing the triumph of the will of a man and while listening to the exclamations of other people, I, myself, began to be less indignant at the price of this miracle.[47]

By the end of his stay in St Petersburg, Custine was ready to leave. He grew weary of life in the city, the oppressiveness he saw all around him in the court and the especially the architecture, which he felt embodied the Tsarist system. In his final verdict on the city he joined a growing number of critics who saw St Petersburg as antithetical to the Russian nature:

I have described to you a city without character, more pompous than imposing, more vast than beautiful, filled with buildings without style, without taste and without historical significance. But in order to give you a complete picture, that is to say a fair one, I must at the same time make you see, in this pretentious and ridiculous frame, a naturally engaging people who, with their oriental genius have been able to adapt themselves to a city built for people who do not exist anywhere; for St Petersburg was built by rich men whose ideas were formed by comparing, without making a profound study, the various countries of Europe. This legion of travellers, more or less refined, more experienced than learned, was an artificial nation, a selection of intelligent and active minds recruited from all nations of the world – it was not the Russian people.

The Russian people are mocking, like the slave who consoles himself for his yoke by quietly making fun of it; they are superstitious, boastful, brave and lazy, like the soldier; they are poetic, musical and thoughtful, like the shepherd; for the customs of the nomadic races will prevail for a long time among the Slavs. All this is in keeping neither with the style of the buildings nor with the plan of the streets in St Petersburg; there is obvious dissension between the architect and the inhabitant. European engineers came to tell the Muscovites how they should build and embellish a capital worthy of the admiration of Europe; and they, with their military submission, ceded to the force of command. Peter the Great built St Petersburg against the Swedes much more than for the Russians. But the nature of the people came to light in spite of their respect for the caprices of the master and in spite of the distrust of themselves, and it is this involuntary disobedience that Russia owes its seal of originality.[48]

Although his remarks carry the condescension of the cosmopolitan aristocrat he was, Custine's account of his time in St Petersburg

continues to offer more insight than many of the sentimental descriptions that were its contemporaries. Custine, even as a foreigner, had grasped the paradox of St Petersburg. He saw the potential of the Russian nation and understood that Russia was moving towards a crossroads. As for St Petersburg, he believed that there was something to all of the legends that one day the city would be swept away, whether by floods or desertion. 'I believe that the duration of St Petersburg will be that of a political system or the constancy of a man,' he said, 'This is something that cannot be said of any other city in the world.'[49]

'POMPEII IS THE MUSE OF ST PETERSBURG!'[50]

Karl Briullov's epic canvas *The Last Day of Pompeii* created an enormous stir when it went on exhibition at the St Petersburg Academy of Fine Arts in 1834. Having claimed the French Academy's gold prize, the painting's much-anticipated arrival was followed by a mad rush to see it. The city's luminaries and public alike were rapt by the horrific power of Briullov's masterpiece. Before them they observed a civilization in the throes of hellish obliteration. In the painting the artist portrayed the citizens of Pompeii, wild eyed with fear and clutching their earthly possessions, cowering before the awesome power of Vesuvius as their world collapses around them. Lightning topples the gods of old as screaming toddlers grasp for their fallen mothers and men and horses are crushed beneath falling rubble. Pushkin was so impressed by this scene that he penned this unfinished ode:

Vesuvius opened its jaws – smoke rolled out – flames
Spread widely, like a battle banner
The earth is agitated – from shaken pillars
Idols fall! The people, chased by fear,
Under a rain of stones, under burning ashes
In crowds, aged and young, flee the city.[51]

Alexander Herzen, a leading Westernizer, critic and early socialist, declared that Briullov, 'who developed in St Petersburg, selected for his brush the terrible image of a wild irrational force destroying the people of Pompeii – that is the moving spirit of St Petersburg!'[52] Briullov's painting was viewed as a prophetic allegory of the future fate of St Petersburg. From its earliest days the curse of Peter the Great's first wife Eudoxia that 'St Petersburg will stand empty,' echoed in the back of the minds of its citizens. This stone creation

The Raspberry Boudoir in the Winter Palace. Visitors were often awed by the grandeur of the imperial palaces. The Marquis de Custine in his travel journals described what he saw as 'barbarism barely disguised under a revolting magnificence'.

built in defiance of nature and history seemed to ask for retribution. Only a decade earlier St Petersburg had seen the worst flood in the city's history, with waters rising over 13 feet in the course of an evening. Disaster had struck in recent memory as well, as only two years earlier in 1831 a deadly cholera epidemic had been visited upon the city, claiming at its height 600 lives per day. Nicholas himself had to calm the rioting in the Haymarket, which resulted from wild rumours circulating among the terrified public. By the end 10,000 were dead.

While Pushkin had even bowed to this apocalyptic paranoia in *The Bronze Horseman*, his St Petersburg remained unshakeable as his faith in the monarchy and Peter's vision of bringing the West to Russia. His successors did not possess such faith. Gogol foretold of a day that 'lightning poured out and covered everything', in St Petersburg, while arch-romantic Vladimir Odoevsky, in his fantastic

tragedy *A Joker from the Dead* (1844), brings his story of love betrayed to an end by sweeping the city into the sea. The poet Mikhail Dmitriev in his poem 'Underwater City' (1847) described the flooding of St Petersburg with only spires visible from above the raging waters. These fantastic predictions would be given further credence by the catastrophic fire in 1836, which destroyed a large area of the city and claimed at least 120 lives, and by a second cholera epidemic in 1848, which took 12,000 lives.[53]

By the middle of the century Russia and St Petersburg were again yearning for change. The rise of the apocalyptic motif was a signal of this growing restlessness. In 1848, the revolutionary wave that swept over Europe had threatened to swamp Russia. Nicholas, true to character once again, clamped down on all dissidents, even banning the writings of Pushkin, Gogol and Turgenev. Westernizers were viewed with suspicion and their

ABOVE Although they also possessed lavish palaces, nineteenth-century tsars began to prefer more intimate and bourgeois accommodation, such as the cottage at Peterhof (1826–9) by Adam Menelaws.

followers harassed. Even their enemies the Slavophiles were singled out as potential troublemakers. But Nicholas could not halt the infection, which had already taken root in his capital. By the 1840s cotton mills and metal working plants had cropped up like mushrooms in the Vyborg and Okhta quarters of the city. With them arrived 12,000 workers housed in the city's first tenements, those of the kind already blighting the cities of the West. Crowding in these humble quarters was endemic, as was the appearance of syphilis and tuberculosis.

While political expression remained impossible during this period, intellectuals found outlets through literature and literary criticism. One such critic became their champion. Vissarion Belinsky, working for the publications *Annals of the Homeland* and *The Contemporary*, challenged the mounting influence of the Slavophiles and their rejection of the St Petersburg ideal. In his famous 1847

response to Gogol's reactionary and conservative religious *Selected Passages from Correspondence with Friends*, Belinsky excoriated him for turning his back on the dominant themes in his writing;

Devotee of the knout, apostle of uncouthness, defender of obscurantism and backwardness, glorifier of the Tartar way of life – what are you doing? Look at your feet! You are standing at the edge of an abyss. . . . Russia sees that her salvation lies not in mysticism, or in atheism or in pietism, but in the progress of civilization, education, humanitarian values. What she needs are not sermons (she has heard enough of them) or prayers (she has babbled enough of them) but the awakening of human dignity, which has been dragged through the mud and dirt for so many centuries.[54]

ABOVE Karl Briullov's 1833 painting *The Last Day of Pompeii* (State Russian Museum, St Petersburg) caused a sensation in a city that felt itself to be dancing on a precipice.

Belinsky's efforts helped spark further organization of intellectual circles. Chief among them was a group of writers, intellectuals and social critics founded by Mikhail Butashevich-Petrashevsky. Known simply as the Petrashevsky, the group gathered regularly to discuss the issues of the day in a free and open forum. Although no singular political ideology prevailed, the Petrashevsky were primarily Westernizers schooled in the philosophy of the Enlightenment as well as being heavily influenced by the works of the French socialist Charles Fourier. Among the group's members was a young writer by the name of Fyodor Dostoyevsky. Dostoyevsky had been discovered by Belinsky, who had published his novel *Poor Folk* in the *St Petersburg Anthology* of 1846. The eminent poet and intellectual Nikolai Nekrasov had exclaimed upon reading his works 'A new Gogol has appeared.'[55]

The Petrashevsky were never as organized as their predecessors, the Decembrists. Their main activities were amassing a library of forbidden literature and expounding their views in journalistic publications. However, the government reaction surrounding the revolutions of 1848 drew attention to their activities. Seeing the rising tide, the Petrashevsky attempted to become more active, but the constant harassment by His Majesty's Third Section reduced their members significantly and even infiltrated the group. The group split under the pressure between those favouring peaceful change and those favouring armed revolt. Dostoyevsky threw his lot in with the latter group. In April 1849, the Government struck, arresting 252 of the Petrashevsky and charging them with a 'conspiracy of ideas'. Of these, 21 members were sentenced to death and imprisoned in the Peter and Paul Fortress. On 22 December 1849 the conspirators were led from their cells to Semenovskaya Square, where their sentences were read aloud to them and a priest performed the last rites. One by one they were tied to posts and hoods were placed over their heads. The drum roll began as the firing squad prepared to fire. Suddenly, a messenger called a halt to the proceedings and read out a last-minute pardon from the Tsar, calling for hard labour instead of execution. Dostoyevsky would describe this nerve-racking experience in his later novel *The Idiot*.

Within six years Nicholas was dead and with him the system he had inaugurated. Russia, humiliated in the Crimean War, had all of its weaknesses and backwardness revealed. Russia desperately needed to modernize economically and politically to face the challenges of becoming a modern nation. St Petersburg was once again the front line of the battle of ideas, reform and revolution that would now commence. A younger and forward-looking tsar was about to ascend the throne and a new day was ready to begin. But the ambivalence remained toward St Petersburg. Would Peter's city be Russia's salvation or its doom? In his essay *St Petersburg and Moscow* Belinsky boldly claimed that St Petersburg was up to the challenge. This city was Peter's dream made reality, a testing ground of new ideas and the receptor of thousands of people coming from the nations of Russia's vast empire as well as from abroad looking for opportunity. What place could be better to direct Russia's future?

St Petersburg is not carried away by ideas; it is a practical and sober man. It will never mistake its flannel frock-coat for a Roman toga; it would rather play at cards than busy itself with the impossible; you will not stun it with theories or speculations, and it cannot tolerate dreams; it does not like to stand in its swamp, but this is still better than to hang in the air without support. . . . In a word, St Petersburg doesn't believe, it demands action. In it each person strives toward his goal and, no matter what it may be, achieves it.[56]

Monuments of Tsarist power, Andreian Zakharov's Admiralty (1810–23) and Auguste Ricard de Montferrand's Cathedral of St Isaac of Dalmatia (1818–58), disguised a growing sense of unease in St Petersburg.

CHAPTER 4:
THE CRADLE OF REVOLUTION

THE TSAR LIBERATOR

On 19 February 1855 St Petersburg rejoiced at the news that Alexander II was crowned Tsar and Autocrat of all the Russias in Moscow. Although he was blessed as Tsar with all of the pomp and ceremony the ancient capital could muster, Alexander was assuming the throne of a nation on its knees. Defeated and bankrupt, Russia was a feudal society in a modern industrial world. It needed a ruler who would be able to shepherd the transition that could no longer be avoided. Having been provided with instruction in economics and a liberal arts education by the renowned poet Vasily Zhukovsky, Alexander was also the bright and shining hope of the nation's progressives, who believed that he would bring to fruition the social and economic reforms the nation so badly needed. Zhukovsky tried to infuse his young charge with a sense of his role as ruler of the largest empire on earth, reminding him that 'History will pass judgment on you before the whole world and it will remain long after you and I have left the earth.'[1]

One of his first acts as Tsar was to pardon the exiles of the Decembrist Revolt and the Petrashevsky conspiracy. This was only the beginning. Within two years Alexander revealed his intention to emancipate the serfs of the empire, which he carried out in 1861 on the sixth anniversary of his coronation. St Petersburg was elated. Crowds celebrated in the streets and theatre performances were interrupted by spontaneous singing of the national anthem. Alexander told a deputation of peasants in Palace Square who came to thank him for their freedom 'With God's help, it fell to my lot to complete the task for your good. Now my children, go and thank God; pray for the eternal repose of my father; prove yourselves useful to the fatherland.'[2]

Alexander continued his reforms in 1863, giving the universities self-administration, which opened the door for the admission of female students. Primary education for the empire's children also began during this time. The Tsar liberator also took further steps to increase the powers of local government and in 1864 ordered the setting up of the *zemstvos*, or local elected bodies, responsible for local administration, policing, public services and health. That same year he furthered Russia's modernization and encouraged enforcement of the rule of law by enacting judicial statutes, which laid the groundwork for the reforming of the court system by allowing it to become open and independent with trial by jury. Later in his reign Alexander would pursue other reforms such the institution of compulsory military service, ending the army's dependence on the conscription of peasants, which to them often meant a lifetime of forced military service.

Alexander also took steps to reform the empire's economy. He introduced the imposition of a national budget, forced the privatization of state industries and encouraged foreign investment and joint ventures. Railways were built at a rate unprecedented under his father. Among his most important tasks was the modernization of Russia's military. This required the production of every kind of armaments and machinery, increasing the demand for iron and steel. St Petersburg, the imperial capital, became the prime location of this drive toward industrialization and modernization. The industries of iron and steel manufacturing, machine production and shipbuilding were joined by a host of smaller businesses from textiles and chemical production to food and tobacco preparation. Paper manufacturing and printing helped fuel the government bureaucracy's need for documentation as well as the increasingly educated public's mounting desire for books and magazines. Technical knowledge and innovation became essential to Russia's future success. Technical and engineering institutes were

LEFT By the mid-nineteenth century St Petersburg began to grow ever denser as a result of population growth and industrialization.
RIGHT *Morning on Nevsky Prospect* (1880), painting by Alexander Beggrow (Museum of the History of St Petersburg).

established in St Petersburg, turning out a host of scientists, inventors and technicians, among them Dmitri Mendeleev, originator of the periodic table. Large banks and international companies made their home in the business-friendly climate of St Petersburg. Carr and McPherson, International Harvester, Singer Sewing Machine Company and Seimens all had substantial presences in the city.

St Petersburg, the baroque and classical city of Peter, Elizabeth, Catherine and Alexander I, with its majestic architecture, monumental squares, grand boulevards and graceful parks, soon found itself changed by its new role. While the court remained as magnificent as it had under previous tsars, the aristocracy was joined by a new group, which, through its wealth and influence, gained entrance into its ranks. The Stieglitz, Putilov, Semyanikov, Poletika and Obukhov families were among this new industrial elite and were quickly accepted into high society. Within the centre of St Petersburg the titans of Russia's new industry and the *nouveaux riches* built splendid mansions and dachas for themselves in a spectrum of revivalist styles from Muscovite to neo-Renaissance. This new wealth increased the demand for fine goods, which were sold along the Nevsky Prospect or served in restaurants such as Contant's, Donon's and Cubat's, or in the dining rooms of the upscale Europa and Grand Hotels.

While the old centre was embellished with the garish palaces of the *nouveaux riches*, the outskirts of the city became the realm of industry. In a wide arch, from the mouth of the Neva across the northern islands of Vasilievsky, Vyborg and Petersburg, down the Schlüsselburg Road, across the Obvodny Canal to the mouth of the Fontanka, industrial complexes created a dirty necklace around the heart of the city. Mills, factories, shipyards and ironworks rose like dark castles on the horizon, spewing smoke, steam and soot into the air, creating an ever-present haze over the capital. Around these factories sprouted scores of tenements, housing for the ever-growing population of workers needed to fuel them. As overcrowding set in, these often substandard dwellings and communities became slums. The St Petersburg's factories produced the materials needed to secure the imperial order and its future, while the slums that surrounded them began to yield a harvest that would eventually dominate and direct that future, the underclass.

New industrial magnates and their families built dachas such as these on the northern islands of the city.

The Stieglitz Museum (1885–95), designed by Maximilian Mesmakher, remains one of the greatest contributions of St Petersburg's *nouveaux riches* to the city's cultural treasures.

POOR FOLK

As Alexander II's program of political and economic reform began the long-awaited and desperately needed modernization of Russia, it created in its wake a glittering world of new wealth and technology. It was also unwittingly producing conditions among the empire's working classes that resembled the Dickensian social nightmares of the West. St Petersburg, the centre of the empire's military-industrial complex and the hub of its heavy manufacturing sector, had throughout its history shown little concern for the living and working conditions of its lower classes, their needs being viewed as secondary to the physical and economic growth of the city. One rare exception during the 1840s involved the appointment of a government commission to investigate the living conditions of the working poor. They often found workers lived in cramped tenements with eighteen to twenty people per apartment. In one extreme case there were fifty people, men, women and children, many infected with tuberculosis and syphilis, living together in a room no bigger than 20 by 20 feet.[3] However, the government did nothing to alleviate these conditions; instead it simply ignored them.

Twenty years later, the liberation of the serfs led to commencement of a massive exodus of peasants from the farms of the rural countryside to the urban centres in search of jobs in Russia's growing legion of factories. With no effective city administration until 1873, with the election of the first Duma, St Petersburg found itself little prepared for the social consequences wrought by industrialization and the influx of thousands of poor workers. Between 1840 and 1880 the number of workers rose from 12,000 to 150,000.[4] These former peasants, many of whom had never been five miles from their homes, found themselves crammed into tenements on the outskirts of town or in the neighbourhoods near the factories.

These tenements were at first constructed of brick. As the need for cheaper housing grew, however, they were soon built with wood. Inside these buildings were flats barely able to withstand the harsh climate of St Petersburg, housing sixteen people each on average. With little or no plumbing, most residents simply threw their rubbish and chamber pots into the central courtyards of the buildings through which they passed daily and their children played. Soon enormous heaps of putrid and stinking refuse collected in these spaces, leading one public health official in 1869 to estimate that there was at least 30,000 tons of human excrement lying untreated throughout the city.[5] As the numbers of new

residents increased, the housing shortage grew desperate. Landlords, hungry to exploit every available space, rented closets, attics, spaces under stairs, or even converted entire buildings into dormitories where residents slept in shifts.[6]

The unluckiest or bravest among the new arrivals found themselves renting below ground in the city's infamous cellars. These dank and awful places were like dungeons, and had never previously been considered suitable for human habitation. As St Petersburg had been built on a swamp, they were never dry. Heavy rains and sewer backups often filled these cells with up to two feet of foetid water and human waste. Yet as the options for shelter decreased, thousands descended into these lonely depths. By 1871 more than 30,000 people were living underground.[7]

For the growing masses, finding accommodation in St Petersburg was only half the battle. Life itself was a constant struggle for survival, as the urban environment grew more hostile to the poorest of its residents. Food, often substandard, was difficult to obtain. The workers' diet was composed mainly of coarse rye bread and soup made from water and pickled cabbage.[8] Many were forced to form cooperatives, pooling their resources to buy the

LEFT As St Petersburg's industrial might increased, factories such as these began to line the Neva to the east along the Schlusselburg Road.
ABOVE RIGHT A nineteenth-century photograph of one of St Petersburg's many industrial slums.

poorest grades of food for communal cooking and consumption.[9] During the mid-nineteenth century drinking water was still extracted from the Neva, which was increasingly polluted from the waste of the city and the factories upriver. One visitor from Scotland was appalled by this. 'The water placed on the table in spring is perfectly pestiferous! . . . Frequently in summer did I meet the nightsman's carts, which discharged their filthy cargo into the Fontanka, so that the air is poisoned. Then in the morning the water for breakfast is procured from [the same place].'[10] Travel guides and government signs advised against such practices but the poor with no other option ignored these suggestions. Illness invariably ensued. The government and charity hospitals overflowed with patients felled by the city's pollution and unsanitary conditions, yet were not equipped to handle the numbers of cases brought to their doors. Peasants, unaccustomed to the polluted environment, fell like flies before the onslaught of disease. Cholera, typhoid fever, diphtheria, smallpox, measles, tuberculosis and typhus claimed thousands of lives each year, giving St Petersburg the appalling distinction of having the highest mortality rate in Europe by 1870.[11]

With life so bleak among the lower classes, many looked elsewhere for solace. The majority of these new arrivals were men who had left their wives and children back in their home villages. In their frustration and loneliness they turned to drinking. The drink of choice was either beer or vodka, which was often so potent as to be fatal. Alcoholism soon became an epidemic, leading the St Petersburg newspaper *Golos* to exclaim 'Drunkenness of late has taken on such horrifying proportions that it forces us to think about it as a social catastrophe.'[12] The prominent diarist Alexander Kikitenko also commented on the situation in 1864:

> Drunkenness is unprecedented, even for Russia. . . . Everywhere, drunken folk wander in crowds through the streets, loll about and huff like cattle. . . . A number of unfortunate accidents, some of them fatal, occur as a result of drunkenness. . . . There have been cases of fatal alcohol poisoning, even among fourteen- and fifteen-year-olds.[13]

As demand for alcohol rose so did the number of the city's taverns, 1,840 by 1865 with 18 drinking establishments on the infamous Stolyarny Alley alone.[14]

With St Petersburg having the highest levels of alcohol consumption in the empire,[15] it inevitably began to experience a wave of crime and public disorder. By the end of the 1860s as many as one in four residents of St Petersburg had been arrested for public drunkenness, disorderly conduct or other related crimes.[16] Hand in hand with such sodden pleasures of the tavern came armies of prostitutes plying their trade. While most of these were peasant girls, their numbers were swelled by impoverished and desperate members of the bourgeoisie and gentry. By the late 1860s and early 1870s, the city had 150 brothels and the number of registered prostitutes – those holding the notorious 'yellow passport' – doubled to 4,400.[17] This figure, however, represented only a small percentage of the true number of prostitutes, who could be found parading their finery up and down the Nevsky and Ligovsky Prospects or more often drunk and cheaply made up on any street corner in the city.

Among the wretched denizens of this carnival of vice walked a young journalist, who quietly observed the desperate bacchanalia of the lower classes while he learned the murky alleyways and dim streets of St Petersburg's dark netherworld. He would transform his knowledge and experiences of these regions into a new literature, which served as a searing indictment of what he believed to be the true consequences of Peter's dream. While his contemporary Charles Dickens' name would later be used to describe the corporeal decline of traditional society during England's industrial revolution, in St Petersburg a new name would come to serve as its equivalent in characterizing modernity's shattering effect on the human spirit. This name was Dostoyevsky.

WHITE NIGHTS AND UNDERGROUND: DOSTOYEVSKY'S ST PETERSBURG

Fyodor Dostoyevsky returned to St Petersburg in 1859 after ten years of exile in Siberia due to his participation in the Petrashevsky conspiracy in the last years of Nicholas I's reign. Originally from Moscow, he had moved to St Petersburg in 1837 to attend the Imperial Engineering School housed in the notorious Mikhailovsky Castle. Writing, however, was his true passion and so he abandoned his engineering career in 1844 to become a journalist. During this time he became intimately familiar with the city, combing its streets for material. Finding fiction more stimulating than pure reporting he began to publish novels in serialized form. In 1846 his first novel *Poor Folk* appeared in the *Petersburg Anthology* and was well received by Belinsky and the noted satirist and poet Nikolai Nekrasov. He followed this up with story *The Double*, a tribute to the style and vision of Gogol.

Initially, the young Dostoyevsky was inspired by the imperial capital and the vision of its founder, Peter I. In his feuilleton *Petersburg Chronicle*, published in 1847, he wrote that St Petersburg was both the head and heart of Russia. 'Even up to the present St Petersburg is in dust and rubble; it is still being created, still becoming. Its future is still an idea; but this idea belongs to Peter I; it is being embodied, growing and taking root with each day, not alone in the Petersburg swamp but in all of Russia.'[18] Dostoyevsky's short story *White Nights* (1848) continued this tribute to the city. In it tells the story of a young dreamer who falls in love with a girl he meets one evening weeping beside a canal. Dostoyevsky sets this story of unrequited love against a backdrop of the city. He portrays a St Petersburg bathed in the soft hues of summer nights, a dreamer's paradise where day and night blend seamlessly together, where fantasy and reality are hardly discernable. This was the St Petersburg of Dostoyevsky's youth, a mystical place where anything seemed possible, where the twenty year old writer who would become a giant of literature, first had his moment of discovery:

I remember once on a wintry January evening I was hurrying home from the Vyborg side. . . . The taut air quivered at the slightest sound, and columns of smoke like giants rose from all the roofs on both embankments and rushed upward through the cold sky, twining and untwining on the way, so that it seemed new buildings were rising on old ones, a new city was forming in the air. . . . It seemed as if all the world, with all its inhabitants, strong and weak, with all their habitations, the refuges of the poor, or the gilded palaces for the comfort of the powerful in this world, was at that twilight hour like a fantastic vision of fairyland, like a dream, which in its turn would vanish and pass away like vapour in the dark blue sky.[19]

Following ten years of exile Dostoyevsky returned a changed man. However, the city that had so enchanted him as a youth had also changed. Upon his return he wrote and published two novels, *The Friend of the Family* (1859) and *The Insulted and the Injured* (1862), re-establishing himself as a writer. But he did not return to the dreamy idealism of his previous work. Years of exile had darkened him. During his exile Dostoyevsky had had a profound shift in his belief systems, rejecting the atheism and Western ideas he had shared with the Petrashevsky circle. Upon his return to St Petersburg, Dostoyevsky found himself on a spiritual journey in search of an elusive faith and its promised salvation.

The emancipation of the serfs in 1861 and its impact on St Petersburg was of deep interest to Dostoyevsky. He watched as thousands of peasants streamed into the city in search of work and fortune. These new arrivals, fodder for the mills, found themselves isolated and cut off from all that was comforting and familiar. They had few skills to cope with such a dramatic change in lifestyle and were soon demoralized, taking solace in the bottle and at the brothels. Others he found had willingly cast off their traditional beliefs in exchange for half-baked philosophies or nothing at all. In 1861 he started the publication *Vremya* (*Time*) with his brother Mikhail to espouse his new-found beliefs in national regeneration through a return to the cultural and religious tradition of Russia's heartland, ideals lost due to the influence of Western political and social ideologies.[20]

The work of another figure rose to prominence in St Petersburg during the early 1860s, providing the foil for Dostoyevsky's religious insurgence. Nikolai Chernyshevsky had studied to be a priest, but transferred to the University of St Petersburg. Like Dostoyevsky he accepted the Western ideals of the Petrashevsky and turned to journalism as a means of spreading his beliefs. He worked with the poet and realist writer Nekrasov, a champion of Dostoyevsky, and became the heir to the great Westernizer Belinsky. Arrested following the student unrest of 1861 for his publication of *Letters Without an Address*, in which he criticized the government and called for political liberties, Chernyshevsky was thrown into the Peter and Paul Fortress, where again, in parallel to Dostoyevsky, he endured a mock execution and exile to Siberia.

It was during his internment in the fortress that he wrote what was to become the most influential revolutionary novel of the age. *What Is To Be Done?* was published almost by accident, escaping the censors and even surviving being lost by Nekrasov only to be

ABOVE Fyodor Dostoyevsky (1872), portrait by Vasily Perov (Tretyakov Gallery, Moscow).

returned following the placement of an advertisement in the policeman's gazette.[21] On the surface *What Is To Be Done?* is a rather poorly constructed novel, which describes the story of a young St Petersburg woman, Vera Pavlovna, who joins a commune of revolutionaries and, through intellectual and sexual liberation, rejects the world of her upbringing. In the book Chernyshevsky sought not just to address the social problems of the day but also to propose radical solutions to them. In traditional St Petersburg fashion he looked West for inspiration. Chernyshevsky encouraged the rejection of the old paternalistic and religious order and the adaptation of the utilitarianism and socialist principles of Charles Fourier.

Chernyshevsky's work became a bible for those disaffected youths in St Petersburg and elsewhere in Russia who yearned for radical social change and political action. The heroes of *What Is To Be Done?* came to believe that through 'rational egoism' or positive self-interest, that is, the realization of their own interests being married to the welfare of society as a whole, a truly egalitarian utopia could be established.[22] The leader of this nihilistic commune was the fictitious hero Rakhmetov, whose 'superior nature' would provide a virtual code of conduct for burgeoning revolutionaries. At once a puritan and an ascetic he eschews earthly pleasures and prepares himself for the coming revolution through rigorous intellectual and physical training. Chernyshevsky's novel influenced many revolutionaries, including Georgy Plekhanov, the father of Russian socialism and the young Vladimir Ulyanov, whom the world would come to know as Lenin.

Dostoyevsky cursed the nihilism preached by Chernyshevsky. He had little faith that human nature, freed from the control of religion and the state, could produce the utopia envisioned by Chernyshevsky and his followers. Dostoyevsky had witnessed what

he believed to be the true measure of man in the wastes of Siberia, a cruel and self-interested beast capable of the lowest crimes, unrepentant and undesirous of forgiveness. But he also became converted by the example of what he believed to be the true 'common' people, those among the criminals who had not abandoned the traditions and faith of the Russian peasantry. He wrote about these opposing portraits of humanity in his *Notes form the House of the Dead* in 1862.[23] Dostoyevsky soon joined the ranks of the Slavophile movement, which believed that the traditional values of the Russian people, as exhibited by the peasantry and the Church, beliefs that were the antithesis of Western ideology, had to be embraced rather than rejected in the pursuit of progress.

In 1862 Dostoyevsky visited Europe for the first time and witnessed first hand the triumph of the Industrial Revolution and its effects on society. It at once fascinated and repulsed him. His impressions were epitomized by his experience in London, where he visited Paxton's great Crystal Palace, the Victorian temple to capitalism and empire. In all of its exhibitions, with their wonders and temptations, Dostoyevsky saw the 'pagan' power of capitalism and its ability to reorganize society economically, physically and spiritually in the pursuit of capital. With bourgeois individualism as a major driving force of this power, his experience further reinforced his beliefs that Western ideas of individual freedom created divisions and isolation among individuals rather than serving as a catalyst to unite them. Back in St Petersburg Dostoyevsky saw his city as 'the most abstract and premeditated city on earth,'[24] which was the greatest expression of individualism on Russian soil. In a drastic change from his earlier tributes, Dostoyevsky now accused Peter's creation of allowing the Western winds to disturb the peace of Holy Russia with devastating consequences.

In 1864 he published *Notes from Underground*, which would be his first literary rather than journalistic rebuttal to Chernyshevsky and his followers. In it, Dostoyevsky painted a portrait of a deranged world of isolation and depravity. For his antihero Dostoyevsky chose an intelligent man driven by his own choice into the dank cellars of the city, a man shaped and scarred by a society of warped values divorced from its roots, rudderless without its faith. Although he yearns to make connections with those around him, his destructive ego and extreme self-loathing inevitably ruins any chance for true human relationships with friends, lovers or acquaintances. For Dostoyevsky his underground man posed a direct challenge to the liberal premise of man's inherent rationality and the belief that he will act in his best interest.[25]

ABOVE *Daybreak in St Petersburg* (1869–71), painting by Fiodor Vasilyev (State Russian Museum, St Petersburg).

CRIME AND PUNISHMENT

This is a city of half crazy people. If we were a scientific people doctors, lawyers and philosophers could make the most valuable investigations in St Petersburg, each in his own field. There are few places where you'll find so many gloomy, harsh and strange influences on the soul of man as in St Petersburg.[26]

Inspector Zamyotov, in *Crime and Punishment*

In *Notes from Underground* Dostoyevsky began to paint an entirely new vision of the imperial capital and its inhabitants, but this vision would reach its fullest expression in his quintessential St Petersburg novel, *Crime and Punishment*. This fused the journalistic and literary sides of Dostoyevsky's talent, providing graphic descriptions of the lives and deaths of St Petersburg's lower classes while at the same time exploring their internal degradation and spiritual turmoil. His hero Raskolnikov is a failed student, an intellectual who has become disillusioned and in debt. Like the underground man he has purposely withdrawn into his cell, in this case an attic. Set in and around the dark heart of St Petersburg, Stolyarny Alley and the Haymarket, Dostoyevsky begins his novel with a claustrophobic illustration of the city behind the monuments, the city of the poor and depraved.

Outside the heat had grown ferocious. Closeness, crowds, scaffolding, with lime and brick and dust everywhere, and that special summer stench familiar to every Petersburger who cannot afford a summer cottage; it all jarred instantly and unpleasantly on the young man's nerves, which were

ABOVE While ice on the Neva was a source of winter celebration for some, the freezing temperatures and substandard housing made life miserable for the city's urban poor.

tense enough already. The intolerable stench of the saloons, especially numerous in that part of town, and the drunks he came upon continually in spite of the fact that it was a working day, contributed to the melancholy and repulsive tone of what confronted him. An expression of the deepest loathing flashed for a moment across his sensitive face.

In his frustration at hearing that his sister is going to marry a local scoundrel for money Raskolnikov decides to murder an elderly pawnbroker, an act which he justifies not only for monetary reasons but as a service to the community as well. But his plan goes horribly wrong when he kills the elderly woman's innocent sister as well, compounding his crime. Although he escapes, he is now isolated from humanity and imprisoned by his guilt and his attempts at the rational justification of the murders. Raskolnikov is further tormented by the appearance of his mother and sister in St Petersburg as well as his encounters with the humble and self-sacrificing prostitute Sonya. Each of them help awaken his true humane nature, obscured by his exposure to the foul influence of St Petersburg. Unable to reconcile himself he is torn between confession (salvation) and suicide (damnation). Finally he chooses to turn himself in, confess his crime and serve out his sentence in Siberia where he ultimately finds repentance, forgiveness and spiritual rebirth.[27]

For Dostoyevsky, as well as for his readers, St Petersburg had become an unnatural environment whose hopeless residents were driven to acts desperation in order to survive. Dostoyevsky even came to despise the architecture of the city, dismissing its eighteenth- and nineteenth-century buildings as 'characterless' and 'pathetic copies' of European styles.[28] 'I'm sorry I don't love it,' he said. Where others saw harmony and beauty he saw nothing but 'windows, holes and monuments'.[29] To him St Petersburg was a window on the West through which all of the wrong things were imported. Later Dostoyevsky would even pay homage to the apocalyptic tradition of St Petersburg literature in his novel *The Adolescent*:

> A hundred times amid the fog I had a strange but persistent dream: 'What if, when this fog scatters and flies upward, the whole rotten, slimy city goes with it, rises with the fog and vanishes like smoke, leaving behind the Old Finnish swamp, and in the middle of it, I suppose for beauty's sake, the bronze horseman on the panting, whipped horse?'[30]

With *Crime and Punishment*, however, the myth of 'Dostoyevsky's St Petersburg' came firmly into being. His sinister characterization of the city, in which striking reality and dark fantasy swirled together in an almost mystical tempest, captured the imagination of many in Russia and even more in the West. Inadvertently, through his genius Dostoyevsky had ensured the immortality of the city he detested.

THE POSSESSED

Both Dostoyevsky and Chernyshevsky helped influence a growing unease among the classes with regard to the social, political and economic consequences of the reforms of Alexander II. Outside the capital former serfs, uneducated and irresponsible, were expected to pay taxes as well as compensation to their former owners, which caused deep resentment and even attacks against former masters and government officials. At the universities, revolutionary fervour, long held at bay, blossomed under the new conditions of relaxed censorship and greater autonomy. Students, the majority of whom were the sons of minor government officials and distressed gentry, felt free to campaign for more changes and greater freedoms. The government reacted by trying to re-impose some of the restrictions it had just lifted.

In September 1861, students, many dressed in peasant garb in solidarity with the newly freed serfs, took over a lecture hall at the University of St Petersburg. This was the first time the students had ever demonstrated in Russia's history. The next day the students returned to find the university closed, so they continued the protest on the streets, even going so far as to lead a procession down Nevsky Prospect, where one participant observed the French barbers waving and shouting 'Revolution! Revolution!'[31] Over the following weeks many were arrested and, much to the students' delight, imprisoned in the Peter and Paul Fortress. As a result of the protests, the university was closed for a year, only opening again in August 1863. During the intervening year a pamphlet began circulating under the title 'Young Russia', written by the student Zaichnevsky, warning of the imminent cataclysm of revolution due to be let loose upon the land. It attacked the monarchy, religion and the family and promised a bloody upheaval:

> Soon, very soon, the day will come when we shall unfurl the great banner of the future, the red flag, and with a mighty cry of 'Long Live the Russian Social and Democratic Republic!' we shall move against the Winter Palace to exterminate all its

A typical tenement staircase in a multi-occupied house. Dostoyevsky's *Crime and Punishment* was among the first literary works to attempt to depict life among the city's lower classes. He believed that many of the poor, poisoned by the noxious atmosphere of the city, were driven to despair or worse to murder.

inhabitants. . . . We shall raise the battle cry: 'To your axes!' and we shall kill the imperial party with no more mercy than they show for us now. We shall kill them in the squares . . . kill them in the avenues of the capital . . . kill them in the villages.[32]

Two weeks later a series of fires broke out across the city. While smaller ones were easily managed and extinguished, the fire in the Schukin Arcade and Apraskin Market turned into a holocaust. The market covered nearly half a square mile in the centre of the city and was stuffed with small wooden shanties themselves filled with goods. Second-hand clothing, books and furniture provided the kindling that allowed the fire to engulf six thousand shops within an hour. The fire rose up 'like an immense snake, rattling and whistling . . . the fire threw itself in all directions, right and left, enveloped the shanties, and rose in a huge column, darting out its

whistling tongues to lick up more shanties and their contents.'[33] The fire spread outwards, igniting houses, timber yards and entire streets, even reaching the Nevsky Prospect and the Ministry of Internal Affairs. The populace fled before the conflagration, singed and terrified like the ancients in Bruilliov's *The Last Day of Pompeii*.

Almost immediately the recriminations flew, aimed directly at the radical students and 'nihilists'. The pamphlet 'Young Russia' and the fires split public opinion and support for the students. Although it was never proven that the students or their supporters deliberately set the fires, one thing was certain: the stakes for both the regime and the radicals had been raised. In St Petersburg radicals were no longer willing to wait for change to be instituted from on high. They were also determined not to allow the development of a liberal constitutional monarchy, which would make way for the emergence of a capitalist bourgeois state. This would require their most daring exploit to date – the murder of the Tsar.

ABOVE The figure of the young radical became a symbol of fear, reverence and fascination, inspiring literary and artistic works, such as Ilya Repin's 1884 *They Did Not Expect Him* (Tretyakov Gallery, Moscow).

The first attempt on the life of Alexander II took place on 4 April 1866 as the Tsar was ending his afternoon stroll in the Summer Gardens. As he came through the gates to his carriage on the Neva Embankment a crowd of onlookers met him. Out of the crowd emerged Dmitri Karakozov, a failed student and radical, who raised a pistol at the Tsar and fired. Luckily for Alexander a young peasant by the name of Osip Komisarov pushed the would-be assassin at the final moment causing the shot to miss. Karakozov was arrested and imprisoned in the fortress, later to be hanged. Komisarov, meanwhile, was awarded a diamond ring from the Tsar and became an overnight sensation, fêted throughout the city as a peasant hero. A year later, during a trip to Paris, Alexander was shot at again by a Russian émigré, but yet again escaped unharmed.

Over a decade would pass before the next wave of terror began. In January 1878 a young female revolutionary, Vera Zasulich, shot and gravely wounded the St Petersburg Chief of Police Fyodor Trepov. This was followed by the fatal stabbing in front of the Mikhailovsky Palace of the Chief of the Gendarmes, Mezentsov, a hated figure among revolutionaries. Revolutionaries began to announce their planned exploits, often warning their victims. Soon they were ready to again make an attempt on Alexander. As one revolutionary put it, 'It was getting strange to beat the servants for doing the bidding of the master and not touching the master.'[34] To accomplish this goal, a small group of revolutionaries formed a group called The People's Will with the expressed purpose of assassinating the Tsar. The group was led by Andrei Zhelyabov, a quiet and intense revolutionary, and his mistress, Sophia Perovskaya, the daughter of the ex-governor of St Petersburg. It was like a page out of Chernyshevsky's *What Is To Be Done?*.

In 1879 they struck. This time the Tsar was walking alone, as was his habit, on Palace Square. Alexander Solovyov fired five times at close range, but once again, the assassin missed his mark, was apprehended and hanged. The group then tried to blow up the imperial train near Moscow. However, the first set of explosives did not go off. The second attempt succeeded, though it destroyed the wrong train. The next plan was unparalleled in its boldness: to attempt to attack the Emperor in his own home, the Winter Palace. A member of the group, Stephan Khalturin, got a job as a footman at the palace and over time smuggled in a horde of dynamite, which he stored in a small chamber two storeys below the Tsar's personal dining room. On the evening of 5 February 1880, at the exact time the Tsar and the imperial family dined each evening, the bomb was detonated. The resulting explosion resounded throughout the city as it tore upwards through the palace demolishing the dining room and a guard's chamber, killing eleven and wounding fifty-six. However, the Tsar, waiting for a guest arriving late from Berlin, had postponed the dinner and once again cheated death at the hands of The People's Will.

Alexander was horrified to have been attacked in his own palace and his family put in danger. 'Am I such a wild animal that I must be hounded to death?' he exclaimed. The atmosphere in St Petersburg and around the Tsar became tense as he ordered a state of martial law and appointed General Loris-Melikov to bring security back to the state. This he did by not only clamping down on revolutionaries but by sacking conservative ministers and relaxing censorship, betting that liberal reforms would offset any attraction to socialism.[35]

The People's Will, however, was undaunted. They were determined and decided to hunt Alexander down on the streets. They studied his movements and habits, noted the shops and parks he frequented, the routes he travelled and when they changed. They planted bombs everywhere. The situation became so bad that when Alexander attended the opera during Christmas 1880, he found the house nearly empty as terrified courtiers feared for their lives in his presence.[36] The next serious attempt was planned to mine one of the streets leading to the parade ground of the Mikhailovsky Palace, frequented on Sundays by the Tsar. The group rented a small dairy shop on the route and began to dig a tunnel underneath the street. All of a sudden plans changed, as Zhelyabov was arrested in connection with another incident. Distraught, Sophia nevertheless decided to continue with the mission.

The morning of 1 March 1881 found Alexander in an exceptionally good mood. Count Loris-Melikov was just completing a new round of reforms, which would allow for elected representatives from around the empire to participate in the Council of State. Alexander noted, 'I have given my approval, but I do not hide from myself the fact that it is the first step towards a constitution.'[37] Its program was to be announced the following day. Alexander left on his usual routine to observe drilling of troops on the Field of Mars. Unbeknownst to him, The People's Will was preparing to pounce, this time with a new weapon. Nikolai Kibalchich, a member of the group and an explosives expert, had invented a hand-thrown bomb, which was filled with sharp pieces of metal surrounding two delicate vials of nitroglycerine which were placed crossways so as to explode upon impact – the first grenade.

On his way back the Tsar altered his regular route by stopping to visit his aunt at the Mikhailovsky Palace. Quickly Sophia ordered the redeployment of assailants along the Catherine Canal, the quickest route back to the Winter Palace. As the imperial carriage thundered on to the embankment the first assailant stepped in the path of the oncoming coach and hurled his grenade under the carriage. A terrific explosion lifted the carriage off the ground and jagged shards of metal shattered the undercarriage, killing two Cossack guards and three of the Tsar's horses. The carriage, which had been a special present from Napoleon III, was actually bomb-proof, and the Tsar shaken but unscathed emerged from the carriage to see what had happened.

Alexander was enraged at the scene of carnage and turned to see the assailant being seized by several policemen. 'What have you done, you madman?' the Tsar shouted as a crowd gathered. An officer approached him and asked, 'Your majesty, are you injured?' The Tsar, looking around at the destroyed carriage and several bodies replied, 'No, thank God.' The assailant, Nikolai Rysakov, heard this as he struggled with his captors and cried out, 'It is too soon to thank God!' Just then a second assailant, Ignacy Hyrniewicki, a radical of Polish extraction, quickly approached the Tsar and tossed a second grenade right at the sovereign's feet. A second explosion rocked the embankment. The Tsar's legs were crushed by the force of the blast and his torn body was thrown back against the canal railing. Although drenched in blood, his midsection nearly eviscerated and blinded in one eye, the Tsar remained alive for the moment and still conscious. He motioned to his officers and hoarsely whispered 'Quickly! . . . Home to the palace to die.'

At lightning speed the Tsar was carried to the Winter Palace, where an anxious imperial family awaited. During the journey, Alexander continued to murmur questions inquiring to the condition of his heir, who was not present at the bombing, and asked for more blankets. When the carriage pulled up to the palace, Alexander had lost so much blood that when the footmen opened the door blood poured out.[38] The Tsar's nephew Grand Duke Alexander Mikhailovich described the pandemonium:

We . . . started a mad race toward the Winter Palace, passing on our way the Preobrazhensky Regiment of the Guards doubling in the same direction with fixed bayonets. Thousands of people were already surrounding the palace

While a devastating blow to the reform movement, the assassination of Alexander II on the Ekaterinsky Embankment was viewed as a triumph for the radicals who believed a return to repression as a step toward the revolution.

. . . there was no need to ask questions; large drops of black blood showed us the way up the marble steps and then along the corridor to the Emperor's study. . . . The Emperor lay on the couch near the desk. He was unconscious. Three doctors were fussing around, but science was obviously helpless. . . . He presented a terrific sight, his right leg torn off, his left leg shattered, innumerable wounds all over his head and face. One eye shut, the other expressionless. . . . Princess Yurievsky burst in, half dressed. Something or perhaps some over-zealous guard had detained her. She fell flat on the couch over the body of the Tsar, kissing his hands and screaming, 'Sasha, Sasha!'[39]

Barely an hour from the time he was taken to the palace, surrounded by his family, including his son the Tsarevitch Alexander Alexandrovich (the future Alexander III) and his grandson the Grand Duke Nikolai Alexandrovich (the future Nicholas II), Tsar Alexander II was finally declared dead. The People's Will had triumphed.

'JUST THE CUDGEL WITHOUT PETER THE GREAT'

Alexander III set the tone of his reign with his first act as Tsar. Upon being declared Emperor he walked over to his father's desk, picked up the newly drafted reform manifesto and tore it up.[40] He then gave the order to swiftly round up the conspirators who planned his father's assassination. Within a fortnight they were all imprisoned. Two weeks later, on 3 April, just over a month after the assassination, five bodies swung from a gallows in Semenovsky Square, with the last conspirator on her way to a life of penal servitude, spared only due to the fact that she was pregnant. While at first revolutionaries celebrated the death of Alexander II and the martyrdom of their compatriots, they were not prepared for the hammer blow of reaction that was to follow.

In his first public appearance as Tsar, Alexander III rode out of the palace accompanied by an entire regiment of Don Cossacks armed with red lances and galloping in attack formation.[41] This show of pageantry and strength was a symbolic act, which declared to Russians that this Alexander would rule over them, not with them. In his ascension manifesto Alexander stated that his goals as Tsar were 'the preservation of order and power, the maintenance of justice and thrift, a return to true Russian principles and the

guaranteeing of Russian interests everywhere.'[42] The new Tsar laid the blame for a decade of instability and the death of his father squarely at the feet of radical and reformist movements and decided resolutely to reverse their influence on his empire.

Alexander III was unlike any ruler Russia had ever endured before. He was a giant of a man with great physical strength, who dressed in loose clothing fashioned on traditional peasant garb and wore a full beard. Intellectually incurious, he was frugal with his finances and eschewed much of the pomp associated with court life. He even refused to move into the Winter Palace, considering it unsafe, preferring to maintain his residence at the smaller and well-guarded Anichkov Palace on the Nevsky Prospect. Eventually, in a move that displayed his distaste and suspicion for the capital, he transferred his family and his court to the imperial estate at Gatchina 40 miles away. Surrounded by layers of security Alexander raised his family in Antonio Rinaldi's grim castle, which had been the favourite residence of Paul I. At Gatchina, the Tsar could live in bourgeois privacy surrounded by his family and favourites, hunting, fishing and cutting down trees, his preferred pastimes.

But Alexander was no hermit; he was a fervent Russian nationalist and had a strong political agenda, which he was determined to implement. Like his grandfather Nicholas I Alexander believed in the trinity of autocracy, orthodoxy and nationality. These pillars of empire had been reinforced by his political mentor and tutor the infamous archconservative Constantine Pobedonostsev. The Procurator of the Holy Synod, Pobedonostsev was referred to by his enemies as the 'Black Tsar' and had instilled Alexander with a strong suspicion of democratic institutions and a deep reverence for his role as Tsar of All the Russias. Upon assuming the throne Alexander replaced all of the progressives in his government with reactionaries and began to construct a modern police state. His security forces would institute a 'White Terror' to quash the radical revolutionary movement and halt the nascent political reforms seeking to form a civil society within Russia. Revolutionary leaders driven out of St Petersburg, Georgy Plekhanov, Pavel Akselrod and Vera Zasulich, all fled to the West.

St Petersburg, however, breathed a collective sigh of relief. After a tumultuous decade of assassinations, explosions and political agitation, the city was ready for a change. The reaction to Alexander II's death had been one of great sympathy and despair and the city Duma even erected a small wooden chapel on the site of the

murder. Alexander III found this inadequate and ordered the construction of a massive church on the site. Begun in 1883 but not completed until 1907, the church was built in the Muscovite Revival style with colourful onion domes in imitation of St Basil's in Red Square. It was called the Church of the Resurrection of Christ, but acquired the ghoulish nickname the Saviour's Church of the Spilt Blood, as inside there remained a patch of pavement, covered with an elaborate canopy, where Alexander II's blood could still be seen.

Although disliked by the new Tsar, St Petersburg flourished under his reign. Economically the city saw its fortunes rise as political stability encouraged further foreign investment and the expansion of industry. The appointments of Ivan Wyschnegradsky as Minister of Finance and Sergius Witte as Minister of Communications saw an incredible influx of French capital into St Petersburg's banks and a four-fold expansion of Russia's railways, including the start of the monumental Trans-Siberian Railway. Many of the capital's elite, enriched by the influx of new funds, quickly adopted the Tsar's slogan of political stability and

ABOVE The stout figure of Alexander III on his steed was indeed the image he projected, strength and stability based on a foundation of conservatism.
RIGHT Fearful of his own and his family's safety, Alexander preferred to reside at the Anichkov Palace in St Petersburg (above) or the heavily guarded Gatchina Palace (below).

order above all else and happily joined in his crusade to ferret out the enemies of the established order. Many even went so far as to form the 'Holy Brotherhood', a secret society to help protect the new Tsar and combat terrorism, which mainly included the members of the exclusive St Petersburg Yacht Club. Their efforts eventually became a farce after members were discovered to have misappropriated funds for Riviera holidays, but, even more embarrassingly, began arresting undercover Okhrana agents, or secret police that they had mistaken as revolutionaries.[43] They were soon afterwards disbanded on the recommendation of the Minister of the Interior.

RED STAR RISING

In the autumn of 1893, the twenty-three-year-old Vladimir Ulyanov stepped off the train in St Petersburg for the first time. Short and stocky with increasingly thinning hair, Vladimir surveyed the capital of legend with his piercing eyes, the city he had heard so much about from the letters of his brother Alexander. He had come ostensibly to work in a law office, a job that had been arranged for him, but Vladimir had other motives. Like many before him he had come to St Petersburg to seek his destiny, which would bring him fame and renown across the empire and around the globe. Unbeknownst to the denizens and lords of Peter's city, however, this man's destiny would lead him one day, like the apocalyptic stories of old, to sweep away the society in which they all existed and on which they all depended. This man was Lenin.

Vladimir was the son of a provincial official and nobleman who came from humble origins. His father, Ilya Ulyanov, was the son of a freed serf and had through his own efforts risen to become the Director of Schools for the province of Simbirsk. He was so successful that the government bestowed upon him the designation of State Councillor, the lowest rank of the hereditary nobility. Young Vladimir Ilyich was a precocious lad who often referred to himself as 'a squire's son'.[44] He was actively religious as well as a good student. Everything in his upbringing pointed to his being bred to join the establishment of the empire; that was until tragedy struck.

Vladimir Ilyich had come to St Petersburg in the footsteps of his brother. Alexander Ulyanov had been executed six years earlier after being implicated in a failed plot to assassinate the emperor. The news of his trial and execution had radicalized young Vladimir. Upon entering the University of Kazan in 1887 he immediately joined a group of students involved in the revolutionary movement. He was later arrested during a student demonstration and expelled

from school. Following his disgrace he spent years on his family country estate, studying law and reading constantly the texts of past and contemporary radicals, including Chernyshevsky's *What Is To Be Done?*, which affected him profoundly. Like his brother, Vladimir was heavily influenced by the violent philosophies of Sergei Nechaev and Peter Tkachev and actions of The People's Will, the revolutionary terrorist organization responsible for Alexander II's assassination. Only later did he approach the works of the man with whom he would be most associated, Karl Marx.

Marxism came to Russia in 1872 when the first copy of *Das Kapital* slipped past the censors, who thought that its dense technical style would be nearly impenetrable for most Russians and believed its theories did not apply to Russian reality.[45] At first this proved true; however, by the end of the decade intellectuals such as Plekhanov had turned to Marx. Having entered a wilderness of doubt following decades of futile terrorism and Tsarist repression, the demoralized radical community found hope in Marx's theories

LEFT The throne room at Peterhof. Alexander III's first act as Tsar was to tear up his father's reform manifesto and to reassert the prerogative of the monarch.
ABOVE RIGHT Alexander III ordered the construction of a church on the spot of his father's assassination along the Catherine Canal. The church was called the Church of the Resurrection of Christ or Our Saviour of the Spilt Blood.

Once again Peter the Great's 'window on the West' became the portal through which new ideas would come to challenge the established order. Later Soviet historians would seek to legitimize the Soviet government's rule and bolster its credentials by making a historic link to the 'revolutionary' reign of Peter and his city. As Peter sought to borrow from the West to modernize Old Muscovy, radicals of the late nineteenth century saw themselves as doing likewise, bringing a new gospel of change to a Russia shackled beneath an anachronistic autocracy.

By the time he had arrived in St Petersburg in 1893 Vladimir Ulyanov was a fully fledged convert to the revolutionary cause. He published his first treatise *The Development of Capitalism in Russia* that same year and upon arrival in the capital joined a Marxist study group. The St Petersburg intelligentsia were taken aback by his rough and provincial appearance and were disturbed by his cutting wit and mocking laugh. But Vladimir's clear leadership ability and his acceptance of the intellectual primacy of their guru, Plekhanov, won him their confidence and even their affection, as was the case with his future wife, Nadezhda Krupskaya. Vladimir became a leading propagandist with the purpose of educating the vanguard of 'conscious workers' who were to organize the proletariat for the future revolution.[47] Vladimir and his compatriots soon found that not all of St Petersburg's workers were inclined to join the revolutionary struggle. Many saw a future for themselves in the economic prosperity of Alexander III's Russia and wanted to move up the ladder not topple it over. The radicals then redirected their energies toward openly campaigning for workers' concerns through what was termed 'mass agitation'. This included the organization of workers' actions and strikes. In 1895, they quickly formed the grandly named Union of Struggle for the Emancipation of the Working Class to begin this process. That was as far as they got. Tsarist officials arrested the group as soon as it was organized. Vladimir was sentenced to a year in prison and then three years in exile in Siberia.

on economic and social development. No longer would they concentrate on organizing Russia's peasant communes as a means to bring socialism to Russia. Now they would turn to the emerging Russian proletariat, whose numbers were most concentrated in St Petersburg. One early Russian Marxist Nikolai Valentinov recalled:

> We seized on Marxism because we were attracted by its sociological and economic optimism, its strong belief, buttressed by facts and figures, that the development of the economy, the development of capitalism, by demoralizing and eroding the foundations of the old society, was creating new social forces (including us) which would certainly sweep away the autocratic regime together with its abominations. With the optimism of youth we had been searching for a formula that offered hope, and we found it in Marxism. We were also attracted by its European nature. Marxism came from Europe. It did not smell and taste of home-grown mould and provincialism, but was new, fresh, and exciting. Marxism held out a promise that we would not stay a semi-Asiatic country, but would become part of the West with its culture, institutions and attributes of a free political system. The West was our guiding light.[46]

After his release from prison in 1896 he boarded the train that had brought him to St Petersburg and took it eastwards into exile. As the city passed by the steamed-up windows, Vladimir, alone with his trunk of books, turned his mind towards the future. Years later he would return to St Petersburg briefly before heading abroad into self-imposed exile. When he finally returned to St Petersburg in 1917, he would not merely organize and agitate, but triumph and rule. The revolution had begun.

ABOVE Vladimir Ilych Ulyanov, known to the world as Lenin, was only in St Petersburg a short time before he was arrested as an agitator and exiled to Siberia.
RIGHT Designed by Alfred Parland, the cupolas on the Church of the Resurrection of Christ or Our Saviour of the Spilt Blood (1883–1907) reflected Alexander III's return to the values of Old Russia in direct contradiction to Peter the Great's reason for the foundation of St Petersburg as a 'window on the West'.

CHAPTER 5:
IMPERIAL TWILIGHT

The accession of Alexander III marked a return to tradition. The new Tsar was a strict conservative, whose views harked back to the Slavophile movement of the mid-nineteenth century, with its romantic and reactionary praise of the values of Old Russia. However, as the weight of repression slowly crushed all political opposition, the other side of the scales lifted, giving rise to a period of cultural renaissance that was without parallel in the nation's history. Alexander would leave his son Nicholas II a Russia that was poised for greatness, yet rife with unresolved political and social resentment. As these boiled over in St Petersburg, events and trends seemed to speed up, as if racing toward a predetermined end. *Fin de siècle* St Petersburg became an idealistic cauldron of cultural expression, in which a heady brew of political, philosophical, artistic and spiritual ideas reacted to create a legacy, epic in scope, that has endured for nearly a century. As twilight fell on the imperial capital, St Petersburg seemed to become ephemeral, the silver light and the coming darkness fading its lines and dulling its senses as if the city itself were already passing into legend.

MUSIC FOR THE TSAR

There is a story that when the composer Mikhail Glinka left St Petersburg for good in 1856, he had his carriage stop at the city limits so that he could get out and spit on the ground in disgust at the city that had denied him respect. After his death in Berlin a year later, his body was returned to 'vile' and 'hateful St Petersburg',[1] where he was buried in a small ceremony. Few would have believed that this man, forgotten at his death, would be recognized by future generations as the 'father of Russian national music'. Glinka had burst on to the scene in 1836 with the premiere of his first opera entitled *A Life for the Tsar*. The opera was based on the tale by Ivan Susanin about a Russian peasant who sacrifices his life to save the first Romanov Tsar, Mikhail I, from the invading Poles. Its nationalistic theme helped it to gain the full support of Nicholas I, who saw it as a cultural extension of his policies. Far more importantly, however, it marked a monumental shift in Russian music. With *A Life for the Tsar* Glinka became the first Russian composer to introduce with amazing effect traditional Russian folk melodies into what was otherwise European-influenced composition.

Yet after this success the composer's career did not flourish. Glinka, small, pasty and dishevelled, was a true St Petersburg

Sunset at the Catherine Palace, Tsarskoe Selo.

nobleman, with a reputation for being a hypochondriac as well as a famous drunkard, never without his trademark glass of champagne. He craved adulation from his friends and yearned for public recognition for his talent. His capricious nature made his marriage difficult and in 1840 he decided to leave St Petersburg for Paris. Before his departure, however, he composed a cycle of twelve songs entitled *Farewell to St Petersburg*, whose subsequent success reversed his decision to leave, so that he could enjoy the limelight once more. Following this achievement, Glinka bet his entire career on his next great opera, the fairy tale *Ruslan and Ludmila*, based on the poem by Pushkin. The opera premiered in 1842 with a gala performance attended by Nicholas I. Half way through the performance disaster struck. The Tsar stood and left the theatre, a devastating verdict for any composer. Glinka fell into a deep depression and left Russia for Europe in 1844, returning to St Petersburg infrequently. While Glinka never did receive the accolades he craved during his lifetime, within Russia the legacy of his music endured.

Life for musicians in St Petersburg was difficult. Those who worked in the capital's various opera houses and theatres were thought of as state employees rather than artists. They were assigned a social position commensurate to civil servants and were compensated as such. Beyond the state institutions there was little opportunity for musicians. Public concerts were forbidden except during Lent, when the imperial theatres were closed, and private salons paid little. Another major factor that exacerbated the lot of the Russian musical world during the early to mid-nineteenth century was that there was no official conservatory of music from which to train new musicians and composers. Most of them were forced to train abroad in the conservatories and salons of Berlin, Vienna and Italy. This continued to bring the latest trends of music from Europe to St Petersburg but did little to foster a Russian national school. It would be up to Anton Rubenstein, a young pianist and virtuoso, to change this.

Having studied and achieved success abroad, Rubenstein was painfully aware of the dearth of music education in Russia and sought support to found Russia's first music school in St Petersburg. He found a strong supporter in Grand Duchess Elena Pavlova, the German born wife of the Tsar's brother Grand Duke Mikhail, who shared his passion for music and became his patron. Together, they founded the Russian Musical Society in 1859, which held regular symphonic and chamber concerts. Eventually, in 1862, the society began to conduct classes and accept students. Such was their elevated status that the society then changed its name to the St Petersburg Conservatory and moved into a new building complex alongside the recently constructed Mariinsky Theatre by Albert Cavos on Theatre Square, the former location of the old Bolshoi Theatre.

Although performing arts had been present in St Petersburg since the age of Peter, much of it was confined to small private theatres such as this one in the Yussupov Palace (right). State support for the arts in the nineteenth century led to the construction of St Petersburg's premier imperial venue, the Mariinsky Theatre (above).

In accordance with St Petersburg tradition the conservatory brought in foreign professors to teach Russian students a curriculum that was steeped in the musical traditions of Western Europe. Having been trained in Germany, Rubenstein particularly favoured German musical theory and practice and employed many professors of German extraction. With such a heavy foreign influence, the conservatory concentrated little on Russian traditional folk or religious music. In fact, Rubenstein was of the idea that Russian national music, though of 'ethnographical interest', was without artistic merit.[2] He even had the temerity to criticize Glinka as an amateur. This attitude enraged the likes of cultural critics such as Vladimir Stasov, who was dedicated to the creation of a Russian national school of arts. He, along with other musical dilettantes in the capital, felt that Rubenstein's conservatory, with its heavy foreign, i.e. German, perspective, was having a stultifying effect on the development of Russian national music.

THE MIGHTY HANDFUL

Stasov was a great supporter of the Russian tradition of the aristocratic music salon from which Glinka had emerged. He felt that only in this environment could creativity be fostered. It was in the musical laboratory of Alexander Dargomyzhky that Stasov's seeds of reaction to Rubenstein's conservatory were sown and germinated. Dargomyzhky was an old-world aristocrat and amateur composer who wrote experimental music to accompany the poetic verse of Pushkin, Lermontov and the French poet Pierre-Jean Béranger, while sitting Glinka-style beneath the warm glow of two candelabra. He surrounded himself with female singers, amateur songbirds whose youth, beauty and fawning admiration made up for any faltering notes. Dargomyzhky, however, was no hack. He was serious about his music and its possibilities. 'I do not intend to debase music to the level of mere amusement. . . . I want the notes to express exactly what the words express. I want truth.'[3] He achieved moderate success in 1856 with his opera *Rusalka*, based on a Pushkin tale, again in imitation of Glinka. The success of *Rusalka* brought new admirers in the form of young and talented musicians and composers who wished to learn more about his expressive style.

In 1856 Stasov presented to Dargomyzhky a young and fiery youth from Nizhni Novgorod who had come to St Petersburg to pursue a career in music: Mili Balakirev. Balakirev had been fortunate enough to meet Glinka and was among his most avid admirers. He sought to carry on the legacy of Glinka through the promotion of a new national music inspired by the musical and literary folk traditions of the Russian people.[4] Balakirev was soon joined at Dargomyzhky's by two more virtuosos who shared his passion and his goals. The first was César Cui, a talented former army officer of French and Lithuanian decent who, like Dostoyevsky, had graduated from the Imperial Engineering School. He had become a fortifications engineer but, like Balakirev, his love for music had brought him Dargomyzhky's. The next to join their number was another officer, this time of the famed Preobrazhensky Guards regiment, by the name of Modest Mussorgsky. Mussorgsky was a talented pianist with a promising army career until Stasov discovered him and, with Balakirev's help, convinced the officer to resign his commission and join them in their project to create a national music.[5]

Due to his penchant for command and boundless energy, Balakirev became the leader of this new group of dilettantes, none of whom had any real musical training. He not only taught Mussorgsky how to compose by studying and playing with him all of Beethoven's symphonies in piano arrangements, but he also familiarized himself with Russian folk music by going out into the countryside, taking a boat down the Volga to record on paper the various songs of the bargemen and haulers. This experience would later lead him to compose *The Song of the Volga Boatmen*. Balakirev also began to expand the group by drawing in Nikolai Rimsky-Korsakov, a seventeen-year-old naval cadet who, after composing a few piano pieces, demonstrated to the group his potential. In 1862 Mussorgsky brought in the final member of the group, Alexander Borodin, the illegitimate son of a Georgian prince, and a practising chemist. Once formed, the quintet became a powerhouse of creative inspiration, generating some of imperial Russia's most evocative and emotional pieces of music. Stasov christened them the *Moguchaya Kuchka* (the Mighty Handful).

The Mighty Handful gathered in salons, including those of Dargomyzhky, Stasov and wealthy sophisticate Nikolai Purgold, to listen and play each others music, helping one another fine tune their art and providing criticism. In 1862, under Balakirev's leadership, they formed the Free Music School as a direct rival to Rubenstein's conservatory, which would foster and cultivate native Russian talent in a free and creative environment. The music that emerged from this experimental school and the Handful drew its inspiration from the countryside of Russia with its villages and estates, the lusty dances of the Cossacks and the Caucasus and the mystical hymns and sonorous bells of the Russian Orthodox Church. It sought to draw closer to the Russian soil by imitating in music the sounds of Russian life.[6]

The death of Dargomyzhky left Balakirev even more in control of the Handful and of the Free School. As he sought to shepherd them all further on a nationalist course, frictions began to arise. Over time this led to the break-up of the original five, as each sought their independence from Balakirev's increasingly dictatorial guidance in order to pursue their own work. Borodin later recalled:

> This is nothing but a natural situation. As long as we were in the position of eggs under a sitting hen, we were all more or less alike. As soon as the fledglings broke out of their shells, they grew feathers. Each of them had to grow different feathers; and when their wings grew, each flew where his nature drew him.[7]

The break-up affected the careers of each of the five differently. The first two members, although heavily influential in the development of the group, produced very little in the way of memorable music. After the break-up, Balakirev was devastated. The composer of two symphonies, his symphonic poems *Tamara* and *Russia*, as well as his dazzling work for piano, *Islamey*, and countless songs, was suddenly without his musical family. Although he left music briefly in 1872, turning to religion then railway work, he later returned to begin composing again and resumed his position at the Free School. César Cui, although the most prolific of the five, was always considered its most mediocre member. He produced ten operas, thirty choruses and some two hundred songs, among other works, none of which is included in popular repertoires of Russian music either in Russia or in the West. Cui was best known as the chief critic of the five, honing their skills and focussing their efforts on the creation of Russian opera, where he felt the national music excelled.[8] Cui eventually became a professional critic writing for one of St Petersburg's newspapers, even having his articles published abroad from time to time.

The last two to join the five, Borodin and Rimsky-Korsakov, became the group's most successful stars, producing among the most beloved music in the Handful's repertoire. Alexander Borodin always considered himself the least dedicated of the Mighty Handful, often referring to himself as a 'Sunday composer', as he worked on his music only when he was not engaged in his duties as head of the chemistry department of the Petersburg Medical-Surgical Academy.[9] Yet his works, which included his great nationalistic opera *Prince Igor* with its mesmerizing *Polovtsian Dances*, his symphonic work *In the Steppes of Central Asia* and his haunting *Nocturne* from the second string quartet, have become classics of the Russian nationalist genre, played by orchestras around the world.

Rimsky-Korsakov became the finest and most successful musician of the original five. As well as completing his operas *The Snow Maiden*, *The Maid of Pskov*, *The Tsar's Bride*, *Sadko*, *The Legend of the Invisible City of Kitezh* and *The Golden Cockerel*, he also produced major orchestral pieces, such as the *Russian Easter Festival Overture*, *Scheherazade* and *The Flight of the Bumblebee*. Rimsky-Korsakov would also go on to complete many of the works of Mussgorsky, Dargomyzhky, Borodin and Cui which were left unfinished after their deaths. He was the only one of the five to cross over and work with members of the imperial conservatory. He made friends with Rubenstein and even took a position teaching practical composition at the conservatory in 1871. His success brought him international fame and imperial recognition during his own lifetime and Rimsky-Korsakov is remembered as one of Russia's masters of orchestration. All of his major works are part of the canon of Russian national music.

THE RADICAL AND THE ROMANTIC

Of the Mighty Handful, none could match the artistic and radical intensity of its towering member, Modest Mussorgsky. Mussorgsky was the embodiment of the nationalist St Petersburg composer, who through his music wrestled with the philosophical and spiritual conflicts inherent in Peter's city. He would come to represent expressionist music at its most audacious while desperately trying to keep his sympathies firmly on Russian ground. In this he was of the same mind as his mentor Dargomyzhky, whose character and music were heavily influenced by the imperial capital, especially its tradition of celebrating dark and comic heroes. Mussorgsky's first operatic endeavour was based on Gogol's play *The Marriage*, and its musical effect was as jarring as its subject matter. Even Dargomyzhky pondered whether Mussorgsky had gone too far.[10] Yet the young composer had broken new ground, setting a trend that would last his entire career.

The young Mussorgsky was also being influenced be the social and political movements active in Petersburg during the 1860s. Like many artists of his generation, he subscribed to the dictums of Chernyshevsky's essay 'Aesthetic Relations of Art to Reality', which preached that 'beauty is life; beautiful is that being in which we see life as it should be according to our own conceptions; beautiful is the object which expresses life, or reminds us of life'.[11] Chernyshevsky called on artists to be realistic and progressive in order to aid societal change.[12] Mussorgsky considered himself a radical, living in a commune and working in the communal atmosphere of the Mighty Handful. When the group disintegrated he despaired at the loss of his 'family'. However, this was not the reality of the composer's character. Mussorgsky was always the most solitary composer of the five and his music the most individualistic, original and forward-looking, perhaps due to the fact that he was the least schooled of the group and thus unencumbered by technical tradition. He longed for realism, attempting to imitate in musical form the sounds of the human voice and the natural sounds of Russian life, a trait for which he was criticized. 'Nothing that is natural can be wrong or inartistic,'[13] he once said. Mussorgsky's *Pictures at an Exhibition* was the first of his works to express this ideal fully, breaking the rules of Western musical composition and doing the most to define what would become known as the Russian national style.[14] The music moves like a

meandering visitor through a picture gallery, being drawn, many times violently, into the powerful images he is viewing. While he claimed himself to be a St Petersburg 'realist', a trip to Moscow in 1859 enchanted him with the glories of Old Muscovy, after which he spent the next thirteen years writing *Boris Godunov* and *Khovanshchina*, as well as the famous *Night on a Bald Mountain*, all influenced by nationalist themes. The heroes he created for the two operas, however, were as conflicted and complex as any of Dostoyevsky's characters, resulting in works that were purely Petersburgian in style rather than jingoistic celebrations of history.

Mussorgsky's life began to unravel in 1874. It was as if his person could no longer bear the constant conflicts between politics and art, old and new Russia, urban and village life, which informed his work. The failure of his opera *Boris Godunov* after its original triumphant premiere drove Mussorgsky to drink, and soon he became a severe alcoholic. 'Mussorgsky is a changed completely . . . his face is swollen and dark in colour, his eyes are dull and he spends days on end in a

St Petersburg restaurant with a cursed bunch of drunkards,'[15] claimed Stasov, commenting on the composer's slide into alcoholism. That same year he also composed an autobiographical cycle of songs called *Sunless*. This cycle was his most Petersburgian of works, which, in the spirit of Gogol and Dostoyevsky, dealt with the artist's isolation and loneliness in Peter's city. Mussorgsky was eventually committed to a hospital, where he was painted by Ilya Repin, a work that shows a broken man, bloated and dying. Four days later his suffering was brought to an end by a fatal stroke brought on by a bottle of cognac, crying 'It's all over! Ah, I am a wretch!'[16]

Through the confrontation of St Petersburg's political and cultural conflicts, Mussorgsky revolutionized Russian national music. His contemporary Peter Tchaikovsky, meanwhile, would come to personify the St Petersburg ideal, unabashedly fusing Western technique with Russian style creating works that transcended nationalism to reach audiences around the globe. The cultural critic Solomon Volkov wrote in *St Petersburg: A Cultural History* (1995): 'Depicting Petersburg and its themes in his symphonies, Tchaikovsky covered a path in a quarter of a century that took the rest of Russian culture one hundred and fifty years to traverse.'[17] He is considered by many as Russia's greatest composer. Works such as the *1812 Overture*, *The Nutcracker*, *Swan Lake*, *Sleeping Beauty* and *Romeo and Juliet* have filtered into international popular culture and can be heard in films, television, advertisements and holiday celebrations. 'Like Mussorgsky, Tchaikovsky through his music also struggled not only with the dual nature of St Petersburg culture, but with his own inner conflicts and darkness which eventually overwhelmed him.'[18]

Tchaikovsky was born in the Ural mining town of Votkinsk in 1840. At the age of ten he and his family moved to St Petersburg, where he was first introduced to Glinka's *A Life for the Tsar*. Interested in music from an early age, he nevertheless entered the School of Jurisprudence, after which he started a career as a civil servant in the Ministry of Justice. It was only in 1861 that he began training at the Russian Musical Society, soon attracting the attention of Rubenstein, who admitted him to the first class of the new St Petersburg Conservatory. Four years later Tchaikovsky's reputation

ABOVE Portrait of Modest Mussorgsky shortly before his death in 1881 by Ilya Repin (Tretyakov Gallery, Moscow).

had grown and his talent was well recognized, at least by some. César Cui described the young composer's graduating composition as 'totally without merit',[19] which devastated Tchaikovsky. On his graduation in 1866, however, Rubenstein offered him a teaching position at the new Moscow Conservatory.

Being a product of the imperial conservatory, Tchaikovsky was an ardent traditionalist and classicist when it came to his composition and he was suspicious and dismissive of the work of the Free School and of the Mighty Handful. Nonetheless in 1868 Tchaikovsky met Balakirev and was invited to meet the rest of the group. While this meeting produced little other than courteous recognition with most of the five, Tchaikovsky would befriend Balakirev and dedicate the theme of *Romeo and Juliet* to him in 1869. This relationship would also bear fruit in Tchaikovsky's *Symphony No. 2*, with its Ukrainian folk themes. On the other hand, Mussorgsky and Tchaikovsky became hostile towards each other, swapping barbs and insults. Tchaikovsky was quoted in print as describing Mussorgsky's *Boris Godunov* as 'musical defecation'.[20]

Although Tchaikovsky expressed a sentimental weakness for the old capital, Moscow, his sympathies and inspiration lay firmly with St Petersburg. 'I admit I have a great weakness for the Russian capital. What can I do? I've become too much a part of it. Everything that is dear to my heart is in St Petersburg, and life without it is positively impossible for me.'[21] Tchaikovsky's music drew its lifeblood from this passion for the many sounds and songs of the city. Tchaikovsky was not politically or philosophically married to the idea of creating strictly Russian music and therefore was free to draw upon various sources such as Italian and French opera, gypsy music or parade marches. His first three symphonies, as well as his *1812 Overture* and *Slavonic March*, show his use of these disparate influences but also his celebration of the city and its imperial ideals. Tchaikovsky was fascinated with the capital's aristocratic heritage and drew upon Pushkin for ideas, turning his works *Eugene Onegin* and *The Queen of Spades* into operas.

In 1877 Tchaikovsky had a mental breakdown as a result of his personal life. Tchaikovsky was homosexual, yet attempted to marry

ABOVE St Petersburg's frequent gloom was the inspiration of Mussorgsky's last composition, his autobiographical *Sunless*.

one of his pupils. This marriage was brief (only nine weeks) and a disaster. Fate, however, intervened with the appearance of Nadezhda von Meck, a rich widow and admirer of Tchaikovsky's music, who became his patron, giving him an income that allowed him to retire from teaching and devote himself to composition. Soon Tchaikovsky's star was in the ascendant; with the success of his opera *Eugene Onegin*, he was received into high society in St Petersburg as well as in foreign capitals where he was invited to perform. Imperial recognition soon followed and Tchaikovsky was asked to write a coronation march for Alexander III. In 1888 he was again given the imperial nod when the Tsar awarded him an annual salary, sealing his position as Russia's composer par excellence. His international fame became so great that he was invited to New York in 1891 to open Carnegie Hall, the same year that he began *The Nutcracker*. Tragically, Tchaikovsky had little time to enjoy his success. On 21 October 1893 he contracted cholera, presumably from drinking untreated water and died four days later.[22]

Thousands poured into the streets to mourn their fallen star, clogging Nevsky Prospect as far as the eye could see. Tchaikovsky's music, more than that of any other composer of the period, exemplified the spirit of late-imperial Russia and late-nineteenth-century St Petersburg. But for all its majesty and romanticism, Tchaikovsky's later music is also tinged with an incredible longing for love and a sense of impending doom. His final *Symphony No. 6 'Pathetique'* served as his musical last testament as well as his requiem. It is in this autobiographical and expressive work that the listener experiences the personal and passionate emotions, struggles and indignities that Tchaikovsky was forced to endure as a homosexual in the late nineteenth century and in which he, as a simple man, finally confronts his eventual demise. 'Pathetique' was his farewell to his beloved St Petersburg, as if he could see the city's approaching doom in the lengthening shadows of imperial twilight. No other Russian composer was affected by or connected to the city in the same way. His biographer Boris Asafyev explained:

> The poison of Petersburg nights, the sweet mirage of its ghostly images, the fogs of autumn and the bleak joys of summer, the cosiness and acute contradictions of Petersburg life, the meaningless waste of Petersburg sprees and the amorous longing of Petersburg's romantic rendezvous, delicious meetings and secret promises, cold disdain and indifference of a man of society for superstition and ritual

right up to blasphemous laughter about the other-worldly and at the same time the mystical fear of the unknown – all these moods and sensations poisoned Tchaikovsky's soul. He carried that poison with him always, and his music is imbued with it.[23]

THE WANDERERS

Music was not the only area of the arts finding itself divided between the nationalist vision of Russian culture and the St Petersburg ideal. From the 1860s, the art world itself began to fracture with the advent of the greater political awareness that was a result of the reforms of Alexander II. Art in Russia had become political propaganda during the previous reign of Nicholas I, who had commandeered the academy and its artists in the service of the state. Subject matter was strictly limited to classical themes and graduates were given ranks. Upon taking the throne Alexander II reversed this and liberalized the university system, appointing a new director of the Academy of Arts to institute changes.

One significant result of these changes was the Academy's attempt to welcome non-academy-trained artists to work in residence. One such artist was Vasily Perov from Moscow, who took up residence at the Academy, producing two canvases. The first, entitled *A Village Sermon*, claimed the Gold Medal that year; his second painting, however, caused a sensation when exhibited in 1862. Entitled *The Easter Procession*, it depicted a group of drunk and disorderly priests and peasant parishioners stumbling out of a village tavern and trying with much difficulty to form a religious procession. The Orthodox hierarchy was horrified at the portrayal of its priests in such a compromising state, while the authorities criticized Perov for representing peasants as disrespectful inebriates. Perov, whose reputation soared as a result of the scandal, had thrown down the gauntlet; Russian art had entered a new era.

In reaction to the fervour over Perov's painting and the student unrest of the previous year, Academy officials decided to restrict the subject matter of the 1863 Gold Medal competition to a single theme: 'The Banquet of the Gods at Valhalla'. This produced a protest by a group of fourteen artists led by Ivan Kramskoi, who petitioned to be allowed to choose their own subjects. Their request was flatly denied. In response the students resigned *en masse* from the Academy, leaving to establish their own artists' commune. The 'Rebellion of the Fourteen' was a great scandal

among the art community and beyond and led to a government-imposed media blackout.

Perov and the Fourteen, like their contemporary the composer Mussorgsky, were greatly influenced by Chernyshevsky's 'Aesthetic Relations of Art to Reality', which stressed beauty in life and stated that 'reality is not only more animated, but also more perfect than imagination'. He also called on artists to explain and 'pronounce judgment on the phenomena of life'.[24] The artists of the 1860s sought to break with tradition not only by depicting for their audiences subject matter taken directly from Russian life but also by enabling them to see beyond the apparent reality to revelation.

The seat of this new movement became the St Petersburg Co-operative of Artists (Artel), with headquarters in a large house on Vasilievsky Island. Here, in the style of Chernyshevsky, the artists of the commune shared everything from basic necessities to art supplies. They socialized, worked and exhibited together, abandoning the competitive nature of the Academy. From the beginning the artists concentrated on depicting realistic images of Russia's peasantry and common folk, themes which soon became in vogue with the art-buying public eager to participate in a more distant way with the reforms of the period. With the help of critic and social progressive Vladimir Stasov, the Artel's work was well publicized and patronized by princes and merchants alike. By the late 1860s it had cornered the St Petersburg art market.

In 1870 the Artel formally disbanded. Influenced by the growing 'Back to the Land' populist movement, Ivan Kramskoi, Vasily Perov, Nikolai Ge, Konstantin Makovsky, Ivan Shishkin, Grigory Miasoyedov and Arkhip Kuindzhi established the Society of Travelling Artists' Exhibitions, with the intention of bringing art to the people by exhibiting paintings in the provinces rather than only in St Petersburg and Moscow. Better known as the *Peredvizhniki* or The Wanderers, they declared in their opening manifesto:

All of us have agreed to a single idea . . . concerning the usefulness of an exhibition by the artists themselves. We think there is a possibility to free art from bureaucratic control and to widen the circle of those interested in art and subsequently widen the circle of buyers.[25]

In this they would succeed. Crowds throughout the Empire flocked to see The Wanderers' powerful and often shocking works in the forty-eight exhibitions they opened between 1871 and 1923.

BARGE HAULERS OF THE VOLGA

There was something eastern and ancient about it . . . the face of a Scyth. . . . And what eyes! What depth of vision! . . . And his brow, so large and wise. . . . He seemed to me a colossal mystery, and for that reason I loved him. Kanin, with a rag around his head, his clothes in patches made by himself and then worn out, appeared none the less as a man of dignity: he was like a saint.[26]

A young St Petersburg artist by the name of Ilya Repin wrote these words from the banks of the Volga where he was spending the summer following his graduation from the Academy. A protégé of The Wanderers, he had endeavoured for two years to gain the permissions and funds to make the trip and had slowly gained the confidence of the local peasantry who initially had been convinced that in sketching and painting their images he would steal their souls. Although he had chosen his subject matter three years earlier, here he finally encountered a group of men whose circumstance and appearance he hoped would encapsulate his vision.

The result of his labours was the monumental canvas *The Barge Haulers of the Volga*. A group of eleven men dressed in rags and bound in leather straps struggle along the muddy bank of the Volga as they haul a jaunty barge upriver against the current. The men, whose figures are bowed from the burden of their work, are stoic characters, their individual personalities brought to life by Repin. In reality they came from distant points of the empire. One had been a soldier, another an icon painter, and leading of the group was Kanin, a defrocked priest. Repin was dismayed at how such men could come to such a position in life. In these men he saw 'Greek philosophers, sold as slaves to the barbarians'.[27] In his finished canvas of 1873, Repin revealed to his audience through these peasants the character of Russia. Bound and shackled to a distant and uncompromising master, her true potential suppressed, Russia waits for relief from her burden, for a release from her torment. But Repin offers hope in the shape of a youth, the brightest of the painting's figures, who, standing upright, adjusts his straps, as if preparing to throw it off.

Barge Haulers of the Volga was received with rave reviews. The realistic and non-sentimental portrayal of Russia's lower classes imbued the painting with a power that was nothing short of awe-inspiring to a public used to classical scenes or propaganda. Vladimir Stasov held Repin up as the artist of the future whose work best represented the

values of the new populist movement in art. *Barge Haulers* remains the quintessential painting of The Wanderers and it launched Repin's career. Repin, however, was not interested in being a tool of the populist movement. He left that year for Vienna and Paris, where he studied and painted alongside the burgeoning impressionists. After initial enthusiasm, Repin found the art scene in Paris superficial and trite and returned to Russia in 1876 when he painted *On a Turf Bench*, one of the first Russian impressionist paintings.

After spending a year in his hometown of Chuguev, Repin moved to Moscow and, like many artists of the late 1870s, came under the spell of the ancient capital. He produced paintings of historic subjects, among them *Tsarevna Sophia Alexeevna in the Novodevitchy Convent* (1879), *The Reply of the Zaporozhian Cossacks to Sultan Mahmoud IV* (1880–91) and *Ivan the Terrible and His Son Ivan on 16 November 1581* (1885). So powerful was the portrait of the demented Ivan holding the limp body of his son he had just bludgeoned to death that many well-corseted ladies in the audience fainted on encountering it.[28] Repin returned to St Petersburg in 1882, after falling out with his Moscow circle. Back in the capital he began to complete his historic paintings while also continuing a cycle of works that were politically dangerous. The paintings *Spurning Confession* (1879–85), *The Propagandist's Arrest* (1880–92), *The Revolutionary Meeting* (1883) and *They Did Not Expect Him* (1884) all depicted scenes from the revolutionary movement, ranging from a prisoner defiantly refusing final confession before execution to the unexpected homecoming of a

released exile to his family home. As Repin never publicly advocated revolution and claimed to merely to be representing true Russian realities he was left at liberty by the authorities.

This was also due to the fact that the new Tsar Alexander III favoured the work of The Wanderers for its strong nationalist sentiment and historical imagery. He became an avid patron of their works and purchased many for his growing collection of Russian Art, second only to Pavel Tretyakov, one of Moscow's merchant princes. Imperial patronage was followed by establishment acceptance. In 1889 The Wanderers were asked to oversee the restructuring of the Academy from which they had resigned in protest twenty-six years earlier. They had returned home. Repin and his fellow Wanderers, Arkhip Kuindzhi and Ivan Shishkin, became professors while others of the group made up a majority of the Academy's board. The Wanderers had now come full circle from rebels to the establishment. Their victory, however, was bittersweet. Just as populist art became the national school, young artists were already chafing, like Repin's young barge hauler, to throw off the weight of its artistic, social and political constraints.

'A GENERATION THIRSTING FOR BEAUTY'

On 5 December 1890 Tchaikovsky's opera *The Queen of Spades* premiered at the Mariinsky Theatre. Alongside the cream of St Petersburg society sat a group of young men held rapt by the opera's tragic themes and vivid portrayal of eighteenth-century

ABOVE Ilya Repin's *Barge Haulers on the Volga*, 1870–3 (State Russian Museum, St Petersburg) defined a generation of artists and their work.

St Petersburg. To them Tchaikovsky was a figure of worship, the symbolic harbinger of the renaissance of the St Petersburg ideal. This small group of dilettantes, lightheartedly identified as the Nevsky Pickwickians, would grow to become St Petersburg's new champions, promoting her virtues through art, music and dance. Together they would lay the groundwork for a glorious cultural sunset of the imperial epoch, whose rays would reach through Russia to the world beyond.

> I intrinsically adored St Petersburg's charms, its unique romance, but at the same time there was much that I did not like in it, and there were even some things that offended my taste with their severity and 'officiousness'. Now, through my delight in *The Queen of Spades*, I saw the light . . . Now I found that captivating poetry, whose presence I had only guessed at, everywhere I looked.[29]

This was the reaction to the opera of the leader of this promising group, Alexander Benois. Cosmopolitan and debonair, he seems to have been bred to his calling. Born into a family of French and Venetian descent, his great grandfather had been Director of Music for Tsar Nicholas I and his grandfather had been the architect of the Mariinsky and Bolshoi Theatres. A true aesthete, Benois was erudite in the fields of music and art and while still a teenager organized the Society for Self-Education, where he and his friends held formal meetings and discussions on the topics of art, literature, music and philosophy. The group was originally made up of Benois, Dmitri Filosofov, Léon Bakst, Eugene Lanceray and Alfred Nourok, but was soon joined by Filosofov's 'country' cousin Serge Diaghilev.

Diaghilev also hailed from a musical family and had spent his early childhood in St Petersburg, where he had the opportunity to meet both Mussorgsky and Tchaikovsky. Although his family moved to Perm, he returned to the capital in 1890 to pursue a career in law. Upon arrival Diaghilev abandoned this pretence and joined the Nevsky Pickwickians as its most uneducated and unpolished member. He was a quick learner and soon with the help of Benois, as well as a three-year sojourn in Europe, brought himself up to speed. Diaghilev never developed a talent the way the others had and, although he attempted to study music, never became accomplished. What soon became apparent, however, was what Diaghilev did possess: boundless energy, enthusiasm and flair for organization and promotion.

The Society was enthralled with art as an expression of eternal beauty, providing a 'mystical experience' rather than delivering a social or political message. The group agreed 'to establish the first principles for Russian Art, Russian architecture, Russian philosophy, Russian music and Russian poetry'[30] – a rather tall order for a group of men in their early twenties. They were, in the words of Diaghilev, 'a generation thirsting for beauty'.[31] They turned their noses up at the works of the Academy, dominated as it was by The Wanderers and their insistence on serious and socially inspired art. The group believed that artists should not be bound by any ideology or state-imposed programme. Such art drove Diaghilev to distraction: 'It's time for these anti-artistic canvases to stop appearing – with their militia men, police officers, students in red shirts and girls with cropped hair!'[32]

The Society was not entirely lacking vision or social responsibility. Benois and the group believed that art could be an uplifting and unifying force, which would make life happier and more beautiful therefore helping to improve society and life in general. To accomplish this they aspired to form connections and collaborations across the various national artistic and cultural media, creating a force that would be on parallel with the arts in the West. Specifically they called for a 'departure from the backwardness of Russian artistic life, getting rid of our provincialism, and approaching the cultural west'.[33] They soon chose a new name, which would be more suitable with their ambitious program: *Mir Iskusstva* (the World of Art).

THE WORLD OF ART

In 1898, after putting on three successful exhibitions of English, German, Finnish and Russian art, Diaghilev set himself toward a new task. Raising money from two of his most ardent admirers and benefactors Princess Tenisheva, wife of the owner of the first car manufacturer in Russia, and Savva Morozov, the Moscow railway magnate, he and Benois launched Russia's first publication dedicated exclusively to the arts. Christened *The World of Art*, after their group, the magazine was a feast for the eyes. High quality and printed in large format, *The World of Art*'s pages were filled with colourful images of current works by Russian and European artists. The subject matter was not limited to paintings; Diaghilev had a broader vision that included literature, art and cultural criticism and a promotion of Russian industrial design. Other sections of the magazine included examples of designs for fabrics, furniture and architectural and interior materials. Diaghilev welcomed and

recruited all representatives of the artistic spectrum to contribute to the new forum – from the realist Repin to the avant-garde Wassily Kandinsky and Marc Chagall.

For Benois, however, the World of Art had another mission – the revival of the St Petersburg ideal and the celebration of St Petersburg as a monument to the fusion of Russian and European creative forces. He believed that the boulevards, canals, bridges and parks were imbued with the spirit of the past, a mesmerizing and inspirational force, which he had first sensed while watching Tchaikovsky's *The Queen of Spades*. Dismayed that poets and authors of the latter half of the nineteenth century had contributed to the decline in the reputation of the city, Benois felt it his duty to try to reverse this trend. In a series of articles entitled, 'Picturesque Petersburg', 'The Architecture of Petersburg' and 'The Beauty of Petersburg', Benois defended the much-maligned imperial capital, countering the typical clichéd criticisms of the city while advocating the use of the city as subject matter for artists. Through

these articles, Benois sought to further his cause for a renewed appreciation of St Petersburg by highlighting the beauty and grandeur of the city's monuments and urban design. The articles were illustrated by Benois and other World of Art artists, such as Léon Bakst and Eugene Lanceray, who produced paintings and watercolours that vividly depicted the architecture and life of eighteenth-century St Petersburg.[34] Benois himself also created thirty-three drawings illustrating Pushkin's *The Bronze Horseman*.

While the World of Art became the catalyst for a renewed discussion over the cultural value of St Petersburg, Benois also used it to campaign for the physical protection of the city's historic fabric. In two articles, 'The Agony of St Petersburg' and 'Vandals', Benois decried the destruction of the city's architectural heritage through demolitions and unscholarly restorations.[35] This sparked the beginning of a preservation movement led by members of the World of Art as well as prominent architects and historians. Under the auspices of the Society of Architect-Artists, the Commission for

ABOVE While The Wanderers portrayed life in all its gritty reality, Alexander Benois sought to revive the art and culture of St Petersburg through the World of Art movement. Portrait by Léon Bakst, 1898 (Tretyakov Gallery, Moscow).

to capture the curiosity and enthusiasm of the public at large and even that of Tsar Nicholas II, who became the magazine's benefactor after the original patrons pulled out. Postcard prints of the magazine's St Petersburg illustrations were all the rage and could be bought at kiosks and bookstores throughout the city. The World of Art folded in 1904, after the imperial patronage ceased due to the outbreak of war with Japan. However, it spawned the production of numerous other publications dealing with art, design and criticism, such as *The Scales*, *The Treasurers of Art*, *The Golden Fleece* and *Apollo*.[39] Another magazine, entitled *Bygone Years*, a direct result of Benois campaign, dealt exclusively with the study of historic St Petersburg. By 1913 it had become the most popular magazine in the capital.[40]

NICHOLAS AND ALEXANDRA

On 1 November 1894, St Petersburg learned of the death of Alexander III at the Livadia Palace in the Crimea; he was forty-nine and had reigned only thirteen years. Alexander III's sudden demise was an unexpected shock to the public, the court and, most of all, his son Nicholas. The shy and sensitive twenty-six-year-old Tsarevitch now found himself the leader of the largest nation on earth, a responsibility he found not only heavy but terrifying. His one shining light in the midst of all of the turmoil was his fiancée, Alix of Hesse Darmstadt, a minor German princess and granddaughter of Queen Victoria. During the funeral, Alix, known as Alexandra Feodorovna, followed the imperial funeral cortège draped in black. Superstitious babushkas in the crowds of onlookers whispered, 'she comes to us from behind a coffin'.[41]

Once married, the young couple moved into the Anichkov Palace on the Fontanka with the Tsar's mother the Dowager Empress Maria Feodorovna and his younger brother and sister. From this cramped apartment of six rooms Nicholas and Alexandra began their marriage and tragic reign, which would become the stuff of legends, a fascinating and romantic tale that symbolized the end of an era. The couple eventually moved to their new rooms on the Winter Palace, signalling the end of the mourning period and the beginning of the social season. From the beginning Alexandra was at odds with the extravagant Russian high society. Brought up in bourgeois comfort in Germany and England, she found them decadent and immoral; they found her prudish and aloof.

Following the mourning period and their coronation, the royal couple retreated to the imperial suburban estate of Tsarskoe Selo. For their residence they chose the Alexander Palace, Quarenghi's

the Study of Old Petersburg was formed, which led in turn to the establishment of the first Museum of Old Petersburg in 1909.[36] Benois became involved in creating and leading the St Petersburg Society for the Protection and Preservation of Russian Monuments of Arts and Antiquity.[37]

While Benois and Diaghilev had succeeded in opening a new front in the debate over the focus of Russian art and culture, not everyone was thrilled with the direction *The World of Art* was going. The magazine's most vociferous opponent was St Petersburg's most influential critic and staunch nationalist Vladimir Stasov, champion of The Wanderers and the Mighty Handful composers. Stasov referred to Diaghilev as a 'decadent cheerleader' and the World of Art a 'courtyard of lepers'.[38] But *The World of Art* had already managed

ABOVE *Portrait of Serge Diaghilev and Nurse* (1905), painting by Léon Bakst (Museum of Theatrical and Musical Arts, St Petersburg). The 'decadent cheerleader' of the World of Art, Diaghilev would broaden the scope of the movement and bring it to the world stage with his Ballets Russes.

austere Roman palace commissioned by Catherine the Great for Alexander I. Within its hundred rooms, Alexandra created an environment that reflected her upbringing and modern European taste. Eschewing the grand staterooms, she concentrated on their apartments, mixing English chintzes with sinuous Art Nouveau for her rooms and heavy Russian revival Arts and Crafts for his. It was in such surroundings that Nicholas and Alexandra were most comfortable and it was here that they would insulate themselves, raise a family and admit only the closest of confidants.

Nicholas's private life raised a few eyebrows and ruffled a few feathers; his public face fared no better. At first the court and the public gave Nicholas the benefit of the doubt but soon saw he was a young man in over his head. Having been raised in the strict etiquette of the Russian court and tutored by the arch-conservative Constantine Pobedonostsev, he was unprepared for the modern ways of fin de siècle St Petersburg or a rapidly industrializing Russia. At one of his first audiences before the court, Nicholas stated while receiving a delegation of zemstvos that their suggestion of greater participation in state affairs were 'senseless dreams' and that as Tsar he intended to 'maintain the principle of autocracy just as firmly and unflinchingly as it was preserved by my unforgettable dead father'.[42] In one stroke, Nicholas had dashed hopes of a political thaw and alienated the majority of Russia's liberals and reformers.

Nicholas had few friends and was constantly bullied by his father's brothers the Grand Dukes, who weighed in heavily on most of his decisions. Uncomfortable in his new position, 'the awful job I have feared all my life',[43] he was often confused about policy and was easily persuaded to change his mind. This created a haphazard government. Such a weak will in a sovereign did not sit well with the likes of Sergius Witte, Minister of Finance, who said of Nicholas: 'A ruler who cannot be trusted, who approves today what he will reject tomorrow, is incapable of steering the Ship of State.'[44] As conflicts with his ministerial staff increased, Nicholas withdrew.

State Councillor Alexander Plovtsov explained: 'The young Tsar feels more and more contempt for the organs of his own power and begins to believe in the beneficial strength of his own autocracy, which he manifests sporadically, without preliminary discussion and without any link to the overall course of policy.'[45]

FIN DE SIÈCLE IN THE NORTHERN PALMYRA

While Nicholas struggled with his new role, his capital was enjoying the fruits of his father's economic labours. As the twentieth century dawned St Petersburg had become a vibrant and cosmopolitan city, prosperous and wealthy, a world-class destination for business and pleasure. Trains brought travellers from Paris, Berlin and Vienna and steamships unloaded passengers from London. The easing of travel restrictions also allowed Russians to travel, who upon returning added a sophistication to the city by demanding the import of goods and services they experienced in the West. Wealthy Russians and foreigners alike could spend they day visiting one of the city's museums, such as the Imperial Hermitage, the Alexander III Museum of Russian Art, the Steiglitz Museum or the private collection of the Stroganov princes. Afterwards they could sample the city's finest cuisine at old favourites, such as Donon's or Cubat's, as well as the new restaurants – Privato, Barel, The Bear and Vienna – before rushing off to a play, an opera, a concert or a cabaret in one of St Petersburg's four opera houses or many theatres.

Ballet reigned supreme. Here, more than anywhere else in Europe the medium of dance had been elevated to an art, rather than simply an adornment to opera. The man responsible for this had been Maurius Petipa, who, having been appointed Ballet Master of the Imperial Theatre in 1862, would hold the position for fifty-six years, producing and choreographing forty-six new ballets, seventeen revivals and thirty-five dances for the opera.[46] He collaborated with many of Russia's great composers, notably

Within the halls of this prestigious institution the rigorous and monastic-like training was conducted, which transformed boys and girls into leaping fawns and gazelles, shooting stars of the stage. Ballerinas held the positions of modern-day Hollywood starlets, gaining fanatical followings and the attentions of the rich and powerful. One ballerina, Mathilde Kchessinka, became the mistress of Nicholas II while he was still Tsarevitch. Nicholas commissioned architect Alexander Gogen to design for her one of the finest Art Nouveau residences in the city. Other greats to emerge from the Imperial Ballet School included Anna Pavlova, Tamara Karsavina and Vaslav Nijinsky, whose scant costume for the 1913 production of *Giselle* with its skin-like fabric that accentuated every curve of his musculature so scandalized the Dowager Empress that he was dismissed from imperial service.[47] Mikhail Fokine and George Balanchine, two luminaries of twentieth-century ballet, were also graduates of the school.

St Petersburg also became a focus of international finance, its business-friendly climate attracting foreign investment. New banks lined the Nevsky to receive this influx of funds and to house the wealth of the new mercantile elite. During the last decade of the nineteenth century Russia had an economic growth rate of 8 per cent, the fastest in the world at that time. Russia lead the world in coal, oil, steel and grain production, eclipsing other countries in Europe and the United States. This flood of new wealth made its mark on the cityscape through a rash of new building. Along the Nevsky Prospect rose new buildings such as the Art Nouveau Eliseev Building and the Beaux Arts Singer Sewing Machine Company Building, while next to St Isaac's Cathedral the sober neo-classical Astoria Hotel and later the new German Embassy foreshadowed the coming of the modern movement.

Not far off the Nevsky Prospect at 24 Bolshaya Morskaya rose the new psuedo-gothic offices of one of St Petersburg's most famous residents, the jeweller Carl Peter Fabergé. Fabergé was the descendant of Huguenot refugees from France who settled in Russia in the early nineteenth century. The son of a goldsmith, he had apprenticed in Frankfurt, Paris and London before returning to Russia in 1872 to assume control of the family firm. Supported by a team of creative and technical geniuses, including his brother Agathon, Mikhail Parkhin, Henrik Wigström, Albert Holmström and August Hollming, Fabergé transformed his father's small firm into one of the most renowned jewellers in Russia and Europe.[48]

Tchaikovsky, with whom he produced *Swan Lake*, *Sleeping Beauty* and *The Nutcracker*. Petipa also ruled over the Imperial Ballet School located behind the Alexandrinsky Theatre on Theatre or Carlo Rossi Street, one of the city's finest architectural ensembles.

At the turn of the century, modernity arrived in St Petersburg in several forms: the Arts-and-Crafts-inspired study of Nicholas II in the Alexander Palace (top); carriages, trams and motorcars on the Nevsky Prospect in 1900 (above); St Petersburg's first up-scale shopping arcade, the elegant Passázh (right).

The event that truly secured this good fortune was in 1885, when Alexander III, having viewed Fabergé's work at the Moscow Pan-Russian Exhibition, commissioned what was to become the paramount symbol of late imperial Russia – the first Imperial Easter Egg. This egg was presented by the Tsar to Empress Maria Feodorovna to celebrate the twentieth anniversary of their betrothal. The eggshell was enamelled in white and opened to reveal a golden yolk, which itself opened releasing a golden hen with ruby eyes. Within the hen lay a further surprise – a miniature replica of the imperial crown. Upon the death of Alexander III, Nicholas II continued the tradition of presenting a Fabergé egg every Easter to his mother but also began commissioning an extra egg for his empress, Alexandra Feodorovna. For two decades each Easter, Fabergé would present the empresses with exquisite

decadent fantasies set in enamel and gold, encrusted with jewels and each with its own surprise, revealing such wonders as delicate flowers, imperial coaches, tiny palaces and miniature portraits. So famous were the eggs that the imperial family agreed to display them for the public at a brief exhibition held at the mansion of Baron von Dervis in 1902.

As St Petersburg progressed into the new century, storm clouds appeared on the horizon. In 1904 Russia found itself embroiled in what many assumed would be a 'small victorious war', partially to defend the empire's far eastern possessions against Japan but also to arouse patriotism and deflect attention from simmering political discontent. Russia, unprepared to fight a war so far from Europe, was humiliated and suffered a crushing defeat at the hands of the Japanese. The fall of Port Arthur in January 1905 marked the end of

ABOVE Monumental skyline: the dome of St. Isaac's Cathedral and the Admiralty spire.

the Russo-Japanese War, but it caused a wave of horror and anger in St Petersburg.

Dormant undercurrents of political and social dissatisfaction began to reveal themselves in small protests and strikes. The yearning for change no longer just included students and workers but also the emerging middle-class professional guilds. In November 1904, without imperial sanction and without interference, the first national Zemstvo Congress took place in St Petersburg, resulting in a petition requesting liberal political reforms. It was the first time a Russian national assembly had ever been convened and its effect was profound, attracting a wide cross-section of political parties and interests, including the nobility. Nicholas, while acquiescing to some of the minor points of the petition, balked at the bolder requests of the *ad hoc* assembly, declaring, 'I will never agree to representative government, because I consider it harmful to the people whom God has entrusted to me.'[49] With this he dropped the match that would ignite the powder keg.

BLOODY SUNDAY

Nuisha!

If I fail to return and am killed, Nuisha do not cry. You'll get along somehow to begin with and then you'll find work at the factory. Bring up Vaniura and tell him I died a martyr for the people's freedom and happiness. I shall have died, if such be the case, for our own happiness as well . . .

Letter written by worker Ivan Vasilev, 22 January 1905

Church bells rang solemnly over the St Petersburg on the morning of Sunday 22 January 1905. Workers from in and around the city gathered their families to pray before the long march toward Palace Square where 150,000 of them and their families intended to present the Tsar with a petition for his protection and an improvement in their working and living conditions. Little had changed among their glum lot since the days of Dostoyevsky, except that their numbers had more than doubled and their conditions worsened. For five days before the appointed day the city had been in the grip of a strike led by the workers of the massive Putilov Works in reaction to the humiliating surrender of the Russian colony of Port Arthur in the Far East and the startlingly inept management of the war. In spite of this, Nicholas II and the imperial family attended the annual 19 January Blessing of the

Waters on the Palace Embankment, carrying out the ritual ceremony barely aware of the growing tension.

The Tsar's officials, however, were well aware of the planned march and had begun to take steps to ensure that the petitioners would never reach the palace. During the night 12,000 troops had been brought into the city, taking up positions on parade routes and in Palace Square. The Tsar himself was no longer residing at the Winter Palace, having returned to his residence at Tsarskoe Selo. The Minister of the Interior, Prince Sviatopolk-Mirsky, insisted that direct communication with the Tsar was impossible and demanded that the march be called off. The organizers refused. The imperial authorities still did not expect hostilities, nor did they expect the march to occur, for they had an ace left to play: the chief organizer of the protesters, Father Gregory Gapon, was a government agent.

Gapon had come into government employ in 1903 as a double agent for the Okhrana, the Tsar's secret police, led at the time by S.V. Zubatov. A former revolutionary turned informant, Zubatov had risen in the ranks of the secret police. He took the concerns of the workers seriously and decided to begin to organize them into unions led by government agents to prevent them from being influenced by socialist revolutionaries. Zubatov chose Gapon to become a leader of this effort due to his passionate concern for workers as well as his unquestionable and religious loyalty to the monarchy. When Zubatov was dismissed after one of his unions lead a strike Gapon assumed control of the unions under the auspices of the Church.[50]

By January 1905 Gapon had become a fiery organizer, convinced of his cause and assured in his faith that the Tsar would respond to the needs of the shivering masses. He no longer heeded the demands of his former masters; his mission, he believed, came from a higher authority. Taking the essences of the reform platforms demanded by Assembly of Russian Factory and Mill Workers and Zemstvo Congress, he drew up a petition to present to the Tsar. Written in grand-sounding formal Russian, it began:

We, workers and residents of the City of St Petersburg, of various ranks and stations, our wives, children and helpless old parents, have come to Thee Sire, to seek justice and protection. We have become beggars; we are oppressed and burdened by labour beyond our strength; we are humiliated; we are regarded, not as human beings, but as slaves who must endure their bitter fate in silence . . . Is it better to die

– for all of us, the toiling people of all of Russia, to die, allowing the capitalists and the bureaucrats to live and enjoy themselves? This is the choice we face, Sire, and this is why we have come to the walls of Thy palace. Order these measures and take Thine oath to carry them out . . . And if Thou does not so order and dost not respond to our pleas we will die here on this square before Thy palace.[51]

Finally realizing the gravity of what was about to occur, the authorities ordered Gapon's arrest, but he escaped and hid with a family of workers.

The marching workers arrived at the meeting points, gathering freely and carrying icons, religious banners and pictures of the Tsar. Speeches were made and the atmosphere was full hope that their faith in God and the Tsar would prevail. As the march began, women and children took the lead to declare the petitioners' peaceful motives and behind the others carried signs asking the soldiers to not fire upon 'the people'. Gapon himself, dressed in a white cassock and brandishing a crucifix, confidently led a column of 50,000 from the south along the Peterhof Prospect heading toward the Narva Gate. Ahead, waiting for him and the surging crowds, was a squadron of cavalry of the Horseguards Grenadiers and lines of infantry arranged beneath the Roman grandeur of the Narva Gate, which served to emphasize their might and authority. Onwards the motley sea of humanity marched, undaunted by this display of arms, singing religious hymns as they reached the Tarakanovka Bridge.

When it became clear that Gapon had no intention of stopping, the cavalry charged. Sabres drawn and raised, they flew into the mass of people. The crowd shrank back from the swinging rapiers, parting and regrouping some taking flight. After two unsuccessful attempts to disperse the crowds the cavalry retreated and the infantry was ordered to take aim. A bugle sounded above the fray, yet the soldiers hesitated, firing volleys into the air, yet the crowd moved forward once again. This time the soldiers lowered their rifles and fired a close range into the approaching procession. The column of marchers shattered as the terrified marchers sought shelter from the flying bullets. Gapon was felled by the corpse of one of his bodyguards. He struggled to get up, his cassock stained with blood. As he surveyed the chaos and the fallen bodies of his followers he cried over and over: 'There is no God any longer! There is no Tsar!'[52]

Throughout the city the situation was getting out of control. Similar scenes of violence broke out as columns of marchers met the Tsar's soldiers determined to prevent them from reaching the Winter Palace. On the Troitsky Bridge on the Petrograd side near the fortress, Maxim Gorky was in the crowd, witnessing the clash of the soldiers and workers that led to the deaths of 100 people. Across town on Vasilievsky Island, the Finnish Lifeguards Regiment and supporting cavalry charged and opened fire on marchers in front of the Academy of Fine Arts. Still along the Nevsky Prospect yet another column proceeded toward Palace Square. It mingled with the well-heeled populace out for Sunday strolls and their ranks were further swelled by the intrepid survivors of earlier clashes. The crowds rolled up to the intersection of Bolshaya Morskaya Street, splitting as their numbers headed toward the General Staff Arch and around to the west to the Alexander Gardens.

Soon 60,000 workers, students and onlookers surrounded Palace Square, which was defended by 2,300 infantry and cavalry as well as artillery. The commander ordered that the crowd to disperse or risk being shot. Still the crowd grew, as they waited for Gapon to come forward with his petition. At two o'clock, when he failed to show, the commander of the guards ordered the cavalry to charge and disperse the crowds. Once again this proved ineffective and the soldiers lowered their rifles at the crowd. On seeing this many on the front line of protesters fell to their knees in prayer. The bugle sounded again and the soldiers sent forth salvo after salvo of bullets and artillery into the fleeing mass, which collapsed into total panic. Men and women were shot in the back; children were shot off statues and out of trees. People in panic trampled themselves and the wounded. A Bolshevik who witnessed the horrible carnage of Bloody Sunday recalled:

I observed the faces around me and detected neither fear nor panic. No the reverend and almost prayerful expressions were replaced by hostility and even hatred. I saw these looks of hatred and vengeance on literally every face – old and young, men and women. The revolution had truly been born, and it had been born in the very core, in the very bowels of the Russian people. [53]

1905

Outside the capital in Tsarskoe Selo, the palace was in shock. The Tsar immediately sacked his Minister of the Interior, but the damage to the throne was done. Empress Alexandra, on hearing of the massacre, could not fathom that the image of the Tsar had been irrevocably broken in the eyes of his subjects. In a letter to her sister Victoria she clearly displays the vast chasm between the cocoon of the palace and the reality of the street:

The poor workmen, who had been utterly misled, had to suffer, and the organizers have hidden as usual behind them. Don't believe at all the horrors the foreign papers say. They make one's hair stand on end – foul exaggeration. Yes, the troops, alas, were obliged to fire. Repeatedly the crowd was told to retreat and that Nicky (the Tsar) was not in town . . . and that one would be forced to shoot, but they would not heed and so blood was shed. On the whole 92 killed and between 200–300 wounded. It is a ghastly thing, but had one not done it the crowd would have grown colossal and 1,000 would have been crushed. All over the country, of course it is spreading. . . . St Petersburg is a rotten town, not one atom Russian.[54]

As St Petersburg lay prostrate under a military lockdown, the rest of Russia exploded into a mass of uprisings, strikes and civil disorder made worse by the complete annihilation of the Russian Fleet at the Battle of Tsushima. The Tsar's uncle Grand Duke Sergei was blown up just outside the Kremlin, in Moscow. In panic, the government appointed a commission investigating the reasons for the tragedy, which for the first time included representatives of the workers.[55] Following this, on 18 February, Nicholas II agreed to the establishment

Blood on the snow; On Bloody Sunday, crowds fled past the Admiralty through the Alexander Gardens after facing the guns of the Imperial Guard.

of the country's first representative body, the State Duma. Nicholas, however, never comfortable with ceding his royal prerogative, reneged on his promise that August and reasserted his authority. The law that he did approve essentially emasculated the new Duma, limiting suffrage and granting the body only consultative powers. The reaction was severe. The Social Democrats, the parent organization of the Bolsheviks, called for a general strike among all the workers of the capital. This time the situation in St Petersburg, as well as in the empire's other major cities, slipped into complete meltdown. All railways halted, factories went on strike, universities closed, theatres went dark and public services, including transport, telephone and electricity ceased. All private businesses and banks ceased operation. Workers took to the barricades, clashing with the army and the police. Order collapsed in St Petersburg, leading to a wave of criminal anarchy, with looting and vigilante violence erupting across the city.

On 17 October 1905 the St Petersburg Soviet of Workers assembled for the first time. With its 562 deputies elected from the Bolsheviks, Mensheviks and Socialist Revolutionaries parties, the Soviet, largely led by Leon Trotsky, began to act as a worker's government, organizing the strikes, publishing its newspaper *Izvestiia*, forming a workers militias and distributing food.[56] Count Witte, father of Russia's economic fortunes, finally confronted the Tsar, handing him an ultimatum: either introduce liberal reforms or appoint a military dictator to crush the revolt. Nicholas demurred and then asked his uncle Grand Duke Nicholas to assume dictatorial power. The Grand Duke, horrified at the suggestion, drew his revolver and threatened to kill himself in the Tsar's office if Nicholas did not give into reforms.[57] The Tsar acquiesced and signed what became the October Manifesto.

ABOVE Following the revolution of 1905, Nicholas begrudgingly signed the October Manifesto which forced the Crown to accept civil liberties and agree to a constitutional government. Detail of throne room in the Winter Palace.

The manifesto granted Russians their civil liberties, established a constitutional order, the creation of a cabinet government led by a Prime Minister and a State Duma elected by the people. With this act Nicholas and the government had bought themselves a reprieve by splitting the liberals and socialists over the possibility of representative government. The city celebrated its victory by ending the general strike and holding a large victory demonstration in Palace Square, a symbolic act which proudly proclaimed that the fallen of Bloody Sunday did not die in vain.

In April 1906, delegates from around the nation flooded into the imperial capital for the first opening of the State Duma. Half of their number were peasants from rural areas, others radical revolutionaries. St Petersburg was at once horrified and bemused as the members arrived dressed in various national costumes and were in awe of the grandeur of St Petersburg. They were a rough lot, carousing in the city's taverns and engaging in political agitation. One old-school St Petersburg liberal described the feelings of many seasoned politicians and intellectuals at the arrival of this barbarian horde:

> It was enough to take a look at the motley mob of 'deputies' . . . to experience horror at the sight of Russia's first representative body. It was a gathering of savages. It seemed as if the Russian land had sent to St Petersburg everything that was barbarian in it, everything filled with envy and malice. . . . In this mass any consciousness of statehood, let alone of shared statehood, was totally submerged in social hostility and class envy.[58]

These deputies, who had just participated in one of the most widespread revolts in Russia's history, were angry and itching for a fight. The court and the government received them with little joy. Nicholas disdainfully opened the first State Duma at the coronation hall of the Winter Palace, with the court to his right and the newly elected delegates to his left. Instead of praising the momentous occasion, the Tsar, humiliated by his loss of power, spoke only of upholding his divine right, the autocracy.

The Holy Devil

The one bright ray of hope that shone down on Nicholas during this tumultuous period of war, revolution and reform was the announcement of the birth of an heir:

Peterhof, 30 July 1904. For us a great unforgettable day on which God's goodness was so clearly visited upon us. At 1:15 this afternoon, Alix gave birth to a son, whom in prayer we have named Alexei. Everything happened remarkably quickly for me at least. There are not words to thank God properly for the comfort He has sent us in this year of hard trials.[59]

After four daughters Olga, Tatiana, Maria and Anastasia, Nicholas finally had a son and heir to ensure the Romanov line. The Tsarevitch was named after Alexis, the father of Peter the Great, a deeply religious man and the last of the Muscovite Tsars. Even the choice of this name was an indication of Nicholas repudiation of Peter's legacy, one that Nicholas believed had brought him and his family nothing but death and the decay of his imperial prerogative.[60]

Soon after his birth, however, a terrible discovery was made. The Tsarevitch began bleeding from his navel, a malady that took three days to stop. As the baby grew to be a toddler he began to bruise very easily. These bruises became painful swellings, which later turned black and blue. The imperial doctors then confirmed to the Empress a suspicion that haunted her more than any other – that Alexis had haemophilia. Haemophilia, a rare blood disease that prevents the clotting of the blood, had been passed down through Alexandra from her mother Princess Alice, who received the gene from her mother Queen Victoria. Alexandra knew exactly what the consequences of such a life for her son would be, as she had lost cousins and a brother to the disease.

To prevent such devastating news from becoming public knowledge, a heavy blanket of secrecy was laid over the court, making the already private world of the imperial couple even more exclusive and secretive, which caused eyebrows to be raised and encouraged rumours. In despair, Alexandra sank further into religious devotion and began to seek the advice of charlatans and faith healers – anyone who might be able to deliver her son from the terrible fate. It was through this desperation that Alexandra came into contact with an eccentric Russian mystic, whose name and person would become synonymous with the decadence of the last days of empire: Grigory Rasputin.

He began his rise to prominence in 1903, when he arrived in St Petersburg. Originally from the Siberian town of Prokovskoe, Rasputin claimed to have had a vision of the Virgin who had told him to become a pilgrim. He walked 2,000 miles from Siberia to

Mount Athos in Greece, after which he became a *starets*, or wandering holy man. During his first trip to St Petersburg Rasputin received the blessing of Father John of Kronstadt, one of the pre-eminent religious figures in the capital. He re-appeared in 1905 and was again received by prominent members of the clergy. Through these contacts Rasputin met the Grand Duchesses Militsa and Anastasia, two Montenegrin princesses married to the Tsar's cousins who were patrons and practitioners of various forms of mysticism fashionable in the waning days of the empire.

The princesses brought Rasputin to Tsarskoe Selo to meet the Tsar and Empress, who were enchanted by his easy demeanour and religious bearing. They saw in him an idealized version of the loyal and faithful peasants of Russia who referred to them as 'little father' and 'little mother' as he did. Most of all, however, Alexandra saw him as figure sent from God to help her and her son. Rasputin, it was discovered, was able to heal the Tsarevitch during a haemorrhage attack by calming him with prayers and perhaps by the use of hypnosis. Whatever the method, Rasputin became a fixture at the palace, his place secured by the Empress.

Outside the palace, Rasputin's reputation among the chattering classes of the capital soon caused a sensation. Unbeknownst to his royal patrons, Rasputin had been driven out of his village for being a philanderer, a scoundrel and a heretic. In St Petersburg Rasputin had set himself up in a well-appointed flat at 64 Gorokhovaya Street, and surrounded himself with a large group of fawning female admirers. He preached to them a dubious theology that taught that to experience forgiveness and salvation one must first give into sin. Rasputin then offered himself up as the instrument to this end. The women eagerly acquiesced to his advances as he gazed at them with his piercing blue eyes and whispered 'You think that I am polluting you, but I am not. I am purifying you.'[61]

By 1911 Rasputin's behaviour had the city in an uproar. The cuckolded husbands of his followers were outraged at the liberties he had taken. Once received in the best salons of St Petersburg, Rasputin now found himself barred from society. Soon accusations of public drunkenness and wanton behaviour reached the Empress, who at first refused to believe the claims, even causing political

damage to those who spoke ill of him. This was until intimate letters appeared in public sent from the Empress to Rasputin, which he had callously given to a friend while boasting of his influence over her. The incident was damaging to Alexandra's reputation and Prime Minister Peter Stolypin ordered an investigation, presenting his findings to Nicholas. The Tsar, unable to choose between his wife's needs and his duty as Tsar, ignored the file. Enraged, Stolypin took matters in his own hands and banished Rasputin from St Petersburg.

That September Stolypin was assassinated in Kiev during a state visit with the Tsar. Rasputin again returned to St Petersburg, where his presence acted like a lightning rod, attracting the attention of the press, the public and the Duma. Rumours circulated that the Empress and the *starets* were lovers. Several prominent members of the Church denounced and even physically attacked him, earning banishment themselves. The new Prime Minister Kokovstov, fearing the sustained damage to the throne, again banished Rasputin, in spite of the protests of Alexandra. It was not until October 1912 that the *starets* was called back to once again heal the Tsarevitch, who had suffered a traumatic attack in Poland. 'God has seen your tears and heard your prayers. Do not grieve. The Little One will not die.' With this telegram Rasputin was restored; this time for good.

THE CHILDREN OF RUSSIA'S DREADFUL YEARS

In the last years of the nineteenth century St Petersburg's intellectual circles were the heirs to the philosophies and literary works of Chernyshevsky and Dostoyevsky. The devotees of the social realism of Chernyshevsky, such as Lenin, Plekhanov and many other prominent socialist thinkers, had taken the path of radical politics and been driven into exile or political limbo. Dostoyevsky, on the other hand, had ignited something altogether different in his disciples – the search for communion with the divine through art, literature and poetry, through which they sought to change the world. While in art and design this manifested itself through the World of Art movement, with its meditation on beauty and the St Petersburg ideal, in literature this spiritual quest saw the emergence of a new set of champions, the symbolists.

ABOVE The 'mad monk', Grigory Rasputin.
RIGHT Nicholas' and Alexandra's bedroom in the Alexander Palace, restored to its 1912 appearance. Powerless to do anything about her son's haemophilia Alexandra in her desperation turned to her faith and later to Rasputin.

Symbolism as a literary movement in Russia had its roots in the works of French writers, among them Charles Baudelaire, as well as the paintings of the English artist Aubrey Beardsley. Concerned with the connection between art and mysticism, symbolists practised the systematic use of metaphorical imagery to express allegorical meaning and to reach ultimate truth. In St Petersburg and Moscow symbolism became informed by the metaphysical idealism of Russian philosopher Vladimir Soloviev, whose views developed in tandem with those from the West.

Soloviev, originally from Moscow, lectured at the University of St Petersburg before he travelled abroad, where he became influenced by the German mysticism of Franz Boehme and Franz Baader. Soloviev's view of artistic beauty was that art was to be used as an instrument for the purpose of universal reintegration. The artist, in creating a work of art, communes with the higher world of the spirit, analogous to the experience of the religious mystic. He also believed that the preordained role of art was to be a theurgic aid in bringing the temporal and spiritual realms together and therefore transform the world.[62] Soloviev claimed that the avatar of this philosophy was his mystical muse, Sophia, a figure who was ideal humanity embodying divine wisdom as well as eternal femininity, and encouraged artists to seek her out. He even claimed to have seen her three times.

The intellectuals of Russia's ancient capital, Moscow, were the first to take up the cause for symbolism, producing a literature that was deeply metaphysical and loosely associated with Slavophilism and Russian nationalism. In St Petersburg it was the unlikely pair of Dmitri Merezhkovsky and Zinaida Gippius who would introduce symbolism to the capital's intellectuals, their salon rising to prominence as the leading centre of creative literary genius. The dark, quiet, shy and scholarly Merezhkovsky complimented perfectly the tall, beautiful and flamboyant Gippius, whose quick wit, flaming red hair and seductive dress earned her the nickname the 'decadent Madonna'. While he was the better critic and theoretician, she was the better poet and the more creative of the two. Along with their protégés, they managed to marry the dark 'Dionysian' undercurrents of Muscovite symbolism with the more 'Apollonian' approach of St Petersburg.[63]

The Merezhkovskys held court at their flat on the Liteiny Prospect, where they hosted the cream of St Petersburg writers, artists and critics every Sunday evening. Stretched out on her chaise longue in a cloud of cigarette smoke, Gippius, her slender body draped in the most avant garde fashions or men's attire, handed down devastating judgments on the works of her guests while peering at her subjects through her lorgnette. For those in St Petersburg who aspired to literary greatness, an audience with this Russian Messalina was mandatory. Moscow symbolist Andrei Bely referred to her as 'a wasp in human attire'.[64] Among their circle was Vasily Rozanov, who was a preacher of sexual transcendentalism, teaching that 'the tie of sex with God is far stronger than the tie of intellect, or even conscience'.[65] Sexual freedom and exploration was a key aspect of the symbolists' search for the connection with God. The Merezhkovskys even engaged in a *ménage à trois* with Dmitri Filosofov of the World of Art, to form a sexual trinity.

The pair further challenged convention by forming the St Petersburg Religious Philosophy Society in 1901, which brought the Russian Orthodox clergy together with the city's leading intellectuals for the purposes of reconciling their metaphysical vision with the established Church. Gippius, ever the firestarter, would attend dressed in an especially provocative black gown whose numerous pleats opened to reveal flesh-coloured silk, giving the appearance that she was naked underneath. The society was shut down by Constantine Pobedonostev after the members condemned the excommunication of Leo Tolstoy and questioned the relationship between Church and State. While the society never achieved its goal it provided a dynamic forum for religious and philosophical debate and had a profound effect on Russian culture well into the twentieth century.

The turn of the century brought greater influence to Gippius and Merezhkovsky as they made in-roads among the Muscovite intelligentsia and fostered relationships with Valery Briusov and Andrei Bely. At the same time they ended their affiliation with the World of Art movement as a result of their divergent interests and views. In 1903 the Merzhkovskys published their own magazine *Novyi Put (The New Way)* followed by *Voprosy Zhizni (Questions of Life)*

ABOVE St Petersburg's 'decadent Madonna', the poetess Zinaida Gippius.

in 1904. But the heady early days of what would become known as Russia's 'Silver Age' were coming to an end. War with Japan tapped into the symbolists' fear of the Asiatic hordes foretold by Soloviev, which would herald the coming of the apocalypse. The bloody revolution of 1905 confirmed their suspicions that the 'end of days' had begun.

THE SILVER AGE

Following the events of 1905, the Merezhkovskys decamped to Paris for a brief sojourn. During their absence a new intellectual power base arose in the form of the decadent 'Tower' of Viacheslav Ivanov. Ivanov, a brilliant scholar, classical philologist and translator, was a follower of Nietzsche and his Promethianism, which saw artists as bringing light to the world. Ivanov wanted more from symbolism than a personal experience; he attempted, through his poetry, to use symbolism as a way to understand the world. He also shared with the Merezhkovskys the desire to see the Church and pre-Christian modes of belief reconciled.

Ivanov ruled the St Petersburg intellectual world from his three-storey massive and eclectically decorated flat at 25 Tavricheskaya, which was known to all as the Tower. Here he held symposia on various themes, such as art, eros, love, death and rebirth. Ivanov opened his Tower to all comers as a haven, and come they did. His Wednesday salons were a welcome respite for an elite that was deeply troubled by the events of 1905. Among his guests was Andrei Bely, recently arrived in St Petersburg on Bloody Sunday. It would be Bely who would introduce Ivanov to his most talented guest, a young poet and protégé of the Merezhkovskys, Alexander Blok.

The son of a lawyer and professor, Blok had formerly been a law student who had become enchanted by the theatre and later poetry. He discovered the philosophy and literature of Soloviev and threw

ABOVE Viacheslav Ivanov's 'Tower' was the intellectual Olympus of the Silver Age. His eclectic salons were attended by such St Petersburg literary luminaries as Alexander Blok and Anna Akhmatova.

himself into study. He fell in love and eventually married the daughter of Dmitri Mendeleev, family friend and inventor of the periodic table, declaring that she was his version of Soloviev's mystical Sophia. Blok's poetry appeared in the Merezhkovsky's magazine *The New Way* and in the Moscow journals, earning him an impressive set of admirers. His poetry is both lyrical and rhythmic, combining an extremely personal insight with the universal, and quotidian elements with mythological motifs. Introduced to Andrei Bely through the Merezhkovskys, he visited Moscow but found the intense mysticism practised by the symbolists there too much and returned to St Petersburg.

After his fall-out with Gippius, who had encouraged Bely to run off with his wife, Blok entered the orbit of Ivanov. He was attracted to the Tower's discussions of religion and mysticism. The night he read poems from *The Snow Mask* his presence was the talk of the town:

> In his long frock coat, with soft necktie tied with elegant casualness, in a nimbus of ashen golden-hair, Blok was at that time romantically handsome . . . He would go slowly to the table with the candles, look around at everyone with his stony eyes and would himself turn to stone until the silence became complete. And he began to speak, holding the verse steady agonizingly well and slowing the tempo slightly on the rhymes. . . . Everyone was in love with him.[66]

Blok secured popular fame with the release of his poem *The Unknown Woman*, which took St Petersburg by storm. Even prostitutes plying their trade with plumed hats claimed that they truly were Blok's unknown woman.

Confident of his influence as master of St Petersburg's intellectual world, Ivanov attempted to unite its various factions within one ambitious publication entitled *Zolotne Runo* (*The Golden Fleece*). Edited by Ivanov, Blok and Grigory Chulkov and funded by Moscow Industrialist Riabushinsky, the magazine brought together for one brief moment all of the Silver Age under one astounding umbrella of art. A cross-pollination of the lavishly illustrated *The World of Art* and the avant-garde *The New Way*, the magazine was illustrated by Alexander Benois, Mikhail Vrubel, Léon Bakst, Nikolai Rerikh, Konstantin Somov and Valentin Serov while its articles were by Blok, Bely, Konstantin Balmont, Briusov, Gippius, Merezhkovsky, Ivanov and Leonid Andreev.

The first issue was an amazing spectacle, but *The Golden Fleece* actually signalled the high water mark of the symbolist movement. Within a year the magazine's harmony collapsed and the symbolist movement fractured irrevocably and became merely one of a number of philosophical and artistic movements. Mercurial from the start, the intellectual world of St Petersburg mimicked the political life of the empire, fracturing into a dazzling kaleidoscope of ideas, images and actions. Beginning in 1905, the Silver Age became ever more brilliant, illuminated by the golden rays cast by the setting sun of the spent empire and contoured by the growing shadows of the coming darkness.

Serge Diaghilev, before departing to take Russia's Silver Age to the world, raised his glass for a bold toast: 'To a new and unknown culture, which will be created by us, and which will also sweep us away!'[67] Diaghilev literally put the show on the road, arriving in Paris to launch his new and inspired form of modern ballet released from the stale strictures of the Imperial Theatre. After sumptuously refurbishing the Châtelet Theatre, Diaghilev in 1909 dazzled Parisians with the full spectacle of Russian art, dance, music and culture. Nijinsky and Pavlova lept across the stage to the choreography of Mikhail Fokine, against vast backdrops by Léon Bakst to the music of Rimsky-Korsokov's *Scheherazade*. Diaghilev would discover and use to great effect the music of Igor Stravinsky, whose *Firebird* (1910) *Petrushka* (1911) and *The Rite of Spring* (1913) captivated and challenged audiences and defined the Ballets Russes. Diaghilev's Ballets Russes were declared as no less than an international triumph.

Back in St Petersburg, new forces were emerging out of the cultural vacuum left by the decay of the World of Art and the symbolist movement. The legacy of Diaghilev and Benois was carried on by art critic Sergei Makovsky and poet Nikolai Gumilev. The pair started the new journal *Apollo* in 1909, which sought to fill the gap of the World of Art, whose creative force had now removed to Paris. *Apollo*'s mission was to refocus artistic and literary energy on the classical and Western traditions in Russian culture as a foil to the corrupting degeneration of the symbolists. Benois was even recruited to work on the publication and the magazine, which soon became the paramount forum for art and literature in St Petersburg.

So confident was Gumilev of his accomplishment that in 1910, much to Ivanov's dismay, he officially declared symbolism dead. Gumilev advocated a return to the purist roots of symbolism epitomized by the French. In its place he established the literary

As the sun set on imperial Russia, St Petersburg's artists and poets sought cultural and religious planes of art and spirituality as a means to bring about the nation's salvation.

PLANCHE N° 13

childhood friend of Gumilev, she was mentored by the director of the imperial lyceum, poet Innokenty Annensky. Akhmatova later married Gumilev, but during a sojourn in Paris had an affair with the artist Modigliani, whose many images of her are now well known. Returning to St Petersburg she was launched at the Tower to high praise and, on the publication of her series of poems *Evening* in 1911, she became a celebrity. Her poems are deeply personal and convey intense inner poignancy through descriptions of Russia's history, as well as the city that would become her universe, St Petersburg.

> My blissful cradle was
> A dark city on a menacing river
> And the triumphal marriage bed,
> Over which young seraphim held bridal wreaths –
> Was a city loved with bitter love.
>
> Solium of my prayers
> You were, misty, calm, severe.
> There my betrothed first appeared to me,
> Pointing out my shining path,
> And my melancholy Muse
> Led me as one leads the blind.[69]

Just as Gumilev was appealing to the elite's nostalgia and advocating a return to tradition, there arose in St Petersburg another alternative scene which sought to throw off convention altogether and turn art and literature on its head. The new *enfants terribles* were lead by the poets Vladimir Mayakovsky and Victor Khlebnikov. These futurists moved to shock the intellectual elite of Ivanov's Tower, as well as the acmeists, by removing meaning altogether from poetry in a swirl of profanity, slang and eroticism. They joined up with fabric heir Levky Zheverzheev's artistically modern Union of Youth in 1910 and released a manifesto in 1912 titled 'A Slap in the Face of Public Taste', which, among other things, called for writers and poets to toss Pushkin, Tolstoy and other writers of the Great Tradition overboard the steamship of modernity.[70]

acmeist movement, which reflected the works of his Poets' Guild. The acmeists believed in the words of the poet Sergei Gorodetsky: 'The rose has once more become beautiful in and of itself. Its petals are beautiful, its fragrance and colour, and not the thoughts, correspondences, mystical love and other things of that sort which were evoked by it.'[68] While the founders of acmeists were Gumilev himself and Mikhail Kuzmin, the movement produced two poets of supreme literary greatness: Osip Mandelstam and the woman whose talent and voice would lift her alongside Pushkin in St Petersburg's literary pantheon, Anna Akhmatova.

Born Anna Gorenko and raised in Tsarskoe Selo, she adopted the surname Akhmatova in reference to Khan Akhmat, the last Tartar overlord of Russia, from whom she believed herself descended. A

These futurists were joined by the painters Mikhail Larinov and Natalia Goncharova, who had all been influenced by the introduction of Matisse to Russia through the collection of Sergei Shchukin. They produced a post-impressionist form of painting called primitivism and founded the artists' circle 'The Donkey's Tail'.

ABOVE Léon Bakst's costume design for Nijinsky as the 'Faun'.

Futurism began to take on a revolutionary flavour. Larinov would declare defiantly: 'We deny individuality has any value in a work of art. We go hand and hand with housepainters. . . . From here begins the true freeing of art.'[71] Futurism in art gave rise to other schools as well, such as the cubofuturism of Mikhail Matyushin, the suprematism of Kazimir Malevich and the constructivism of Vladimir Tatlin.

The frantic activity of the various artistic and literary movements moved alongside the decline of symbolism, which was still championed by Ivanov. Symbolism always had a component of eroticism, which was displayed in the pioneering books in 1907 – *Wings* by Mikhail Kuzmin and *Thirty-Three Abominations* by Lidia Zioveva-Annibal, both members of Ivanov's circle. These were the first erotic books to tackle the subjects of homosexuality in men and women. Their content was both shocking and titillating to Russian audiences, whose desire for such material was beginning to increase exponentially. It was Mikhail Artsybashev's *Sanin* that helped turn Russia's desire into lust and sexual revolution, its tale of sexual debauchery and free love tapping directly into the growing undercurrent of decadence slowly seeping into the general populace long fed by widespread prostitution. Sanin was followed by a tsunami of erotic and pornographic novels and materials and even promoted the establishment of sex clubs among the educated youth.

Quietly producing alongside this spectacular explosion of creative ardour among the artists and literati of late-imperial St Petersburg was another group of writers who stayed true to the legacy of Chernyshevsky, eschewing the mystical and the nostalgic for the social realism of the nineteenth century. The *Znanie*, or Knowledge Group, came out of the publishing house of the same name. Writers such as Alexander Kuprin, Leonid Andreyev and Ivan Bunin concentrated on generating novels and poetry that confronted the social ills of the day. The star among this group was the revolutionary celebrity Maxim Gorky. Already a respected member and fundraiser for the socialist revolutionaries and the Social Democratic Labour Party, he was already acquainted with Lenin and Leon Trotsky by 1907. Gorky was very popular among the radical movements and produced several successful novels, among them *Mother* (1907), *A Confession* (1908), *Okurov City* (1909) and the *Life of Matvey Kozhemyakin* (1910). Gorky's work, with its attempts to create ideal revolutionary heroes, would later became the prototype for the literature of the Soviet state.

1913: THE LAST HURRAH

February 1913 marked the 300th anniversary of the Romanov Dynasty. Having been battered by the events of 1905, the imposition of the Duma and the Rasputin scandals, the court saw an opportunity to reconnect Russia's imperial family with their subjects. St Petersburg threw itself into the preparations. Festoons of white, blue and red were swagged across public buildings, strings of twinkling lights illuminated the main thoroughfares and portraits of the sovereigns graced the city's squares. The Mariinsky Theatre put on Glinka's *A Life for the Tsar* and the nobility and dignitaries of every far-flung province filled the cities' hotels and guesthouses, adding to the already raucous gaiety. St Petersburg was throwing its last and greatest party to celebrate the longevity of a dynasty that had run out of steam and purpose.

Nicholas and Alexandra were unable to grasp this last chance to connect with their capital. Years of worrying and suffering over the Tsarevitch's haemophilia had transformed the Empress into a sad and distant shadow of herself. St Petersburg only served to remind her of her youth long past. As the crowds cheered and Nicholas waved she stood coldly by a forced smile across her face. The receptions exhausted her to the extent that she often nearly fainted. No grand imperial balls were held at the palace and when Alexandra attended the ball at the Hall of the Nobility she refused to dance. The citizens of St Petersburg watched with resentment as she slowly withdrew from their celebrations and took their Tsar with her.

As the celebrations passed, the momentary respite of hope and nostalgia fell away, leaving only the stench of strife and desperation. By January 1914 there were again one and half million workers on strike throughout the empire. In St Petersburg the labour situation was getting worse as workers rioted and barricaded the streets. Alexei Tolstoy, in his book *Road to Calvary*, captured the feeling of a city and society aimlessly slipping into oblivion, as the last rays of the imperial sun slipped beneath the horizon and plunged all into darkness:

> Tormented by sleepless nights, deadening its misery with wine, gold and loveless love, the shrill and feebly emotional strains of tangos for its funeral dirge, the city lived as if in expectation of a fatal and terrible day of wrath. There were auguries in plenty, and new and incomprehensible things were emerging from every cranny.[72]

FOLLOWING PAGES Twilight on the Neva.

Chapter 6:
Leningrad:
From Red Piter
to Hero City

And confined to this savage capital,
We have forgotten forever
The lakes, the steppes, the towns,
And dawns of our great native land.
Day and night in the bloody circle
A brutal languor overcomes us . . .
No one wants to help us
Because we stayed home,
Because, loving our city
And not winged freedom,
We preserved for ourselves
Its palaces, its fire and water.

A different time is drawing near,
The wind of death already chills the heart,
But the holy city of Peter
Will be our unintended monument.
'Petrograd 1919', Anna Akhmatova[1]

The Stray Dog

It was after midnight as the young woman walked quickly across Mikhailovskaya Square, turning as she passed the great yellow palace beyond and casting a glance at the statue of Pushkin. On the corner a warm light emerged from an opened door leading to a basement haunt. Sporadic sounds of laughter and shouting, punctuated by the tinkling of the piano, filled the night air as a small cadre of youths, well dressed yet very drunk, spilled out on to the street. The woman seemed not to notice as she slipped silently behind them down the steps to the entrance. Once inside, having signed and scribbled a few lines in the thick pigskin volume, she was enveloped by the air, pungent and alive with a heady cloak of tobacco, alcohol, perfume and sweat. In its undulating waves it carried art, ideas, music and sex. Scanning the crowded room she could see handsome futurist Mayakovsky, Ilya Sats experimenting on piano, her husband Gumilev sitting close, too close, to a pretty songbird and Kuzmin, the Russian

By the turn of the century St Petersburg had become a city full of monuments of glories past whose future remained a impenetrable riddle.

Beau Brummell pontificating to a young guardsman. 'Good evening Anna,' announced Boris Pronin, the owner of this decadent grotto, 'we have been waiting for you.' All eyes turned as on stage Vsevolod Meyerhold, master of the imperial theatre bowed deeply in her direction. Anna Akhmatova, the queen of The Stray Dog, had arrived.

Established in 1912, by 1914 The Stray Dog had become the new centre of avant-garde activity in the city. As many of the various circles seemed to sense an approaching apocalypse, they abandoned their salons, even the heights of Ivanov's Tower, and co-mingled in this crowded basement and awaited the end. Acmeists, futurists, cubists, constructivists and what were left of the symbolists gathered together in a last period of debauched harmony. Artists and workers were allowed in free of charge but the wealthy, the bourgeois or the connected had to pay royally for admission. Under its vaults painted with flowers and birds the denizens of the club held exhibitions, performance arts, concerts and readings. For Akhmatova, at the height of her fame, The Stray Dog represented the best and worst of all aspects of her life, yet she looked back on it as the happiest of her days. 'We are revellers, we are all whores. How

unhappy we are together.'[2] But as expressed in her eerily prescient poem 'July 1914' she sensed that all of this was fleeting and that a great period of trials was about to begin.

WAR'S DARK SHADOW

The event that all of Europe anticipated and feared, the spark that would ignite the great conflagration and bring forth the coming storm for Russia, occurred in the backwater provincial capital of Bosnia Herzegovina. On 28 June 1914, the heir the throne of the Austro-Hungarian Empire, Archduke Franz Ferdinand was assassinated at the hands of Serbian terrorists. Austria, encouraged by Kaiser Wilhem II, presented an ultimatum to Serbia which it could not accept. As Austria declared war and began the shelling of Belgrade, the government in St Petersburg was in an uproar. Nicholas, caught between Slav nationalists in support of Serbia, his General Staff calling for mobilization and his cousin the Kaiser, tried desperately to avert war. Russia found itself in a quandary it was unable to avoid: to launch into a war in support of its allies for which it was unprepared or lose face and risk political instability. Never a strong-willed ruler, Nicholas vacillated before finally issuing the order for general mobilization of Russia's armed forces on 31 July. On 1 August Germany declared war on Russia.

Nicholas appeared on the balcony of the Winter Palace before a crowd of thousands of his subjects, who held placards, icons and images of the Tsar. He then announced that Russia was now at war and took the oath recited by Alexander I in response to the Napoleonic invasion of Russia: 'I solemnly swear that I will never make peace so long as one of the enemy is on the soil of the fatherland.' As the crowds waved flags and cheered, St Petersburg abandoned itself to fate and prepared for war. The strikes, which had bedevilled the city's industry, halted as thousands joined the armed services. In the Duma even political battles were put aside as the socialists fell in line in support of the war and the assembly dissolved itself so as to not let politics get in the way of the war effort.[3]

On the streets the mob exploded into a frenzy of anti-German sentiment, attacking German shops and establishments. Petersburgers with German-sounding names chose more Slavic-sounding ones. The fury reached its crescendo with the sacking of the German Embassy on St Isaac's Square as the police chief and Military Governor of the city looked on. Nicolas signalled his support for this spate of violent patriotism by changing the name of the imperial capital from St Petersburg to the Slavonicized Petrograd. To many cooler heads this

ABOVE Nathan Altman's 1914 portrait of Anna Akhmatova (State Russian Museum, St Petersburg) portrays the sphinx-like poetess in crystalline splendour during a period she would recall as the happiest of her life.

was an omen. Not only was the city's name taken from the Dutch, not the German, but this move seemed to indicate a repudiation of the St Petersburg's founder, who never intended his window on the West to become a Russian city.

To many of St Petersburg's intellectuals, the war signalled the beginning of a great national and spiritual renewal. Many artists and writers, including Gumilev and Mayakovsky, joined up for the war effort, while others, such as Blok, were later drafted into it. To others, however, the war portended something altogether more sinister: the beginning of the end. Blok referred to the coming war as the 'incinerating years' and Gorky solemnly predicted 'One thing is clear: we are entering the first act of a worldwide tragedy.'[4] Zinaida Gippius, exasperated at her colleagues' support for the war, declared that they had all gone

insane: 'For us, who had not yet lost common sense, one thing was clear. War for Russia, in its present political condition, would not end without revolution.'[5] Akhmatova's reaction was still deeper; she offered all she held dear as a sacrifice to ensure Russia's safe passage through armageddon.

> Give me bitter years of grave illness.
> Gasping, insomnia, fever,
> Take away my child and my friend,
> And my mysterious gift of song –
> That's how I pray at Your Liturgy
> After so many days of suffering,
> So that the storm cloud over dark Russia
> Will turn into a cloud in a glory of light.[6]

ABOVE A modern-day military review in front of the Winter Palace recalls the summer of 1914 as imperial Russia plunged headlong into the catastrophe of World War I.

Progress in the war did not go well. The elation that greeted news of Russia's initial successful invasion of the Austro-Hungarian Empire led by General Brusilov was soon diminished by the disastrous rout at the Battle of Tannenburg. Russia's military inadequacies became painfully clear as defeat followed defeat and casualties mounted, totalling 1,800,000 by the end of 1914. By 1915 the majority of Russia's trained standing army was obliterated, leaving freshmen, officers and untrained recruits to bear the weight of the continuing struggle. Russia's peasant soldiers had little notion of national patriotism and still less idea of why their nation was at war. They served because they were drafted. Brusilov even commented that many of them did not even know that a country such as Germany existed.[7]

At Stavka, the Russian military headquarters, efficient management of the war was stifled by courtly politics and incompetence. Those close to the Tsar were promoted at the expense of those who were successful in the field, allowing aristocratic officers with nineteenth-century sensibilities to commit blunder after blunder. The army itself was hindered by poor mobility owing to poor railway systems and few mechanized transports. By winter, shortages were rife in everything from armaments to foodstuffs as the supply systems failed under the weight of the demand. Hospitals, which were already overflowing with the wounded, soon had to deal with epidemics of cholera, typhus, typhoid, dysentery and scurvy, which felled scores of soldiers due to the unsanitary conditions at camp. The German offensive in May 1915 drove the army into full-scale retreat, destroying what little morale was left among the troops. The number of desertions skyrocketed as the soldiers voted with their feet and went home.

In Petrograd, the city swelled with wounded and deserters. They brought the horror of the front with them to the citizenry of the capital, who turned their heads away and continued to party. The *ogarochny* (literally, those who burn the candle at both ends) became the lords of the city, which had lost its will to live. This ultra-decadent class filled the most expensive restaurants along Nevsky Prospect and spent lavishly and wastefully on extravagant parties, turning their grand houses into gambling dens and brothels. Through these golden halls wandered diplomats, spies, corrupt officials, war-profiteers, criminals and above all Rasputin, who held court at the gypsy restaurant the Villa Rode.[8] Outside in the streets the war was devouring all available resources, making shortages a regular occurrence in the capital. Prices shot up as speculators sold to the highest bidders. Eventually, when they were unable to buy food or fuel for their families, the workers of Petrograd, toiling away to provide armaments to prop up the war they neither wanted nor understood, began to strike.

Down in The Stray Dog, the futurist poet Mayakovsky, disgusted as he watched the round-the-clock Sodom and Gomorrah of the bourgeois and the elite in the last throes of their ascendancy, decided to shriek his dissent against the war and against everything the elite stood for:

> To you, living through orgy after orgy
> Who have bathtubs and warm toilets!
> Aren't you ashamed to read in newspaper columns
> About the presentation of St George Crosses . . .
>
> To please you, loving vulgar women and good food,
> Would I give you my life?
> I would rather serve pineapple water
> To whores at the bar!

In late 1915 the Tsar asserted himself. He attempted to placate political criticism by sacking his most reactionary ministers. Under pressure, he then reconvened the Duma to help deal with the collapsing war effort. Instead, the Duma assailed the incompetence of the government and began to manoeuvre to take power. Their efforts were led by a young radical lawyer Alexander Kerensky, who had begun working tirelessly for the overthrow of the monarchy.

ABOVE Even before 1914, a dark malaise had fallen over St Petersburg, as expressed by such works as *The Kriukov Canal* (1910), coloured wood engraving by Anna Ostroumova-Lebedeva (State Russian Museum, St Petersburg).

Nicholas, distressed at the failure of his commanders and overwhelmed by the political criticisms, decided to take personal command of the army. While this decision was supported and encouraged by his Prime Minister Goremykin, the Empress and, through her, Rasputin, Nicholas met the vociferous opposition of his mother, the imperial family, his cabinet and the Duma. Undeterred, the Tsar left in late August for the front. Within days, the Duma moved to demand reform and to establish a semi-parliamentary state. The cabinet agreed. Nicholas, furious and unwilling to yield his power, closed the Duma and in doing so dashed any hopes for the survival of his dynasty.

The hazy atmosphere of political confusion, social unrest and apocalyptic fear that gripped the city in 1916 was further enforced by the release in book form of Andrei Bely's *Petersburg*. This novel represented not only the last gasp of the symbolist genre but also the last great literary contribution to the St Peterburg myth. In it Bely paints a picture of a city of misty shadows where locations shift. It is a city divided and in conflict between its palaces and great monuments and its blackish-grey cubes covered in a greenish-yellow fog, through which a seething swarm of bodies daily crawls to reach the factories and where the Bronze Horseman rides again as harbinger of the apocalypse.

Through a story that ostensibly revolves around the confused efforts of a student duped by revolutionaries to assassinate his father, a high ranking official, Bely managed to represent all of the various contrasting forces that bound the city in conflict with itself and were hurling it towards its ultimate destruction. Bely, allying himself to the tradition of Gogol and Dostoyevsky, was of the opinion that St Petersburg's illegal or unnatural state was the cause of these perpetual conflicts. Ever a symbolist, however, Bely also saw St Petersburg as stuck on the border between the heavenly and earthly planes, on the border between the West and Asia. As a student of Soloviev, he also believed that Asia would eventually swamp Europe and wipe St Petersburg, with all of its contrasts, off the face of the earth, freeing Russia from this alien yoke to pursue its naturally ordained course.[9]

THE MURDER OF RASPUTIN

With Nicholas at the front anxieties about the nation fell to the Empress, who became increasingly reliant on the advice of Rasputin. Rasputin's increasing presence at the palace and interference in government affairs, coupled with his very public debaucheries, horrified and alarmed the imperial family and the conservatives.

Criticism of the dynasty was on everyone's lips and revolution was spoken about openly, as if it were already a *fait accompli*. The Tsar even began to receive advice from members of his own family and the nobility to allow the Duma to name a government.[10] Nicholas again tried to make small concessions, by naming A.F. Trepov as Prime Minister. Alexandra hated Trepov and her influence, supported by Rasputin, hindered his negotiations with the moderate factions of the Duma, which was increasingly coming under the control of the radical Trudovik and Menshevik parties.

In Petrograd members of the imperial family allied with the political elite, realizing that revolution was now inevitable, decided began to hatch various plots to remove Nicholas and place another Romanov on the throne and set a government of confidence. This idea of a coup supported by the privileged elite was a vain effort to preserve their way of life through revolution from above before it came from below. While none of the main plots succeeded, one of their efforts did – the assassination of Rasputin.

The plot was led by one of late imperial Russia's most flamboyant characters, Prince Felix Yussupov. The prince, from Russia's wealthiest princely family and married to the Tsar's niece, was a known homosexual who virulently despised Rasputin. It was rumoured that Rasputin had tried to seduce him on his wedding day.[11] Yussupov recruited two other members of the imperial family the Tsar's cousins Grand Duke Dmitri Pavlovich and Grand Duke Nicholas Mikhailovich. Finally the royal trio turned to the conservative leader of the Duma, V.M. Purishkevich, an outspoken critic of Rasputin. The plan they hatched was as naive as it was ambitious: kill Rasputin and arrest Alexandra, thus removing all negative influences from the Tsar and enable him to listen and to restore order before it was too late.

On 30 December Rasputin was accompanied by the prince to the Yussupov Palace on the Moika on the pretext that he was to meet Princess Irina and treat her for some unspecified illness. Rasputin received a warning of a plot the day before, but ignored it, although he did place money into his daughter's account, which some say was indication that he may have had a premonition of his death. At the palace Yussupov led Rasputin down into a cellar apartment which he had opulently decorated for the visit. Plush oriental carpets, chandeliers, a rock crystal crucifix and an elegant table set with plates of sweets and goblets of wine. Unbeknownst to him the

cakes and wine were laced with poison. The monk drank, yet did not die. The prince, who had begun to panic, conferred with his co-conspirators. This time he returned with a pistol.

Back downstairs Rasputin had grown woozy. The prince returned and referred him to the crucifix standing on a nearby table. As Rasputin admired the object, Yussupov shot him in the side. Shrieking in pain Rasputin fell to the floor, presumably dead. The conspirators quickly moved to prepare for the removal of the body. Once ready they returned to the cellar. They could not believe their eyes: the body was gone. Meanwhile Rasputin had struggled to the courtyard and was limping through the snow trying to escape. 'Felix, Felix, I will tell the Tsarina everything!' he shouted, as he made for the embankment. Purishkevich then drew his own pistol and fired twice missing both times. Cursing, he took aim once again and this time made his mark. Rasputin was struck in the back and in the head before he collapsed. To make sure the job was done Purishkevich walked over to the Rasputin and kicked him in the temple.

Rasputin's body was then weighted with chains, driven far from the palace and dumped into the Neva. Two days later the body washed up. Alexandra, upon hearing of her confidant's death, was paralyzed with fear and rage. The plot was soon revealed and, in spite of the objections of the imperial family, the prince and the Grand Duke were banished on the orders of the Tsar. Alexandra, looking for some sign of hope from her lost friend, then received the monk's last will and testament. Part of it read:

> Tsar of the land of Russia, if you hear the sound of the bell which will tell you that Gregory has been killed, you must know this: if it was your relations who have wrought my death then no one of your family, that is to say, none of your children or relations will remain alive for more than two years. They will be killed by the Russian people.[12]

REVOLUTION!

February 1917 in Petrograd was brutally cold. Winter storms turned to blizzards, blanketing the roads leading to the capital. Villagers shut themselves up in their houses and waited to deliver their foodstuffs to the city when the weather cleared. By 20 February supply trains had ground to a halt and rumours quickly spread throughout the city that rationing was about to begin. Panic ensued among all strata of society as bakery shelves were cleared, endless queues formed and prices soared. Fuel shortages had also caused the closure of the Putilov Works, filling the streets with workers with nothing to do. To the south in Tsarskoe Selo, Tsar Nicholas, attempting to handle the fallout of Rasputin's murder, came under terrible pressure from politicians and his family to announce the formation of a government responsible to the Duma. Once again the Tsar fled the Alexander Palace and headed for the front, leaving the capital in the hands of the Empress, his Prime Minister Protopopov, who swore that he was advised by Rasputin's spirit, and the inept Military Governor General Khabalov.

On 23 February, the day after the Tsar's departure, the sun burst out above Petrograd, temporarily loosening the grip of ice and cold on the city. Taking advantage of the change in weather, Petrograd's populace left their apartments and flooded on to the streets, mingling with soldiers and workers. The weather was particularly fortuitous for the socialist organizers of the International Women's Day March that was planned for that day. Groups of well-dressed society ladies, female students, women workers and peasants gathered and began a peaceful procession down the Nevsky Prospect toward the Municipal Council. Their slow procession was encouraged by the delighted cheers of their supporters. Across town, on the Vyborg side, female textile workers also took to the streets on strike, demanding bread for their families. The men of the various metal works along the Neva as well as the workers of adjoining factories followed suit, joining their ranks. By the afternoon 100,000 workers had joined the strike and began to move toward the Liteiny Bridge. The police quickly blocked their way and managed to drive the crowd off using sabres and cudgels. In front of the Municipal Council Building, however, the police were less successful in ending the demonstration, as mounted Cossacks were not inclined to attack women, regardless of orders.

The following day the hungry workers again sought to reach the city centre, largely with the hope of looting the well-stocked stores of the wealthier quarters. Socialist agitators were there to urge them on. 'Comrades, if we cannot get a loaf of bread for ourselves in a righteous way, then we must do everything: we must go ahead and solve our problem by force. . . . Comrades, arm yourselves with everything possible – bolts, screws, rocks, and go out of the factory and start smashing the first shops you find.'[13] By mid-morning, upwards of 200,000 workers had taken to the streets, heading for the Nevsky Prospect. This time, the crowds simply brushed police forces aside or avoided roadblocks by crossing the frozen Neva. Throughout the city workers skirmished with police and Cossacks. However, on

The Winter Canal.

the Nevsky Prospect a carnival atmosphere erupted as Petrograd's middle classes came out to embrace the workers. In Znamenskaya Square, an enormous rally was held with cheering crowds shouting 'Down with autocracy! Down with the war!'[14] Orator after orator mounted the plinth of the monumental statue of Alexander III and railed against the government and the Tsar. Again the police stood back and did nothing, even as a potent symbol of the autocracy was hijacked by agitators, a fact not lost on the roaring throngs.

A general strike was declared on 25 February, spilling more than 200,000 workers on to the streets. The city came to a standstill as trams halted, cabs refused to pick up fares and newspapers remained undelivered. Among the crowds red flags began to appear and protesters chanted 'Down with the Tsar!' Once again the response of the Cossacks was timid. They even watched idly as the chief of police was dragged from his horse, beaten and shot in the middle of the Liteiny Bridge. Further away, on the Nevsky Prospect in front of the Kazan Cathedral, during a face-off between protesters and the Cossacks, a young girl emerged from the crowd, approached the Cossack commander and presented him with a bouquet of red roses, symbols of peace and revolution. The commandant leaned down from his horse and accepted the flowers with a smile. The crowd went wild with jubilation.[15] There were even cases of Cossacks attacking mounted police. As for the city's garrison, it clashed several times with the demonstrators, yet was equally conflicted over its duties to quell dissent. The city regiments were largely made up of peasants recruited to replace career soldiers who had been sent to the front. They saw the workers and demonstrators as their own kind and refused to intervene.

As the disorder in Petrograd grew, the ministers met to plan strategy. They sought to avoid open conflict with the crowds, believing that if bread could be provided the demonstrations would peter out. Their sentiments were echoed by socialists and Bolshevik leaders, who were not ready to see these disturbances as a revolution. Even Zinaida Gippius saw it as merely a 'bread riot'. The Tsar, however, was not amused by the reports, viewing the marches and riots as detrimental to the execution of the war effort. He ordered the military to put down the demonstrations by the following morning. With this command, the Tsar provided the final spark that lit the powder keg. Having no clear picture of how precarious the situation in Petrograd really was, being continually lied to by inept and embarrassed officials, Nicholas had guaranteed revolution.

That night the city was alive with activity. Police abandoned the workers' districts as mobs looted and burned their stations. Thousands of troops started to move into position to discourage any further demonstrations. At the Alexandrinsky Theatre, however, a final eerie act was being played out. As gunshots broke the stillness of the winter night the cream of Petrograd society – Grand Dukes, aristocrats, diplomats, intellectuals and artists – assembled in the gilded stalls and boxes for the sold-out premiere of Meyerhold's production of Lermentov's *Masquerade*. The play tells the tale of a jealous husband who is tricked into believing his wife has been unfaithful and poisons her. The story, in the great apocalyptic tradition of St Petersburg, is set against a backdrop of a doomed elite society on the verge of being swept away, an ironic mirror of the assembly of the great and good in the audience. Lavishly designed by Alexander Golovin and stunningly orchestrated by Meyerhold, the play brought back to life, for fleeting moment a glimmer of imperial St Petersburg, which was rapidly sinking beneath a tide of revolution. Later one spectator recalled:

> So close, in the same city, next to those starving for bread – this artistically perverted, brazenly corrupting, meaninglessly frenzied luxury for the sake of prurience. What was it – the Rome of the Ceasars? What were we going to do afterward, go to Lucullus to eat nightingales' tongues, and let the bastards howl, seeking bread and freedom?[16]

The following morning the city awoke to find itself militarized. The bridges across the Neva were raised, barricades and roadblocks had been erected with checkpoints and machine gun emplacements. As the crowds assembled in the working class districts and headed towards the centre, they were fired upon by the soldiers. Throughout the day, casualties abounded all over the city as clashes erupted at several flashpoints. The horrible day reached its bloody crescendo with a particular incident in Znamenskaya Square, where a training regiment shot and killed fifty demonstrators. Emboldened by the bloodshed, the crowds began to realize that the situation had altered into something far more serious and quickly rebounded. Soon the peasant soldiers were faced with having to decide whether to stand with the people or with the Tsar. Protesters approached, beseeching them not to shoot their mothers and sisters, but to join them. The Pavlovsky Regiment was the first to mutiny, firing on a squadron of mounted

police until they were apprehended and disarmed. Their leaders were captured and sent to the Fortress of Peter and Paul, the last prisoners of the regime. As evening fell on 26 February the disturbances seemed to have been quelled. On the Fontanka, the palace of Princess Radziwill was brilliantly lit for her previously planned soirée, her guests dancing as the champagne flowed. The French Ambassador Maurice Paléologue commented that it called to mind the grand maisons of Paris in 1789.[17]

During the night the soldiers of the Volynsky Regiment, which had been responsible for the Znamemskaya massacre the day before, unanimously decided to go over to the demonstrators. At dawn they quickly sent word to other regiments, including the Preobrazhenskoe Regiment, founded by Peter the Great, who in turn rebelled and joined the workers. With soldiers now leading the crowds they attacked the city's arsenals and armed scores of workers and citizens. They also moved to occupy strategic locations such as railway stations and the telephone exchange. The 'bread riot' had suddenly been transformed into an armed revolt.

As the day progressed the violence escalated. More regiments mutinied, killing their officers and fighting loyal soldiers. Armed crowds began to hunt the police, who responded with snipers and machine guns. Bands of soldiers raced through the streets in stolen cars waving red flags and firing into the air as they drove from location to location battling the police. Armed mobs descended on

ABOVE The Alexandrinsky Theatre and the Catherine Monument, scene of the last theatrical performance of imperial Russia.

places of authority, attacking police stations and court buildings, burning and looting as they went. Ambassador Paléologue observed the chaos:

> Frightened inhabitants were scattered through the streets . . . At one corner of Liteiny, soldiers were helping civilians to erect a barricade. Flames mounted from the Law Courts. The gates of the Arsenal burst open with a crash. Suddenly the crack of machine-gun fire split the air; it was the regulars who had just taken position by the Nevsky Prospect. . . . The Law Courts had become nothing but an enormous furnace; the Arsenal on the Liteiny, the Ministry of the Interior, the Military Government Building . . . the headquarters of the Okhrana and a score of police stations were in flames, the prisons were open and all of the prisoners had been liberated.[18]

The Peter and Paul Fortress, symbol of Tsarist political oppression, was also occupied and the Red Flag waved above its ramparts. In the streets the public organized itself to help the revolutionary soldiers by feeding them, housing them and lighting bonfires. Doctors cared for the wounded, shopkeepers opened their stores as shelters and children ran errands for them. This was truly a people's revolution as citizens of all classes were participating in the fray with police and the authorities.

Gorky and other leaders of the political intelligentsia were displeased, as the disorders seemed to spin out of control. They denied once more that this unruly mob was the long-awaited revolution. Alexander Shilapnikov, the leading Bolshevik in Petrograd, said 'There is and will be no revolution. We have to prepare for a long period of reaction.'[19] With Trotsky in New York and Lenin in Zurich, the Bolsheviks remained aloof, awaiting developments. At the Tauride Palace, however, the Duma moved

ABOVE The raising of the bridges on the Neva: a typical occurrence late at night, on the morning of 26 February 1917 it signalled revolution.

cautiously to try to fill the power vacuum. They formed the cumbersomely named 'Provisional Committee of Duma Members for the Restoration of Order in the Capital and the Establishment of Relations with Individuals and Institutions' so as to not appear as if they were assuming power too quickly. The committee was headed by the President of the Duma Mikhail Rodzianko and it included, among others, Prince Lvov and Alexander Kerensky. On the other side of the aisle the Mensheviks led the formation of the Provisional Executive Committee of the Soviet of Workers Deputies, with Nikolai Chkheidze as chairman and Matvei Skobelev and Kerensky again as deputies. Vladimir Nabakov (the writer's father), who was working at the palace, described the atmosphere:

> Soldiers, soldiers and more soldiers, with tired dull faces; everywhere were signs of an improvised camp, rubbish, straw; the air was thick like some kind of dense fog, there was the smell of soldiers boots, cloth and sweat; from somewhere we could here the hysterical voices of orators addressing a meeting in the Catherine Hall – everywhere crowding bustling and confusion.[20]

As a revolutionary government began to take shape in Petrograd, the Tsar, still monarch and autocrat, began to get nervous as more reports began to flow in. Earlier in the day he had dismissed a cable from Rodzianko as nonsense until the evening of 12 March, when the news of the mutiny reached him. He ordered General Ivanov to move north and subdue the city and establish himself as military dictator in Petrograd. Nicholas then ordered his train to head back to Tsarskoe Selo as he was eager to secure the protection of his family. Unbeknownst to him, his cabinet had already resigned and turned themselves over to the Duma, which for their own protection interred them in the Fortress.

On 13 March, the tone of the revolutionary forces grew darker, as mutinous soldiers commingled with criminals, heavily armed vigilantes and rowdy drunken mobs. The violence in the streets began to spiral out of control. At the Naval base of Kronstadt, sailors tortured and massacred their officers. In Petrograd, the crowd, fuelled with anger and alcohol and armed to the teeth, began to lash out at all signs of privilege and authority. On the streets, well-dressed citizens ran the risk of harassment or worse. The police, now openly hunted and brutally executed by the crowds, began to flee the city or turn themselves into the Duma, which they hoped would save them.

Criminals released from prison quickly formed gangs and set about looting shops, taverns and wine merchants. Next they turned to the houses of the wealthy, robbing and raping inhabitants of palaces and mansions. The prima ballerina Mathilde Kchessinka, Nicholas's former mistress, narrowly escaped before the mob ransacked her Art Nouveau mansion. One clever aristocrat Countess Kleinmichel saved her mansion from looting by posting a sign that read: 'No trespassing. This house is the property of the Petrograd Soviet. Countess Kleinmichel has been taken to the Peter and Paul Fortress.'[21]

At the Tauride Palace, the seat of power in the city, the two representative bodies had divided into two wings of the palace. In the right wing was the Temporary Committee of the Duma and in the left wing was the newly established Petrograd Soviet of Workers and Soldiers Deputies. The first had authority and no power; the second had power in the streets but no authority. Kerensky noted that in this arrangement, 'two different Russias settled side by side: the Russia of the ruling classes who had lost (though they did not realize it yet) . . . and the Russia of Labour, marching towards power, without suspecting it.'[22] Both houses were united in the determination to bring the streets under control as events were quickly slipping into anarchy. The Temporary Committee ordered the soldiers to return to their barracks. Suspicious of retribution, the Petrograd Soviet issued Order Number One: a list of demands and conditions for the soldiers' compliance. Drawn up by the Bolshevik Sokolov, it stated that the military was responsible only to the Soviet, that soldiers were citizens when not on duty, that they be treated with respect and that officers no longer had the right to speak down to them nor to expect a salute or honorific titles.

Meanwhile there remained pockets of soldiers loyal to the Tsar throughout the city: the Winter Palace, which held 1,500 loyal troops, the Admiralty, where Khabalov was still headquartered, the General Staff Building and the Astoria Hotel. The Astoria, where numerous officers and their families were housed, was the scene of a bloody battle when revolutionary soldiers tried to take over the building. The Tsar himself was beginning to encounter the revolution as his train had to be re-routed through Pskov due to the fact that the line to Tsarskoe Selo had been occupied by rebellious troops. Upon his arrival in Pskov Nicholas was informed that the Imperial Guard and His Majesty's Regiment in full regalia swore allegiance to the Duma as well as the elite Marine Guard, which was led by Grand Duke Cyril. After swearing allegiance, Cyril returned to his palace and hoisted the Red Flag. With these acts Petrograd fell to the revolution.

ABDICATION

Nicholas, despairing at the news of the mutiny of his elite corps and realizing that only a massive assault on the city would crush the revolution, decided reluctantly to give into pressure and permit a government answerable to the Duma. Not long after one of Nicholas's aides sent the order, Rodzianko replied by wire from the chaos of the Tauride Palace. His message read:

> His Majesty and yourself apparently are unable to realize what is happening in the capital. A terrible revolution has broken out. Hatred of the Empress has reached a fever pitch. To prevent bloodshed, I have been forced to arrest all the ministers. . . . Don't send any more troops. I am hanging on by a thread myself. Power is slipping from my hands. The measures you propose are too late. The time for them is gone. There is no return.[23]

In Petrograd events were moving rapidly. On the morning of 15 March the Duma and the Soviet had contentiously agreed to form a cabinet with Prince Lvov as Prime Minister, Kerensky as Minster of Justice and Alexander Guchkov as Minister of War. Part of the deliberations was an agreement that the Tsar abdicate in favour of his son Alexis, with his brother Grand Duke Michael as regent. In Pskov the Tsar was presented with a transcript of a discussion between Rodzianko and his commander-in-chief General Alexeiev, which described the situation and recommended abdication. This was followed by several telegrams from his chief commanders. One after the other they advised the Tsar that the only option to prevent the country from sinking into anarchy and avoid the collapse of the war effort was to abdicate.

Having tried all his life to defend his imperial prerogative, Nicholas was dumbfounded. But he trusted his generals, and his patriotism would not allow Russia's defeat in order to save his crown. He at first agreed to abdicate in favour of his son but after consultations with doctors about Alexis's haemophilia, abdicated for him as well. Nicholas, exhausted and in despair, wrote in his diary: 'For the sake of Russia, and to keep the armies in the field, I decided to take this step. . . . Left Pskov at one in the morning. All around me I see treason, cowardice and deceit.'[24]

In Petrograd the announcement that Nicholas II had abdicated in favour of his brother Michael was met with fervent indignation by the crowds of soldiers who packed the Soviet and the grounds of the palace. 'No more Romanovs!' they cried. The Grand Duke, now Tsar Michael II, listened to arguments for and against his ascension, but finally it came down to security. The Duma, he was told, could not ensure his safety. Michael, seeing the writing on the wall, promptly declined the throne and abdicated. With this act three centuries of Romanov rule came to end and the imperial sun had finally set. Petrograd rejoiced upon the announcement of Nicholas's abdication and the fall of the dynasty. As the Duma, closely watched by the Petrograd Soviet, got down to work, the revolution began to bury its dead. On 25 March, 180 martyrs of the revolution were laid to rest in the middle of the Field of Mars. The Glorious February Revolution was heralded as a political and spiritual purification of the Russian people, an almost Christian effort, which would sweep away all the social ills of the past. As people walked through the streets they saluted each other with the traditional Easter greeting altered for the revolution: 'Russia has arisen!'

LONG LIVE THE REPUBLIC!

> Russia is free, but not yet purified. The first cry of a baby is always a joy; even one realizes that both mother and child still might die.[25]
>
> Zinaida Gippius

Soon after its assumption of power it became painfully clear that the diarchy that balanced the Duma and the Petrograd Soviet was unworkable. For the time being the Soviet felt free to let the Duma run things as its time to assume power had not arrived. It fell on the Duma to run the country, while the Bolsheviks set about infiltrating military units and local Soviets. Meanwhile, the Provisional Government led by Prince Lvov could barely function, as the gentlemanly former president of the Zemstvo Council was unused to political manoeuvring and party politics. He had assumed that he was taking over a government of national unity, but he could barely keep his ministers from attacking each other.

Lvov was an optimist and believed in the Russian people. He and his supporters desired the creation of a liberal democratic state and viewed the Provisional Government as caretakers whose power eventually would be turned over to an elected Constituent Assembly. As liberals they refused to support old forms of political control and oppression, such as the police, prisons, courts and the death

The assumption of power in February 1917 of the state Duma housed in the Tauride Palace (above) led to the end of the Romanov Dynasty and the house arrest of Nicholas and his family in the Alexander Palace (below).

penalty, nor would they consent to violently suppressing demonstrations. They were also over-sensitive about their legitimacy and over-cautious about producing perfect elections. As they allowed ideals to cloud their common sense, they played into the hands of the Bolsheviks, who could sit back and criticize the government for not calling elections sooner.

Petrograd was suddenly free, having been granted the rights of assembly, press and speech. All legal restrictions of religion, class or race were removed and universal suffrage was introduced, including for women. Meetings spontaneously broke out on street corners, in cafés, theatres and squares, as the citizens of Petrograd spoke their minds freely for the first time. In the factories the new

freedoms gave rise to a growing labour militancy as factories organized their own elected committees. These elected bodies immediately set about exacting concessions from employers with the help of the government, which was eager to keep the war effort moving. Factories also formed their own militias, later known as the 'Red Guard' in order to protect the gains of the revolution. Labour militancy became a major problem for the government as growing expectations of workers soon outpaced employers and the government's ability to deliver. In their disillusionment workers went on strike and fell under the influence of the Bolsheviks.

The Bolsheviks themselves were struggling to adjust to the stunning pace of events. Newly freed Bolsheviks, such as Joseph

ABOVE The first monument of free Russia: the Tomb of the Martyrs of the February Revolution on the Field of Mars.

Stalin and Lev Kamenev, arrived in Petrograd to guide the Central Committee. They struck a moderate tone and showed support for the Provisional Government. Lenin, in exile in Zurich, only learned of the revolution on 2 March and was viewed in Petrograd as largely out of touch. Fearing a loss of influence, Lenin arranged to be transported to Sweden by the German government, which was actively fomenting revolution as a means of undermining Russia's involvement in the war.

From Sweden Lenin travelled to Finland and, in a feat of dramatic staging, arrived in Petrograd's Finland Station on 3 April on board a train festooned with red bunting and banners as a military band thundered the 'Marseillaise'. Greeted by an honour guard and a crowd of enthusiastic supporters, Lenin threw down the gauntlet, claiming leadership of the Bolsheviks and his intentions as he declared: '[the Provisional Government] are deceiving you, just as they deceive the whole Russian people. . . . The people need peace. The people need bread, the people need land. . . . Sailors, comrades, you must fight for the revolution, fight to the end, for full victory of the proletariat. All hail the world Socialist Revolution!'[26] He then headed by motorcar to the Kchessinka Mansion, now the headquarters of the Bolsheviks. There he began to lecture from the balcony announcing his programme; all power to the Soviets, peace with Germany, and nationalization of land, banks and industry.

The Lenin who returned to Petrograd after years of self-imposed exile was not the earnest yet affable man who first arrived in 1893. Years of living in Siberia and abroad had hardened him. He knew little of Russia having never spent very much time in the provinces or among the people. For years he lived off the proceeds of his mother's estate and had never been gainfully employed. His knowledge of history was spotty other than about revolutions and he had read few of the classics of Russian literature other than the works of Chernyshevsky and Turgenev. What gave Lenin his aura, what inspired men and women to follow him, was his utter and unwavering devotion to his quest for power. As a professional revolutionary he was a man driven. Like Rakhmetov, the hero of Chernyshevsky's *What Is To Be Done?*, Lenin lived an ascetic life like a revolutionary monk. Eschewing personal pleasures he lived in spotless spartan quarters, exercised regularly and devoted his little free time to writing and study.

Lenin was a completely unsentimental man. Gorky described him as having an ignorance of work and human suffering, which had developed into a 'pitiless contempt, worthy of a nobleman, for the lives of the ordinary people. . . . Life in all its complexity is unknown to Lenin.'[27] Once, after listening to a symphony, Lenin exclaimed 'I cannot listen to music, it excites my nerves. I feel like talking nonsense and caressing people who, living in such a filthy hell, can create such beauty. Because today one must not caress anyone: they will bite off your hand. One must break heads, pitilessly break heads, even if, ideally, we are opposed to all violence.'[28] The Mensheviks asked how anyone could compete with someone who thought about revolution twenty-four hours a day. Yet the Bolsheviks, soldiers and workers responded to him because of this cool aloofness and his towering personality. To them he became like a Tsar of old, not only leader of the party but also its god, inspiring fanatical faith and unfaltering loyalty.

As the spring bled into the summer, the Provisional Government struggled to survive. Determined to carry on the war, the government found itself in constant conflict with the revolutionary soldiery who, in the middle of April, rose up once again. Twenty-five thousand soldiers marched on the Mariinsky Palace, seat of the Provisional Government on St Isaac's Square. The leaders of the Petrograd Soviet, again not ready to assume power, ordered the soldiers to disperse. Fearing that a collapse into civil war would result in a situation they would be unable to control, the Soviet decided to throw its weight behind the government and consent to allow its members to form a cabinet with it. The troubles did not end there. In early June peace in Petrograd was again under fire as anarchists seized the presses of a right-wing newspaper. They called on soldiers, sailors and workers to support them, who happily began to respond to the call to arms. Again the Soviet was forced to intervene on behalf of the government, stemming the rising revolutionary tide and allowing the anarchists to be crushed.

The constant turmoil of four months of revolutionary conflict began to take a toll on Petrograd physically and socially. 'This is no longer a capital, it is a cesspit,' exclaimed Gorky. 'No one works, the streets are filthy, there are piles of stinking rubbish in the courtyards. . . . It hurts me to say how bad things have become. There is growing idleness and cowardice in the people, and all those base and criminal instincts which I have fought all my life and which, it seems, are now destroying Russia.'[29] The brutal violence on the street, which was leading to unchecked crime, vigilante justice and mob violence, horrified Gorky and other intellectuals.

After many years of planning they watched in dismay as the peasantry co-opted their revolution. These workers, soldiers and sailors from the Russian heartland, Asiatic Russia, rejected the entreaties of the Westernized intelligentsia in order to settle scores rather than erect a new society. Gorky lamented:

The Russian people, having won its freedom, is in its present state incapable of using it for its own good, only for its own harm and the harm of others, and it is in danger of losing everything that it has been fighting for for centuries. It is destroying all the great achievements of its ancestors; gradually the national wealth, the wealth of the land, of industry, of transport, of communications and of the towns is being destroyed in the dirt.[30]

General Brusilov's initial military successes on the front with Austria quickly dissolved. Kerensky as Minister of War, who had benefited from the military victories, now found himself compromised as the army was forced to retreat. The Bolsheviks, urged on by Lenin, sensed this and moved to act. On 4 July a mutiny headed by the 1st Machine Gun Regiment broke as soldiers protested about their units being sent to the front. The revolt split the Bolsheviks, who were unsure that they could control the gathering storm as anarchists began agitating among the soldiers. Soon the soldiers began to demand that all power be transferred to the Soviet. Stalin, leading the Central Committee, initially came out against the armed rebellion as it could not be sure of the loyalty of the majority of regiments, but later reversed this.

Groups of workers joined the fray and began to demonstrate as well, for it seemed to all that the assumption of power by the Soviet had begun. The demonstrators flooded into the Soviet chamber calling for power. Lenin remained behind the scenes, waiting for the events to unfold. However, in a rare case of cold feet, he would not give orders to take over. Without leadership the revolt faltered. Kerensky realized the Bolsheviks were behind the putsch and released papers implicating Lenin as a collaborator with the Germans. Troops of the Petrograd garrison and from the front arrived and occupied Petrograd, ending the revolt. Kerensky now ordered the arrest of all Bolshevik leaders. Lenin once again escaped over the Finnish border. The party, with its leader gone, under attack in the press and by the government, its supporters disarmed and disheartened, had reached an all-time low.

Following the July Days, Prince Lvov had had enough. Caught between armed revolt and the struggle between the right and the left, the prince was unable to reconcile the various parties and, for the sake of national unity, resigned. Kerensky was named as his successor. Kerensky, vain and arrogant, cultivated the image of himself as a national leader called upon by the people to save Russia. He was aided in this by several members of the intellectual elite led by the Merezhovskys, who sought a romantic figure to rally around. Kerensky, seeking to make a dramatic statement, moved himself into the Winter Palace and set himself up in the apartments of Alexander III. With the Bolsheviks neutralized, the ever-paranoid Kerensky began to see threats from the right. On 31 July, in total secrecy, he moved the Tsar and the imperial family from their house arrest at Tsarskoe Selo to the Siberian town of Tobolsk. He then dismissed the commander-in-chief General Brusilov and replaced him with General Lavr Kornilov, an ambitious patriot popular with the right. Kornilov, himself a popular figure, soon began to eclipse the Prime Minister, whose own reputation was in decline.

The Kornilov Affair

The fall of Riga in August 1917 placed the Germans within striking distance of Petrograd. Kerensky, growing weaker politically, became ever more suspicious of his commander-in-chief as Kornilov's public persona grew and the people yearned for order. A series of miscommunications provided Kerensky with the excuse to assume dictatorial powers and dismiss Kornilov. Kornilov, believing he was being tricked and that Kerensky's government had fallen to the Bolsheviks, ordered troops to march on the capital. The Prime Minister-cum-dictator, isolated by the right, was then forced to appeal to the Soviet for help. The Soviet Executive Committee, now transferred to the Smolny Institute, sprang into action, mobilizing their soldiers and workers to defend Petrograd against the invader. The Bolsheviks took the opportunity to rehabilitate themselves politically and several of their leaders were released from prison. The Soviet also sent agitators to meet the oncoming troops who, upon being told that Kerensky was still in power, halted their advance. The city thus delivered and Kornilov neutralized, Kerensky had survived, but only just. He had totally lost support of the right and lost face with the army. Concessions granted to the Soviet had severely diluted his power, which ended beyond the corridors of the Winter Palace. Lenin, encouraged by gains in the city Duma and the military revolt, then decided to act.

'Kerensky is now entirely in the hands of the maximalists and the Bolsheviks. The ball is over. They have not yet raised their heads, they sit. Tomorrow of course, they will get on their feet – to their full height.'[31] Zinaida Gippius was not alone in predicting that the Bolsheviks had not yet shown their hand. Petrograd itself was abuzz with anticipation. The citizens of the city, tired and disillusioned, began to ignore the political manoeuvrings with which they could no longer keep up. The Bolsheviks became increasingly nervous as Petrograd, citizens and workers alike sank into apathy and seemed in no mood for yet another uprising.

RED OCTOBER

The lads have all gone to the wars
To serve in the Red Guard –
To serve in the Red Guard –
And risk their hot heads for the cause.

Hell and damnation,
Life is such fun
With a ragged greatcoat
And a Jerry gun!

To smoke the nobs out of their holes
We'll light a fire through all the world,
A bloody fire through all the world –
Lord, bless our souls!

From *The Twelve*, Alexander Blok (1918)

Yellow and brown leaves danced across the slick, wet streets, carried on the first breaths of winter. Exhausted Petrograders, sick of war, tired of shortages and fed up with revolution, abandoned the streets for the warmth of their homes. As the city fell silent and the hours grew late on 24 October, the final phase of the coup that everyone expected yet no one cared about began. The classical edifice of the Smolny Institute, blazing with light, shone through the naked trees like a great beacon in the dark sea of Petrograd. Cars came and went delivering messages to and carrying orders from the Bolshevik leadership to the faithful in the streets. Orders were given to seize key points of administration, finance, communications and transport in order to isolate the Provisional Government in its headquarters, the Winter Palace. The Fortress garrison joined the Bolsheviks and the guards regiments decided to remain neutral. Slowly and without incident, the Red Guard relieved the government soldiers who were either disarmed or simply went home. Finally just after midnight, bewigged and bandaged, Lenin entered the party's headquarters in a disguise for fear of being arrested at this crucial hour. Upon his arrival he assumed control over the orchestration of events, which would herald Red October. The next morning posters began appearing nailed to posts or plastered on walls.

TO THE CITIZENS OF RUSSIA!

The Provisional Government has been deposed. Government authority has passed into the hands of the organ of the Petrograd Soviet of Workers and Soldiers Deputies, the Military-Revolutionary Committee, which stands at the head of the Petrograd proletariat and garrison.

The task for which the people have been struggling – the immediate offer of a democratic peace, the abolition of landlord property in land, worker control over production, the creation of the Soviet Government – this task is assured.

Long Live the Revolution of Workers, Soldiers, and Peasants!

The Military-Revolutionary Committee of the
Petrograd Soviet of Workers and Soldiers Deputies.[32]

Alexander Kerensky awoke on 25 October in his lavish bed in the Winter Palace having retired late and slept little. Upon learning that troops he had requested the night before were not forthcoming, he realized the game was up and began to plan his escape. The telephone lines to the palace had been cut and the railroads seized, but he managed to requisition a car from the American Embassy filled with gas pilfered from the English Hospital. Dressed in the uniform of a Serbian officer, he took off toward Pskov, where he hoped to rally enough troops to retake the city. With the Stars and Stripes waving, the Red Guard soldiers let the motorcade of the most wanted man in Russia pass, mistaking him for an American official.

Back at the Winter Palace, the ministers of the Provisional Government could do nothing but wait, defended by only a paltry force of 3,000 loyal troops, consisting mainly of a few officers, Cossacks, teenagers and a women's shock battalion. People flowed in and out of the palace constantly, including Bolshevik spies. It was

FOLLOWING PAGES: LEFT A defiant Lenin still points toward the future in front of the Smolny Institute; RIGHT ABOVE *Lenin Addressing the Red Army of Workers on 5 May 1920* (1933), painting by Isaak Israilevich Brodsky (Private Collection); RIGHT BELOW Palace Square, scene of the final triumph of the Bolsheviks.

so easy to gain entry to the palace that reporter John Reed flagged himself through with an American passport. The palace was supposed to have fallen by this time, however Bolshevik troops in charge of the task were late. Lenin, still in disguise, was furious, as he wanted to declare the fall of the Provisional Government before the opening of the Second Congress of Soviets scheduled for 10am that day. The assault was ordered again, yet the Bolshevik commanders again had a hard time mustering the Red Guard, who were reluctant to place themselves under fire. In fact at dawn on 26 October they had already attempted an assault but retreated in disorder at the first shots. When later replaced by the pride of the revolution, the vicious sailors of Kronstadt, they too beat a hasty retreat at the first signs of government resistance.

At 6:50pm the government was handed an ultimatum. They did not respond, naively believing that the Bolsheviks would be condemned for their violent overthrow. As the evening wore on only a small force of Bolsheviks stood before the palace. At 9:40pm the cruiser *Aurora* fired a booming yet blank round from the Neva. With this signal the cannons of the fortress began to fire at the palace. Fortunately the antiquated cannons and the garrison's incompetence caused the majority of the shells to land in the river. The Bolsheviks frantically continued to attempt to muster the forces needed to take the weakly defended palace. As the hours passed the loyal troops defending the government tired of waiting for support slowly abandoned their posts and fled into the night.

The legendary storming of the Winter Palace depicted in paintings, literature and film, including Eisenstein's brilliant *October*, with hordes of soldiers, sailors and workers charging across the square, is today known to be fiction. Bolsheviks actually entered through the through open windows and doors on the undefended Hermitage side. Once inside they proceeded to damage and loot the interiors, destroying the apartments of the former imperial family and raiding the imperial wine cellars, igniting an uncontrollable bacchanalia, which would last for days. When several hundred more entered through the main gates

The cruiser *Aurora* remains a popular site of revolutionary pilgrimage for its role during the Bolshevik coup.

facing the square, the palace was already occupied. At 2am on the morning of 26 October, the ministers of the Provisional Government assembled in the White Dining room were arrested and taken to the Fortress.

At the Smolny Institute the Congress of the Soviets was in an uproar as the moderate socialists staged a walk out due to being underrepresented. Lenin, having stacked the deck, had split the opposition, Mensheviks assuring the Bolsheviks total domination of the Soviet. At 3am it fell on the new Minister of Enlightenment, Anatoli Lunscharsky, to read the proclamation declaring the fall of the Provisional Government, which was received with thundering applause. The following evening a triumphant Lenin put the final stamp of approval on the revolution climbing the podium in the ballroom of the Smolny Institute before a rapturous audience of delegates and announcing the formation of the Soviet of People's Commissars.

In the midst of these 'Ten Days that Shook the World', Petrograd simply shrugged its collective shoulders and carried on as normal.

Work continued, trams and taxis raced down the broad avenues and commerce resumed. Few were aware that a darkness was settling on the city and the country, which would last for nearly a century. Zinaida Gippius commented contemptuously on the lack of fear or struggle during the whole episode, concluding 'Petersburgers are in the hands of the two-hundred-thousand-man band of the garrison, headed by a group of swindlers.'[33]

RED PITER

'If St Petersburg is not the capital, then there is no St Petersburg.'

From *Petersburg*, Andrei Bely.

In celebration of their victory over the Provisional Government, victorious Bolsheviks and their supporters went on a rampage of looting. The finest shops and houses were targeted by the mobs, their interiors smashed, their treasures stolen, but it was the city's

In fact largely a non-event, the celebrated storming of the Winter Palace became a integral part of revolutionary history and lore. *The Storming of the Winter Palace* (1927), painting by Rudolf Franz (Museum of Russian Art, Kiev).

wine cellars which were most sought after. The invasion of the cellars of the Winter Palace began a drunken orgy, which went unabated for several days as each new cellar sparked an instantaneous party. Guards and fireman sent to stop the mob joined them and got drunk, the restaurant Donon's had to hire a machine gunner to preserve its collection and one shocked French aristocrat described the behaviour of the hordes 'as if guerilla warfare was being waged for the right of entrance to the kingdom of Bacchus.'[34] As the chaos and crime seemed to spin out of control the Bolsheviks set up the All-Russian Extraordinary Commission to Combat Counter-Revolution and Sabotage, better known as the Cheka, at 3 Gorokhovaya Street. Headed by the hardened veteran revolutionary Felix Dzerzhinsky, the Cheka was originally mandated 'to fight the enemies of Soviet authority', but their purview was expanded to include 'all bandits, thieves, speculators and other criminals who undermine the foundations of the socialist order'.[35]

By December winter had fallen upon Petrograd like an arctic fusillade, with four blizzards hitting the city in one month. Petrograd descended into famine as food supplies petered out, railways ceased to function and the city starved. Factories were forced to institute limited working hours as materials, fuel and electricity were scarce. Desperate to keep warm, people began to burn whatever they could for firewood, breaking up furniture, pulling up fences, cutting down trees in the parks and tearing down houses. These problems were compounded as the city's water systems failed and the results were outbreaks of typhus, cholera, dysentery and influenza, which killed thousands.

'Petrograd is a dying city,' exclaimed the disgusted Gorky as he surveyed Petrograd. 'Almost every day they pick up people who have dropped from exhaustion right in the streets. The dogs eat them. The city is unbelievably dirty. The Moika and Fontanka are full of rubbish. This is the death of Russia.'[36]

The former ruling classes were forced to sell their possessions or even their bodies at rock bottom prices on the streets. The Bolsheviks also forced former officers and aristocrats to perform menial tasks such as street cleaning to humiliate them. Trotsky explained, 'Our grandfathers, great-grandfathers and fathers all had to clean up the shit and filth of your grandfathers and fathers. Now you are going to do the same thing for us!'[37]

February 1918 saw the city in complete panic as Lenin ordered the evacuation of the capital in the expectation of a German invasion intended to occupy the capital and overthrow the Bolshevik regime. Again order collapsed as the Soviet Government debated and argued the terms of peace with Germany. German planes dropped bombs on Petrograd and on the next day, 3 March 1918, Lenin signed the Treaty of Brest-Litovsk. Within days, Lenin, wary of the Germans and the threat they posed to Petrograd and his regime, ordered the removal of the capital to Moscow. This was also a symbolic gesture, for, by bringing the capital back to its ancient seat Lenin was turning his back on the West, on the legacy of Peter and all his great city stood for.

During the Civil War Petrograd struggled on. In his memoirs Osip Mandelstam quoted Anna Akhmatova's description of the city during this time:

All the old St Petersburg signboards were still in place, but behind them there was nothing but dust, darkness and yawning emptiness. Typhus, hunger, executions, darkness in the flats, damp firewood, people so swollen as to be unrecognizable. In Gostiny Dvor one could pick a large bouquet of wild flowers. The famous Petersburg wooden paving is rotting. From basement windows of Kraft's one could still catch the smell of chocolate. All the cemeteries were in ruins. The city had not simply changed, it had in fact turned into its opposite.[38]

By 1920 the city's economy had completely collapsed as hyperinflation soared, production plummeted and the port remained dormant. The barter system took over as paper money became worthless. Workers left the factories in droves looking for work in the black market economy or other ways of providing for themselves as wages fell. Citizens of the city were forced to travel out to the villages with items to barter for food. The Bolshevik officials left in charge of the city soon gave in to the temptation for corruption, even in one case diverting public supplies to a black market, which they personally operated out of the back of the Smolny Institute.[39]

The city began to bleed people. Between 1918 and 1921 the city's population fell from 2.3 million to 720,000.[40] Some fled to Moscow following the government but most were peasants who had moved to the city for work in the factories or in the garrisons. Thus vanguard of the revolution, after exacting its revenge, simply abandoned Petrograd and melted back into the villages. The number of Bolsheviks even fell from 50,000 to 13,000.

Petrograd seemed well on its way to becoming a ghost town. Silence fell upon the city as trams stopped running, cars ceased to race down the avenues and factories ground to a halt. Over time the pollution above the city faded and the skies cleared, revealing a brilliant azure sky. At night the city was engulfed in darkness, a universe lit only by the twinkling of candles and the fires of stoves. The poet Vladislav Khodasevich remarked 'St Petersburg became more uncommonly splendid than it had ever been and might ever be again. . . . There are people who look better in their coffin: so it was, it seems, with Pushkin. Doubtlessly, so it was with St Petersburg.'[41]

Four years to the month after the revolution the city rose up again in a call for bread. On 22 January 1921, the city again went on strike demanding bread. Demonstrations broke out and sailors joined the protestors. Crowds clashed with Bolshevik troops and martial law was declared. The Cheka rounded up hundreds of ringleaders, mostly moderate Mensheviks. Nonetheless the revolt grew to become the first internal threat to the Bolshevik regime in the city. The epicentre of the revolt was based on the naval island of Kronstadt, whose sailors demanded new elections excluding all parties and greater freedoms. They declared that the Bolsheviks no longer had the interests of the people at heart. By 2 March they were in full mutiny. Trotsky himself was dispatched to deal with the crisis, organizing the battery of Kronstadt from Oranienbaum and air strikes on the naval base. These measures had little effect on the sailors hardened by years of war, revolution and privation. Taking advantage of frozen Neva, the Bolsheviks attempted to storm the island, yet the sailors turned the guns on the ice and drowned thousands. Trotsky then ordered an overwhelming force of 50,000 to attack. Breaking through the island's defences, 10,000 Bolsheviks were killed. Kronstadt, again in the hands of the Bolsheviks, paid dearly for its mutiny. Two thousand five hundred sailors were executed, while the rest were sent to concentration camps in the White Sea.

POETS AND PALACES:
THE PRESERVATION OF PETROGRAD

While the rest of his comrades moved to Moscow, Maxim Gorky, bard of the revolution, stayed behind in Petrograd. Gorky still considered the city the cultural capital of Russia and endeavoured to keep artistic and intellectual life alive in the city. Lenin scolded him for this, complaining that Petrograd was infested by

[an] embittered bourgeois intelligentsia, understanding nothing, forgetting nothing, and learning nothing, and in the best case – and the best case is a rarity – is perplexed, desperate, groaning, repeating old prejudices, fearful and frightened of itself. . . . Here as an artist, you cannot observe or learn anything.[42]

Still he persevered, organizing a publishing house to employ out-of-work writers and intellectuals and establishing two artistic and scholastic associations based in the Eliseev Mansion on the Moika and the Vladimir Palace. These havens served to keep the salon culture alive during this period. The associations held lectures, readings and discussions, as well as provided housing and food for the city's writers and scholars.

Another figure of the new regime who remained in Petrograd was Anatoly Lunacharsky, a former playwright, head of the Commissariat of the Enlightenment. From the outset he worked tirelessly to preserve the city's treasures. Upon accepting his duties he released a proclamation:

Citizens, the former overlords have gone and left us a great heritage which now belongs to the people. . . . Preserve this heritage, preserve the pictures, the statues, the buildings: they are the incarnation of your might and of the spiritual might of your ancestors. . . . Do not touch a single stone, preserve the monuments, the buildings, the antiquities, the writings; they are the soil of which your new people's art will grow.[43]

In January 1918 Lunacharsky passed an ordinance stating: 'All buildings and structures, as well as art and historical monuments, are considered property of the republic, valid immediately, regardless of what institution or organization, including churches, cathedrals and monasteries, owns or uses them at present.'[44] Lunacharsky next appointed curators of the former imperial residences to ensure the protection of the collections within them. These indefatigable curators paved the way for the opening of the palace museums to the public in June 1918. On opening day thousands of awe-struck visitors would file through the sumptuous interiors of the former palaces of the Tsar.

Lunacharsky also tapped the old intelligentsia to help him in his work. Alexander Benois, who, through the World of Art before the revolution, had praised the cultural legacy of the city, had joined

Gorky and impresario Feodor Chaliapin to form the Council for the Protection of Cultural Treasures under the former Provisional Government headed by Feodor Golovin. Benois became the head of the department when the name was changed under the Bolsheviks to the Collegium for the Preservation of Monuments and Museum Affairs before joining the Hermitage staff. Another sophisticate of the *ancien regime*, Alexander Plovstov was instrumental in saving the palace of Pavlovsk from looting.

Perhaps his greatest success was the protection of the imperial Hermitage collections as well as the inclusion of the Winter Palace in the new State Hermitage. Lunacharsky also empowered the curators to seize looted artworks, which resulted in the return of half of the items looted from the palace found in antique shops and in the baggage of émigrés.[45]

The new regime's attitudes towards heritage were far from consistent. While Lunacharsky and his agency worked for the preservation of the former imperial palaces and museums, the Bolsheviks turned their energies toward another source of private wealth, the Russian Orthodox Church. Seeing the Church as the 'opiate of the masses' as well as a major rival to their newly attained power, in 1922 Lenin ordered the local Soviets to remove all objects of value from churches, even those items which were consecrated. Icons by the hundred were torn apart and used as firewood, their silver and gold melted down, their precious stones sold off to fund imports of machinery and to fund new industrial enterprises.[46]

Petrograd's literary establishment continued to have apprehensions about the new regime. The Merezhkovskys were the first to realize that artistic freedom and the Bolsheviks' goals were incompatible and decamped to Paris. The former acmeists and members of The World of Art rejected the new system and its cultural ambitions as too lowbrow. The futurists, on the other hand, moved to embrace the revolution, seeking to dominate as its chief artistic expression. Futurists Mayakovsky, Meyerhold, Malevich, Tatlin, Altman, Rodchenko and Tolstoy left for Moscow to secure favour with the new government, while acmeists and symbolists Akhmatova, Blok, Gumilev, Bely and Mandelstam remained.

Although he remained in Petrograd, Blok was at first enthusiastic about the revolution, seeing in it, as Soloviev predicted, the great cleansing of Holy Russia. He published his poem 'The Twelve' on 3 March 1918. It depicts the wild nighttime ride of a patrol of Bolsheviks through the wintry streets of Petrograd. The poem was a hit but drew the ire of many who thought his conclusion of Christ

leading the troop was a betrayal. Bely also originally embraced the new regime, republishing *Petersburg* for the new post-revolutionary audience and joining Blok with his work with Proletkult (Proletarian Culture), a group which had emerged to challenge cultural elitism by encouraging the celebration of proletarian culture and bringing culture down to the level of the people through lectures, classes and readings in factories and other plebeian arenas.

However the honeymoon did not last long, as the ideological demands of the Bolsheviks were too much for these artists to bear. The stifling atmosphere caused Blok to become disillusioned and complain of 'suffocating'. He died of heart failure in 1921. For the intelligentsia, his death became an allegory of Pushkin's, symbolizing the impossibility of the artist's co-existence with a cold and unsympathetic system. While Blok had tried to live with the Bolsheviks, the unabashedly elitist Nikolai Gumilev was openly contemptuous of the new regime, even going as far as writing monarchist poetry. For his troubles he was arrested and shot on the trumped-up charge of complicity in counter-revolutionary activity. Anna Akhmatova, who never accepted the new faith of revolution, wept at Blok's grave. She wept not only for him but also for her husband Gumilev; but mostly she wept for St Petersburg and the price that she and all of her kind would pay as they sailed further into the abyss.

> A different time is drawing near,
> The wind of death already chills the heart,
> But the holy city of Peter
> Will be our unintended monument.[47]

SPECTACLES IN THE JAZZ AGE

The arrival of 1920 in many ways brought relief to Petrograd. Lenin declared the start of the New Economic Policy (NEP), which relaxed revolutionary regulation, allowing freedom of commerce for the independent operation of small businesses and farms. This had a dramatic effect on Petrograd as food became plentiful and the economy picked up. As a result of the NEP the population would rise over the next decade from 720,000 in 1921 to 1,775,000 in 1929. Overnight a new class of rich entrepreneurs emerged from the wreckage of the old system and again the city was alive with restaurants, clubs and fashionable people. American movies and jazz were all the rage as Hollywood stars became household names and cabarets became the hot spots of the city.

The neo-Byzantine Naval Cathedral Kronstadt (1908–13). The crushing of the mutiny on the island naval base of Kronstadt secured Soviet control over Petrograd.

As the mood improved in Petrograd, the city's new overlord, party chief Grigory Zinoviev was determined to raise the city's profile as the Cradle of Revolution and a headquarters of World Socialism. He also sought solidify Petrograd's reputation as a centre of revolutionary culture by supporting the efforts of the artists of the avant garde. They had proven their talent during the May Day and October Revolution celebrations of 1918, during which the artists, led by Nathan Altman, draped the city in red banners, hung enormous canvases of cubo-futurist paintings of workers, soldiers and peasants and even put a red cap on the tower of the Duma.[48]

Temporarily out of fashion, the avant garde roared to the forefront again in 1920 with the production of new mass spectacles, which awed the audiences and raised eyebrows in Moscow. The triumphant crescendo of their work was undoubtedly Nikolai Evreinov's production of *The Storming of the Winter Palace*. An audience of over 100,000 spectators on Palace Square, which had been draped with Altman's monumental canvases, watched as the cast of thousands re-enacted the October Revolution using booming orchestral music, klieg lights, acrobatics, motorcars, cannon from the *Aurora* and a grand finale of fireworks. This and the five other spectacles that year served to mythologize the revolution as the beginning of the new age while trying to resurrect the spirit of the revolution in the hearts of the participants and spectators.[49]

As the avant garde flexed their collective muscles they moved to take over institutions such as the Academy of Arts, which Alexander Rodchenko, Vladimir Tatlin and Varvarna Stepanova reorganized along futurist lines. They also commandeered the Imperial, now Lomonosov, Porcelain Factory, which began to produce 'propaganda porcelain' with designs by Kasimir Malevich. Tatlin secured himself a space in posterity with his drawings and model for the Monument to the Third International. Its iconic constructivist design was truly revolutionary. A spiralling mass of steel beams encasing three revolving glass geometric structures it was planned to hold the various bodies and functions of the Communist International or Comintern. Such a digression from the traditional classical designs of most architects symbolized the total break with the past, as Tatlin's tower with its unadorned materials and transparent structures became the avatar of the ideals of the revolution. Planned for construction in Petrograd, Tatlin toyed with spanning it across the Neva in an effort to outdo Peter by taming nature.[50]

On 12 May 1926, at the former Assembly of the Nobility, the revolution heard for the first time the music of a nineteen-year-old composer, Dmitri Shostakovich. Having entered the Petrograd Music Conservatory in 1919, the young Shoshtakovich was heavily influenced by the music of Tchaikovsky and Mussorgsky as well as by many of the contemporary composers who visited the city, such

ABOVE *Festivities Marking the Opening of the Second Congress of the Comintern and Demonstration on Uritsky (Palace) Square in Petrograd on 19 July 1920* (1921), painting by Boris Mihajlovic Kustodiev (State Russian Museum, St Petersburg).

as Bela Bartok and Alfredo Casella. His *Symphony No.1* electrified audiences with its references to the greats of Russian music, yet introduced them to a new world of modern music, which would a year later be exported from the city to the concert halls of Berlin and on to America. Nikolai Malko, a student of Rimsky-Korsakov and the conductor of the symphony, declared, 'I have the feeling that I have turned a new page in the history of symphonic music and discovered a major new composer.'[51] Indeed he had.

LENINGRAD

> In Petrograd the great proletarian revolution had its first, decisive victory. . . . Like an unscalable cliff, Red Petrograd stood high all these years, and remains today the first citadel of Soviet power. . . . The first workers' and peasants' government in the world was created in this city. . . . Let this major centre of the proletariat revolution from this day forward be connected with the name of the greatest leader of the proletariat, Vladimir Ilyich Ulyanov Lenin.[52]

With this pronouncement the Second All-Union Congress of Soviets changed the name of the city for the second time in its history. The name change was organized by party boss Zinoviev in an attempt to further his own political ambitions to make the city a world capital of Communism by linking the city forever with the name of the late revolutionary leader who died in January 1924. As if the ghost of Peter objected to the new appellation, in September the city was struck with a devastating flood. Many saw the event as punishment and pointed out that it occurred nearly one century after the flood that inspired Pushkin's *The Bronze Horseman*.

In Moscow power was shifting again as Joseph Stalin secured his position as party leader and his intention to follow Lenin's philosophy of perfected socialism in one country over the export of revolution. This served to undermine Zinoviev's effort at making Leningrad a world socialist city. Zinoviev, who had believed himself a possible heir to Lenin, fell out of out of favour with Stalin, who sent the virile and charismatic Sergei Kirov to consolidate his power over the Leningrad party. Setting himself up in the Hotel Europa on Nevsky Prospect, Kirov engineered the election, which swept Zinoviev and his followers from power to become party boss of Leningrad in 1926. Zinoviev was subsequently expelled from the Politburo and the Comintern.

As party chief, Kirov oversaw the end of the NEP in Leningrad and the commencement of the first Five-Year Plan. Leningrad, the country's main industrial base, became the centre of a massive industrialization and modernization campaign, which, to the horror of intelligentsia, was partially financed by the sales of Russian art treasures from the Hermitage and the imperial palaces. In 1921 Lenin had set up the Antikvariat to sell Russian imperial treasures to the West in exchange for desperately needed hard currency. During the 1920s and 1930s thousands of pieces of furniture, jewellery, paintings and objects from private and imperial collections, including the famous Fabergé eggs, found their way into the hands of American millionaires Armand Hammer, J. Paul Getty, Mathilde Geddings Gray and Marjorie Merriweather Post, as well as foreign monarchs such as King Farouk of Egypt and Queen Mary of Great Britain. The Hermitage was further forced to part with many of its artworks for the new

ABOVE RIGHT Vladimir Tatlin's constructivist icon, the Monument to the Third International (1920).

Pushkin Museum in Moscow, in exchange for which it received a vast collection of impressionist works and other works confiscated from the city's princely families.

Kirov's efforts paid off, as Leningrad became the centre of Soviet industrial design and execution. Industrial production in the city skyrocketed to unprecedented heights as tractors from the Putilov and October Works were churned out in the thousands along with telephones and hydrogenerators. To fuel this expansion labour was desperately needed. The peasants once again flooded into the city, increasing the population over the decade from 1929 to 1939 from 1,750,000 to 3,119,000. The city, in welcoming the newcomers, struggled to build new housing, schools and transport.

Soviet planners largely spared Leningrad's historic city centre from significant changes due to a comprehensive preservation policy and lack of resources for new construction. These factors helped them to decide to build the new administrative centre of the city along the largely undeveloped International, later Moscow Prospect in the Moscow-Narva District. The Leningrad Soviet commissioned the design and construction of several new projects

in the constructivist or functionalist style, which eschewed traditional classicism and ornament, placing function over form. Beginning in 1925 a series of new projects took shape. Architects Alexander Gegello and Alexander Nickolsky designed the Moscow-Narva District (Gorky) House of Culture, a theatre notable for its functional monumentality. The pair, along with G.A. Semonov, designed new workers' housing along Tractor Street, and Armen Barutchev designed a department store and 'kitchen factory' so women workers did not have to cook at home. David Krichevsky, in a playful take on Soviet symbolism, designed the Tenth Anniversary of October School in the shape of a hammer and sickle, but it was the Moscow-Narva (Kirovsky) House of the Soviets, designed by Noi Trotsky, that was the true outstanding modern monument of the era, with its low, streamlined base punctuated by a sharply angular ten-storey tower, the first skyscraper in Leningrad. Further afield, Soviet architects Igor Fomin and Evgeny Levinson drew upon the work of Moisei Ginzburg and Le Corbusier for their design of the Apartment House of the Leningrad Soviet.[53]

ABOVE Sergei Kirov (left), a favourite of Stalin and Leningrad party boss helped revive the city's fortunes. After his assassination on 1 December 1934 monuments throughout the city were named after him such as the famous Kirovsky Zavod (centre), formerly the Red Putilov Works, and the new Moscow-Narva (Kirovsky) House of the Soviets (right) by Noi Trotsky (1941).

In the city centre the Soviet busied itself with converting many of the palaces of the rich into communal flats or requisitioning them for professional organizations. While the Soviet preserved Leningrad's palaces, many of the city's churches were wantonly destroyed: the Znamenskaya Church on Znamenskaya Square, the Trinity Cathedral on Trinity Square, the Cathedral of Andrew I on Vasilievsky Island, the Church of the Dormition in the Haymarket, the Church of the Saviour on the Water on the English Embankment, Resurrection Church on the Fontanka, the Annunciation Church, the German Reform Church and many others were demolished or unrecognizably altered. Other larger and more significant churches such as St Isaac's Cathedral and the Kazan Cathedral were converted into museums of religion and atheism. Sovietization continued throughout the city as scores of small chapels and Tsarist monuments were removed or destroyed and street names and squares were renamed to honour the revolution.

Alongside the physical and social transformation of the city, cultural changes also began to occur. Following Lenin's death in 1924 ideological purists begin to attack Leningrad's avant-garde expressionism as being anti-proletariat. The burgeoning film industry in Moscow also took some shots with its films Eisenstein's *October* and Pudovkin *The End of St Petersburg*, each taking a swipe at the St Petersburg myth. The two directors in their efforts even went so far as to damage the Winter Palace. Pudovkin recalled: 'I bombarded the Winter Palace from the *Aurora* while Eisenstein bombarded it from the Peter and Paul Fortress. One night, I knocked away part of the balustrading of the roof, and was scared I might get into trouble, but, luckily enough, that same night, Eisenstein broke 200 windows in private bedrooms.'

By 1929 the mass spectacles had returned to Leningrad. However, these new holiday spectaculars were no longer the avant-garde productions of previous years; in fact, they were beginning to mimic the processions and celebrations of the old world. Yet Communism as the new religion was replacing Orthodox icons and banners with images of revolutionary leaders and slogans of International Communism.

In 1929 Lunacharsky was ousted. With the last defender of the old cultural intelligentsia out of the way open season began on Leningrad's literary and artistic community. Many fled during this period: Balanchine in 1924, Benois and Alisa Rosenbaum in 1926. Rosenbaum would then dedicate her life to fighting Communist ideology as author Ayn Rand. The leader of the futurists, Vladimir Mayakovsky committed suicide in 1930. Others, however, chose to challenge the purist attack openly. The Association for Real Art (*Oberiuty*) was formed by a group of intellectuals and publicly protested against the collectivization of art and literature. Such disobedience was no longer tolerated under Stalin and the group was forced to disband, its members branded class enemies and eventually arrested and killed. By 1932 all independent literary associations were closed down.

Other artists also suffered, such as young music star Dmitri Shostakovich, whose *Lady Macbeth of Mtsensk*, the first in a prepared trilogy in praise of the Soviet women, was an enormous success until a surly Stalin saw a portion of it and condemned it. In Moscow rising star Andrei Zhdanov, Stalin's cultural henchman, ushered in the era of socialist realism, which called for a heroic portrayal of the revolution, the people, the glory of work and the ideal socialist world. This shift marked the death of modernism and the triumph of traditionalism and classicism in art, music and architecture. This was acutely felt in Leningrad in the designs for the construction of new districts, particularly in the Moscow Narva District, which would be dominated by the totalitarian classicism of the House of the Soviets. Designed by Noi Trotsky and his team, the 70-foot-long structure with a 3,000-seat audience hall was intended (yet never realized) to be the headquarters of the Leningrad city government.

ABOVE Igor Fomin and Evgeny Levinson's Apartment House of the Leningrad Soviet provided modern housing for the Communist élite.
RIGHT The Stalin era marked a return to classical architecture albeit with monumental proportions.

THE TERROR

Stalin was always suspicious of Leningrad, viewing it as an threat to his rapidly consolidating power. As the 'Cradle of the Revolution' and home to the party's old school establishment, these revolutionary veterans were not inclined to worship the upstart Georgian. Originally Stalin had sent Kirov to subdue the city. However, Kirov himself had risen to the status of a Bolshevik hero, so popular that he even won more votes in the elections to the Central Committee. Fearful for his position, Stalin organized the assassination of his former comrade on 1 December 1934. Kirov was dispatched with one bullet to the back of the head. Immediately Zinoviev, the former party boss of Leningrad, was arrested and later executed. To fill the void in Leningrad, Stalin sent the trusty Zhdanov, now a high-ranking member of the Central Committee, and began to hatch an even more insidious plan, the elimination of the old Leningrad party as part of a larger purge of the national party itself. Leading the Terror in Leningrad would be Nikolai Yezhov, chief of the soviet secret police, the NKVD, which was the predecessor of the KGB. He ruled his army of death from the organization's headquarters at the infamous address 4 Liteiny.

Following Kirov's murder, 30,000 Leningraders were rounded up and sent to concentration camps. This initial purge was later expanded to encompass the remnants of the former nobility, who were rounded up in 1935. Over the intervening years the entire Leningrad party apparatus was wiped out and replaced by hacks loyal to Stalin. As the purges continued unabated they would dangerously thin the officer corps of the military and wipe out the Red Army's senior command. Professionals such as factory managers, engineers and scientists were arrested or fired and replaced by unskilled party hacks who were barely capable of carrying out their responsibilities. Hundreds of key workers at the Putilov Works were sacked and arrested. At the Hermitage, fifty curators were arrested and twelve shot as spies. The Kresty prison was once again filled to the brim. Conditions in this and other prisons were far worse than they ever were under the Tsars. Soon every family in Leningrad was touched by the Terror having had a member arrested or knew someone who had disappeared into the back of the sinister vans known as Black Marias. Between 60,000 and 70,000 Leningraders disappeared during the terror denounced as enemies of the state. Mass graves of terror victims have been found outside the city at Levashyovo (24,000) and the Rzhevsky firing range near Toksovo (30,000). There were deposited the bodies of men, women and children murdered by the NKVD.

In Leningrad the hand of oppression fell hard as Stalin attempted

ABOVE Soviet planners sought to impose a Soviet character on the city with monumental buildings such as Noi Trotsky's Leningrad House of the Soviets (1936–40) (left), while the NKVD carried out a murderous purge of its citizens, many of whom disappeared into prisons and dungeons never to be seen again (right).
RIGHT The modern day headquarters of the KGB, the successor organization of the NKVD.

'To the Victims of Political Repression'. Anna Akhmatova stood for hours outside the Kresty prison in hopes of getting word to her son.

to close the window to the West once and for all. During the Terror, travel abroad ceased, foreign books and periodicals were banned and even contact with foreigners was suspect. As the Terror widened, its dark forces were aimed at artists and writers. Shostakovich was forced to write his *Symphony No. 5*, entitled 'a Soviet artist's answer to justified criticism', as an act of contrition to supposed acts of sedition. His was a light sentence. In 1934 Anna Akhmatova's best friend the poet Osip Mandelstam was arrested and eventually died in the Gulag. The futurist visionary Malevich, having been isolated by the party, died in poverty in 1935. His death was followed a year later by that of Gorky, who was found dead of mysterious causes. The great avant-garde director Meyerhold and the poet Benedikt Livshits were both arrested, tortured and executed. Akhmatova's son Lev Gumilev would find himself arrested in 1933, in 1935 and again in 1938. Akhmatova herself faced ostracism and isolation. 'The new people remain, and will remain, cold and unmoved by the whining of a woman who either was born too late or did not die in time.' Akhmatova would spend hours in line waiting to try to hear word of her son or perhaps catch a glimpse of him. To her fellow citizens, however, her presence and dark sorrowful countenance gave them hope. As Stalin declared that 'life had become better, life has become merrier,' Akhmatova sat and composed her great testament to the Terror, 'Requiem'.

> And if ever in this country
> They decide to erect a monument to me,
>
> I consent to that honour
> Under these conditions – that it stand . . .
>
> Here, where I stood for three hundred hours,
> And where they never unbolted the doors for me,
>
> This lest in blissful death
> I forget the rumbling of the Black Marias,
>
> Forget that detested door slammed shut
> And an old woman howled like a wounded animal.
> And may the melting snow stream like tears
> From my motionless lids of bronze,
>
> And a prison dove coo in the distance,
> And the ships of the Neva sail calmly on.[54]

WAR!

At noon on 22 June 1941, the city's loudspeakers awoke. As if to clear their collective throats, the speakers' crackling feedback prepared the way for an announcement of startling import delivered by the Commissar for Foreign affairs Viacheslav Molotov:

> Men and Women, Citizens of the Soviet Union! The Soviet Government, and its head Comrade Stalin, have instructed me to make the following announcement: At 4am, without declaration of war and without any claims being made on the Soviet Union, German troops have attacked our country, attaked our frontier in many places and bombed from the air Zhitomir, Kiev, Sevastopol, Kaunas and other cities. . . . The government calls upon you, men and women, citizens of the Soviet Union, to rally even more closely around the glorious Bolshevik Party, around the Soviet Government and our great leader, Comrade Stalin. Our cause is just. The enemy will be crushed. Victory will be ours.[55]

The news of the German invasion of the Soviet Union broke like a thunderclap over the city of Leningrad. The parks and avenues of the city were crowded on this luminous summer day, which would last way into the early hours of the morning during the long White Nights. Those adults over the age of twenty-five knew exactly what this meant, their memories imprinted with shortages, rations, queues and privation. Quickly women raced to the shops to buy whatever they could lay their hands on. Banks were flooded as people drained their accounts; the pawn shops, jewellers and antique dealers were besieged as people sought to convert their cash into hard assets of jewels, gold and silver.

Leningrad was not wholly unprepared for the German attack. Rumours had circulated all summer about the impending invasion. Germans had pulled their foreign workers and ships out of Soviet ports and Soviets spies passed messages of troop massing and deployment on the border. Leningrad grimly had had a taste of this coming conflict during the brief Winter War with Finland between January and March 1940. In an attempt to push back the border with Finland only twenty miles away Stalin on 1 February ordered the Red Army to invade. The fighting was brutal. The Finns fought valiantly, harassing and slowing the Russian forces, moving swiftly on skis from one place to another and inflicting heavy causalities on the invader. Trainloads of wounded flooded into Leningrad, who upon arrival passed on stories of an incompetent and ill-equipped fighting force weakened by the purges. Over a year later Leningraders knew what they were up against and began to brace themselves for the worst.

It is well recorded that in the days leading up to the invasion Stalin refused to allow his commanders to prepare for battle. He could not believe that he would be so grossly betrayed by Hitler. This miscalculation would have catastrophic consequences, for when the Germans raced across the border, Panzers blazing, the Red Army scrambled to organize a defence. Stalin himself had a nervous breakdown and was not seen for weeks. As the German Army Group North led by Field Marshal Ritter von Leeb swept into Soviet-occupied Lithuania and brushed aside the paltry force led by General Kuznetsov the road to Leningrad lay open. Leningrad was key to Hitler's Barbarossa campaign, a target whose capture would seal Moscow's fate and secure the destruction of Russia.

As the news filtered in, Leningrad got to work. Zhdanov, caught off guard on holiday in Sochi, returned and ordered the evacuation of many of Leningrad's most important factories, while converting others to a wartime footing. Meanwhile, in the Hermitage, Director Iosif

Orbeli ordered the forty most precious paintings of the museum taken down and hidden in the basement vault, which contained the museum's priceless collection of Scythian gold. By 7 July 160,000 People's Volunteers made up of every section of Leningrad society from worker to child were recruited to begin preparing a system of defences around the city. They dug in shifts around the clock barely stopping as Germans flew over and strafed them. By the time they finished they had completed three rings of defences consisting of 15,875 miles of open trenches, 340 miles of anti-tank trenches, 400 miles of barbed wire fences, 190 miles of obstacles and 5,000 gun emplacements.[56] Inside the city groups organized volunteer squadrons of air raid guards and firefighting brigades.

Organized evacuations began first with children, of whom over 200,000 were evacuated before the blockade. They were followed by necessary workers needed to operate evacuated machinery from factories and cultural institutions, such as the Philharmonic, the Mariinsky Opera and the Ballet. On 1 July the first train of twenty-two cars of Hermitage treasures, including entire collections of Old Masters, such as Rembrandt's *Return of the Prodigal Son* and *Descent from the Cross* and Titian's *Mary Magdelene*, the Scythian gold, the

As the German onslaught advanced toward Leningrad hundreds of these pillboxes for machine gunners were constructed throughout the city within days.

sarcophagus of Alexander Nevsky and Houdon's seated statue of Voltaire, left the city for Sverdlovsk in the Ural Mountains. A second train would depart nineteen days later. The Hermitage's efforts were echoed in all of the suburban palaces, where the heroic labours of palace curators such as Vladimir Ladukhin, Anatoly Kuchmov and Anna Zelenova ensured the preservation of thousands of objects many packed using the clothes of the former imperial family.[57]

THE 900 DAYS PART 1:
THE IRON RING CLOSES

From the outset the German designs for Leningrad were no less than complete annihilation. When posed with questions regarding the fate of the population the response from Berlin was equally ominous: 'The problem of the life of the population and the provisioning of them is a problem which cannot and must not be decided by us. In this war we are not interested in preserving even a part of the population of this large city.'[58] Such questions to the high command became more pertinent as the Germans advanced through the Baltics, captured Pskov and reached the outer ring of Leningrad's defences by mid-July, sending armies of refugees northwards towards the city.

The city's defence, led by Zhdanov, General Kliment Voroshilov (a protégé of Stalin) and General Markian Popov, struggled against the onslaught, throwing every available unit at the advancing Germans and the new attack by the Finns to the north. The Germans advanced rapidly along the Baltic surrounding the Russian 8th Army at Oranienbaum. Elsewhere to the south and east they were only able to slow the advance temporarily; the reinforced Germans broke through the Luga line in mid-August and by the end of the month captured Luga, Novgorod, severed the rail line to Moscow and reached the banks of the Neva southeast of the city on 29 August.

The last rail line to the city was cut on 31 August, sending Leningrad into panic. The Germans again pushed ahead, splitting the Russian 48th Army east of the city, crushing its southern flank and capturing the town of Schlüsselburg on 9 September. Across the river, the ancient fortress of Schlüsselburg, Peter the Great's 'hard little nut', which had held the likes of Peter's first wife, Empress Eudoxia, the ill-fated Tsar Ivan VI, several Decembrists and was the place of execution of Lenin's brother, remained in Russian hands, as it would throughout the war. With the fall of the town, however, the German forces had accomplished their objective, sending the message to Berlin, 'the iron ring around Leningrad has been closed'.[59] The Nine Hundred Days had begun.

At the Smolny, Zhdanov was busy preparing city for the final battle declaring over the radio, 'The enemy is at the gates!' Stalin had sent Molotov and Malenkov to Leningrad to assess the situation in order to decide if the city would be abandoned. The two reported back to Stalin the staggering reality of the situation. Under the command of Zhdanov and Voroshilov Leningrad's defence was a shambles, with the Germans and Finns encircling the city outskirts and inadequate supplies for a sustained siege. Stalin, however, understood just what the abandonment of the city would mean: the release of German troops to the central front for the assault on Moscow, a risk he could ill afford. Leningrad would be held.

The city itself had already abandoned itself to total war. The Baltic Fleet had moved into position along the gulf and up the Neva. In anticipation of house-to-house fighting street signs were painted over and windows blacked out. The set decorators of the Mariinsky Theatre set to work creating hundreds of *papier mâché* tanks and cannons. On 3 September citizen brigades began to construct a system of barricades, machine gun nests, pillboxes and booby traps. The outlying districts became fortresses, streets and pathways littered with concrete anti-tank obstacles called 'Dragon's Teeth' and their houses structurally reinforced and occupied with snipers. On 13 September Zhdanov began to carry out orders from Moscow to mine the city's infrastructure, factories, the Baltic Fleet, cultural and administrative institutions, military installations, supply depots, port facilities and rail hubs, so in the event of a German breakthrough the city itself would rain death upon the invader as a last show of defiance.

Meanwhile the Germans began to open up their artillery on the city. Shelling began on 4 September and aerial bombardment commenced two days later. Signs soon appeared warning Leningraders to avoid walking on the north sides of the streets. Planes buzzed overhead and air raid sirens howled sending the population scurrying into basements and bomb shelters. The worst raid occurred on 19 September, which involved 264 aircraft followed by a 197 plane attack on 27 September.[60] The Hermitage was hit thirty-two times by shells and twice by bombs, other monuments damaged in the bombing were the Engineers Castle, Gostiny Dvor, the Russian Museum, the Tauride Palace, the Mariinsky Theatre and the Church of the Spilled Blood. One of the worst raids caused the destruction of the Badyev food warehouses near Vitebsk Station. In the ensuing conflagration four acres of warehouses burned, the fire devouring thousands of tons of foodstuffs. Aerial bombardment continued throughout the autumn

until the onset of winter made such sorties ineffective. Shelling, however, continued through November, eventually declining to holidays only to conserve munitions and let starvation do its work.

As the military situation outside Leningrad turned desperate Stalin recalled the disgraced Voroshilov and replaced him with General Georgy Zhukov. By 10 September the Germans, headquartered at Gatchina, continued to advance through Peterhof, Strelna as far as the Kirov works to the south-west and through Tsarskoe Selo and Pavlovsk to the south, while attempting to link up with the Finns in the east. Zhukov response was simple: 'Attack! Attack! Attack!', so that not an inch would be surrendered without a fight. He ordered that every available fighting force, no matter how small, would move forwards no matter what the cost. Zhukov steeled the resolve of his commanders and soldiers by promising to have them shot if they retreated.

All of Leningrad was mobilized. Anyone capable of holding a rifle was sent to the front. The badly weakened and exhausted Red Army and inexperienced volunteer corps threw themselves at the Germans. As they drove forward they fired screaming Katyushas, rocket-propelled missiles, to devastating effect as the Baltic Fleet, its guns now in range of the advancing foe, pummelled the enemy lines. The Germans, while slowed, had not been stopped. It was then that fate smiled upon the city. Hitler, having waited patiently for von Leeb to take the city, desperately needed his Panzer divisions for the final assault on Moscow. On 17 September the 41st Panzer Corps were ordered to head to south toward the Moscow front. With the Russians resisting every inch and winter quickly approaching, Army Group North had no choice but to dig in for siege. On 22 September Secret Directive No.1a 1601/41 arrived from Berlin entitled 'The Future of the City of St Petersburg':

1. The Führer has decided to erase the city of St Petersburg from the face of the earth. I have no interest in the further existence of this large population point after the defeat of Soviet Russia. Finland has also said the same about its disinterest in the further existence of this city located directly on its border.

2. The previous demands by the fleet concerning the maintenance of dockyards, harbours, and similar important naval facilities are well known to the OKW; however, the satisfaction of these does not seem possible in view of the general line of conduct with regard to St Petersburg.

Lined up like soldiers on parade, rusty field guns used in the defense of the city serve as reminder of the epic 900-day siege of Leningrad.

3. We propose to closely blockade the city and erase it from the earth by means of artillery fire of all calibre and continuous bombardment from the air.[61]

THE 900 DAYS PART 2: THE LONGEST WINTER

While the battle for Leningrad raged on the outskirts, inside the city another battle was being fought. Dmitri Pavlov, Commissar of Trade for Russia, arrived in the city to take over supply and distribution of food and fuel. His was a Herculean task and one of the most crucial to the survival of the city. In September food had barely been rationed and authorities had allowed supplies to be consumed wantonly. Upon assessing the situation he found that for 2.9 million civilians and 500,000 soldiers there was only a month's supply of food. With all routes to the city cut, transport of supplies over Lake Ladoga was the only solution. However, with German bombers sinking supply boats at will, they would have to wait until ice formed on the lake. In the mean time Pavlov instituted severe

rationing and began a hunt for food that left no stone unturned. Women were sent out into battle zone to harvest the fields on the outskirts, agents were sent to the inner villages to bargain for food, private hordes were seized and private commerce in food was halted. Pavlov also inaugurated a ration card system, which distributed food according to social station. Fraud was soon rampant as hungry citizens attempted to get extra cards by reporting theirs lost. In response the government refused to grant replacements and threatened those guilty of fraud with death. Soon to lose a card essentially meant death by starvation; theft of cards was tantamount to murder.

Regardless of the shelling and the rationing, the city's residents did their best to carry on, adjusting to the siege the best they could. They threw themselves into the various wartime volunteer activities or spent extra time at work to keep their minds off the steadily encroaching hunger, which grew like a cancer in their bellies. Scientists and scholars, engineers and cooks also set to work in the development of substitute foods such as cottonseed oil cake.[62] At the Hermitage workers continued their research and Orbeli even opened a planned exhibition on the Uzbeki poet Alisher Navoi. People congregated in bookshops and the public library remained open. As the days passed, public events became fewer and fewer and Leningraders, weak with hunger, stayed home. Together they listened to the radio and poet Olga Berggolts, who became the voice of Leningrad. Many of the city's prominent citizens and artists were invited to speak. Shostakovich and Anna Akhmatova among them. Yet what most remember about the radio was what aired when there were no presenters: the ubiquitous sound of the metronome on the radios and loudspeakers, ticking away the seconds, minutes and hours until the siege would finally be delivered, while in the cold the shelling continued.

The first snows of the season fell in mid-October as the temperature sank below freezing. Day by day the populace grew hungrier, thinner and colder. There was no more kerosene and the cold joined hunger as the constant obsession of people's minds. Hunger-related sicknesses such as dystrophy, diarrhoea and scurvy became rampant as a result of the fillers in the bread ration, which was stuffed with cellulose, tree bark, sawdust and leather. Horses, dogs, cats, even rats and mice began to disappear from the cityscape as they died of hunger or were butchered for meat. People began to die. One survivor recounted 'Today it is so simple to die, you just begin to lose interest, then you lie in bed and you never again get up.'[63]

ABOVE As siege guns roared and bombers thundered across the sky, Hermitage employees bravely continued their work in the cellars beneath the palace in an effort to preserve the museum's treasures.
RIGHT With little food or fuel during the bitter winter of 1940–1 Leningrad began to die, filling the city's cemeteries the point that citizens simply abandoned their shrouded dead at the gates.

The fall of Tikhvin on 8 November was a devastating blow to the supply situation as the town was a vital rail link, which brought supplies from the interior to the ports on Lake Ladoga. With the lake still unfrozen and no supplies coming in famine loomed. Hitler triumphantly declared 'Leningrad's hands are in the air. It falls sooner or later. No one can free it. No one can break the ring. Leningrad is doomed to die of famine.' Supplies quickly ran out. Rations were cut to 10½oz for workers, 5½oz for everyone else. By 20 November this fell to 9oz for workers, 4½oz for everyone else.

By December the temperatures in Leningrad fell to 9°F, sinking to −4°F by early January. Central heating ceased and the hunt for fuel was on. As during the revolution and Civil War, wooden fences and houses were torn down and dismantled for firewood. Inside apartments, people cooked and tried to warm themselves on *burzhuiki*. These makeshift stoves barely kept the heat above freezing, were smoky and often caused fires. Others abandoned their flats for central hallways less exposed to the outside and

were always dressed. Water froze in glasses and frost formed on the walls. With no fuel and no workers the city's industries shut down, followed by Leningrad's main power plant. With no electricity trams stopped and the municipal water system froze, forcing people to melt snow or cut through ice to the canals and rivers to get fresh water. People threw their waste into the streets and courtyards. In December the poet Vera Ibner observed the state of things to come. A passer by bundled in scarves and coats trudged by dragging a child's sled on which, wrapped tightly in a shroud, lay a body.

As winter set in Leningrad began to die. People died in the quiet of their flats or while walking in the street. Children died. Whole families died. People would not report deaths in order to be able to take advantage of their ration cards by hiding bodies. Men and boys who were still required to carry out labour died quickest while women held on. Flu, typhus and dystrophy also began to claim lives. In December there were 52,881 recorded deaths followed by 199,187 in January and February. People

ABOVE With no fuel or power, the city's trams, trains, and cars halted. Cold and starving Leningrader's retreated into their homes leaving the city a deserted landscape of silent monuments.

began dying at rates of up to 10,000 a day. More and more sleds appeared hauling their swaddled cargo towards the local cemeteries; when these were full they were forced to go further out. Those who were to weak simply dropped the bodies in the street. One Leningrader recalled:

> The nearer to the entrance to Piskarevsky I approached, the more bodies appeared on both sides of the road. Coming out of town where there were small one-storey houses, I saw gardens and orchards and then an extraordinary formless heap. I came nearer. There were both sides of the road such enormous piles of bodies that two cars could not pass. A car could go only on one side and was unable to turn around. Through this narrow passage amidst the corpses, lying in the greatest disorder, we made our way to the cemetery.[64]

Soon the city began to take on the visage of a Hellish arctic landscape. The nights lasted forever, their black stillness only broken by the howl of the winds and the fires that burned freely as the fire brigades had ceased to function. The ninth circle of this icy hell was undoubtedly the infamous Haymarket. Here in this traditional center of despair and depravity, immortalized by Dostoyevsky and Gorky, ruled the fat and oily rosy-cheeked princes of the Black Market. These thieves and rogues preyed upon the defenceless populace unhindered by a nonexistent police force. What Leningraders feared the most was that these dark lords of the underworld maintained their health not through bread by the consumption of human flesh. The Haymarket was the only place in the city to obtain meat. Few asked where it came from, especially since animals were nowhere to be found. Rumours of cannibalism abounded. People disappeared regularly and on the streets parents drew their children closer. Corpses were found missing limbs. Human heads were found in the streets. It seemed as if the Bronze Horseman had given way to four new riders, the sound of whose hooves signalled the Apocalypse.

THE 900 DAYS PART 3: THE ROAD OF LIFE

There was only one hope that could deliver the city from certain disaster. The vast Lake Ladoga was the only route around the German lines through which supplies could be brought. As winter

set in ice began to form, stopping boat traffic, but it was not yet thick enough to support the supply trucks needed to relive the city. Whole teams of scientists observed and calculated in an effort to predict when the ice would be ready. Finally, on 17 November, the first scouting party crossed the lake and reached the town of Kobona. Desperate to save the starving city the authorities ordered the opening of the lake to traffic on 20 November. With Tikhvin still in German hands and the Kobona road clogged with traffic, the supply of food arriving in the city hardly made a difference. The recapture of Tikhvin on 9 December returned railway supply to the lake. Within days six routes across the lake were opened. The Road of Life was in full operation.

During these desperate weeks between November and January the city was only two days away from starvation. The failure of a truck to deliver its load could mean the difference between life and death. The city's fate was in the hands of the workers of the ice road. The heroic effort went into overdrive; trains brought in more and more supplies, better trucks rode round the clock across the sixty

ABOVE RIGHT December 1940 saw the appearance of a scene which would come to define the city's suffering: a woman dragging a child's sled on which lay the shrouded corpse of a deceased loved one.

ice routes, dropping supplies off and picking up evacuees. Throughout the month of January Leningraders barely held on. Many would die later from the damage done to their bodies by such privation. Relief came by late January as supplies increased and rations doubled. People had food and fuel again. Evacuations started in earnest. In January 105,000 were evacuated, and 500,000 more over the following four months.

As the pressure of starvation began to ease, the Leningrad authorities began to realize the next looming disaster, which faced them with the onset of spring. Mountains of trash, filth and excrement clogged the courtyards and alleyways of the city. Bodies remained under the snow and ice. If this mess were not cleaned up in the waning weeks of the winter the city's already weakened population would face epidemics by the spring thaw. Beginning on 15 March, 100,000 Leningraders filtered into the streets to begin the clean up. Over the next two months triple that amount would be recruited to clean 12,000 courtyards, 3,000,000 square yards of streets and 1,000,000 tons of filth.[65] By April a degree of normalcy had returned to Leningrad as corpses were buried, damaged buildings were patched and painted, and people planted gardens all over the city, even in the major parks.

In late March Leningraders tuned their radios to a music performance in Moscow. Their own Dmitri Shostakovich, reluctantly evacuated in October, was premiering his *Seventh Symphony*, entitled 'Leningrad' in honour of his beleaguered home

city. The triumphant theme gave them hope and the international attention it received provided worldwide attention on the siege. The ice road across the lake closed on 24 April but soon resumed as a water route. 528,000 more people were evacuated and 250,000 reinforcements arrived. By July 1942, 1.1 million remained in the city, relieving rations and fuel supplies. By the end of the year only 637,000 would remain, barely 25 per cent of the city's pre-war population. To those who remained the city felt deserted.

Summer and Autumn of 1942 still proved difficult for the Russian forces defending Leningrad as they were still unable to pry the Germans out of their positions. With the onset of winter, however, Russian commanders felt more confident with extra reinforcements and well-fed troops. In December they formulated a plan to raise the siege of Leningrad. On 12 January 1943 Operation 'Iskra' or 'spark' was launched, resulting in the Russian forces breaking through the German lines and creating a corridor to the mainland between Lake Ladoga and the German lines, effectively breaking the iron ring. Olga Berggolts proclaimed across Leningrad, 'The blockade is broken. . . . We shall triumph! . . . We know we have much to live through and much to bear. But we'll endure everything. Now we have felt our strength!'[66]

The winter of 1942–3 was not nearly as bad as the nightmare of the previous winter. Braving the German guns through the 'corridor of death', the first supply train arrived directly into Finland station in early February to be followed by hundreds more. By 22 February consumption in the city had almost returned to pre-war levels. The Germans, however, were not defeated yet and opened up a fierce shelling campaign that lasted from July through September. Through all of this more troops arrived via the 'corridor of death' so that by the autumn the Red Army consisted of more than double the German troop strength, forming the largest concentration of troops on a short front in all of Russia, more even than at Stalingrad. By January the Russian generals were ready to once and for all end the siege of Leningrad.

On 15 January 1944, a tremendous roar of thousands of cannon shook the city as the Russian artillery announced the start of the final push to liberate Leningrad. Many of these shells were produced in the city's factories now up and running. On the shells were written phrases such as 'For our children's anguish', 'For our murdered friends' and 'For the blood of Leningrad's workers'.[67] Following the tremendous fusillade General Leonid Govrov

ABOVE During December 1940 and January 1941 the supplies slowly making their way across the frozen ice of Lake Ladoga kept Leningrad from starving. This heroic passage was dubbed the Road of Life.

launched a three-pronged attack from the Oranienbaum, Pulkovo and Volkhov fronts, shattering the enemy lines and driving the Germans into retreat. Within days Tsarskoe Selo, Pavlovsk, Peterhof, Gatchina, Ropsha, Novgorod and Mga were all liberated. An ebullient Zhdanov announced on 27 January that the longest siege in modern history had ended. Leningrad was free.

INSULT TO INJURY

On the first anniversary of the lifting of the siege, the city of Leningrad awarded the Order of Lenin by the Presidium of the Supreme Soviet and 470,000 citizens were decorated for bravery and service. On 1 May 1945 Leningrad was bestowed the title 'Hero City'. But in the midst of all of the parades and celebrations, Leningraders recalled the tremendous price they had paid to save their beloved city. More people had died in the siege of Leningrad than in any other catastrophe or epidemic to strike a city in modern history. It is estimated that over 1 million civilian and nearly 500,000 military deaths occurred during the siege. Of these 600,000 are buried in mass graves of 20,000 each at Piskarevskoe Cemetery. Today, a monument of Mother Russia stands before an eternal flame with the words of Olga Berggolts inscribed on the monuments base:

> Here lie Leningraders,
> The men, women, and children of the city,
> Along with the fighting men of the Red Army,
> All gave their lives,
> In defending you, O Leningrad,
> Cradle of the Revolution.
> We cannot list the names
> Of the noble ones who lie beneath this eternal granite.
> But of those honoured by this stone
> Let no one forget, let nothing be forgotten.

As early as 1943 plans for the reconstruction of Leningrad were prepared, complete with designs for the construction of a modern city. In the plan historic buildings were to be restored, grand new housing estates and boulevards would rise from the rubble and new industry would emerge from the ruins. The new city would accommodate a population of 3.5 million. The victorious leaders of Leningrad, flushed with victory, wanted the city to revive Zinoviev's dream of Leningrad as Russia's second capital and window to the

A mournful sculpture of Mother Russia offers a garland to the heroic dead of Leningrad at Piskarevskoe Cemetery.

West. They promoted the Hero City myth and planned to use it to leverage benefits in the post-war era.

Outside the city the curators of the palace museums found themselves confronted with a nightmarish landscape. The palaces they had worked so hard to preserve were shattered ruins, burning shells surrounded by mines. One American reporter wrote of the scene 'All Peterhof is gone . . . It isn't a ghost town like Kiev, Kharkov, Poltava, Orel or Kursk . . . it is a desert strewn with wreckages from which, perhaps, has been been blown some of the most exquisite and most joyful art man has created'.[68] Many doubted the probability or wisdom of restoration. Yet Anatoly Kuchmumov former Alexander palace curator and post-war Director of Museum Monuments persevered, convincing his superiors to appeal to Moscow and to Stalin. When presented with photographs of the ruins of the palaces, Stalin surprised even his closest advisors by agreeing to fund the initial restoration efforts.[69] The Herculean effort to reclaim Russia's built heritage from utter destruction started gradually but would pick up momentum during the 1950s, becoming symbolic of Leningrad and Russia's resurrection. The palace of Pavlovsk would open in 1957 followed by the Catherine Palace in Tsarskoe Selo in 1959, minus the famous Amber Room, which had been removed by the Germans and lost, the palace of Peterhof in 1964, Gatchina in 1985 and the Alexander Palace in the 1990s. The restoration of all of these sites still continues.

In Moscow, however, the suspicious temperament and jealous rage of Stalin and his henchmen sought to bring the city to heel. Zhdanov was brought to Moscow and forced to accept a reduced share of resources for Leningrad, including reduced funding for the grand reconstruction plans, which were scaled back. Leningrad's humiliation was compounded as other cities restoration efforts were given priority over the Hero City. Yet Stalin wanted more. Having returned to Moscow and desperate to secure his power, Zhdanov helped Stalin launch a crusade against the Leningrad intelligentsia and non-Soviet culture. He attacked the newly returned Akhmatova, whose 'Poem Without a Hero' had yet to be published, satirist Mikhail Zoshchenko, seige-survivor Olga Berggolts, writer Boris Pasternak and composers Shostakovich and Prokofiev. Akhmatova's son was again sent to prison; Orbelli was dismissed from the Hermitage. Zhdanov's death in 1948 provided Stalin with a pretext to proceed with a second purge of the Leningrad Party apparatus. The infamous 'Leningrad Affair', cooked up by Lavrenti Beria and Georgy Malenkov, implicated and led to the execution of Zhdanov's right-

hand Alexei Kuznetsov, former mayor and Leningrad Party chief Peter Popkov, and P.A. Tyurkin, who managed the Road of Life. Thousands were prosecuted and disgraced. The purge spread even to implicate Zhdanov himself. His papers were seized and his memory and role expunged from the party history.

Stalin then moved to hinder the post-war economic recovery of the city by directing the specialization of its industries, leading to the decline of the city's overall economic importance at the expense of other cities. Stalin's final act of vengeance against the city went further than just humbling the city politically, he moved to erase the Hero City myth and the memory of the siege. He ordered the closure of the Museum of the Defence of Leningrad and the suppression of all accounts of the siege that emphasized its heroic nature. Even the great mass cemeteries remained neglected without formal dedications and monuments until 1960.

Stalin's death in 1953 did not entirely revive Leningrad's status or its prospects. The city did rebuild, albeit on a less ambitious scale, with the addition of a new metro system, the completion of the House of the Soviets, the Victory Park, New Finland Station and Kirov Stadium. Post-war industrialization helped the city swiftly repopulate. Peasants flooded into the city once more to take the places of the thousands that had died or been evacuated never to return. These new Leningraders at first had little attachment to their city, unlike the reverence held for it by the survivors. By 1950 Leningrad had reached pre-war levels of production and vast new housing complexes were constructed. The city began its sprawl, which continues to this day.

Perhaps the final chapter to the tragedy of Leningrad's wartime legacy ended on VE Day in 1975 with the dedication of Sergei Speransky and V. Kamensky's *Monument to the Heroic Defenders of*

LEFT 'Here lie Leningraders . . .'. The mass graves of Piskarevskoe Cemetery hold 600,000 citizens and soldiers. 'All gave their lives, in defending you O Leningrad. . . . Let no one forget, let nothing be forgotten.'
ABOVE RIGHT While many of the city's monuments were spared, the suburban palaces of Peterhof (above), Tsarskoe Selo, Gatchina, Strelna and Pavlovsk lay in ruins.

Leningrad, as Leningrad finally sought to reclaim its position and its status as the Hero City. This awe-inspiring monument, which is situated to the south of the city centre at the foot of Moskovsky Prospect on Ploschad Pobedy, the precise site of the furthest advance of the enemy, provides a triumphant gateway to the city and celebrates not only the heroism of the defenders but the agony of the citizens during the siege. Its soaring tower, encased in red granite believed to have been removed from Hitler's Reich Chancellery, is flanked by two formal compositions by M.

Aniushkin, depicting soldiers, workers and civilians marching to the city's defence. Behind the tower, however, sunken beneath the ground, is a more sacred space surrounded by a great broken ring lit by gas torches lighting the various honours bestowed upon the city. In its centre is another structural group, which illustrates the terrible suffering by the city's women and children and through them mother Russia.

But it was left to Anna Akhmatova, muse of St Petersburg, to use the experience of the siege to encapsulate all of the city's

ABOVE While much of the city's post-war plans were abandoned as a result of political rivalries, projects such as the Leningrad Metro were superb additions to the city's infrastructure and architectural heritage.

literary heritage, its myth and the history of its tumultuous half-century into a work of such power that it defined the city for the next generation of writers. In her magnum opus 'Poem Without a Hero' Akhmatova marries the city's legacy and myth with her own biographical narrative. While telling the story of a tragic lovers' triangle, which included veiled references to the legacies of Pushkin, Gogol and Dostoyevsky, Akhmatova also inserts figures and talents from her own life: Blok, Mandelstam, Gumilev and Meyerhold. Parallel to this Akhmatova is also telling the story of St Petersburg, guiltily identifying her bohemian pre-revolutionary life with the city's persona as the Babylon of the Snows while later participating in the suffering and exaltation of the city's purgation by terror and fire to prepare it for its final conversion into the martyred Hero City. 'Poem Without a Hero' was Anna Akhmatova's monument and finest testament to her greatest love, St Petersburg.

ABOVE Sergei Speransky's and V. Kamensky's long-awaited Monument to the Heroic Defender's of Leningrad (1975) serves today as the modern gateway to the city.

Chapter 7:
The Window Opens

Glasnost Arrives

It is hard for those of us who have been raised in the Western democracies since the end of the Second World War to imagine that, as recently as the 1970s, poets and intellectuals in Leningrad were being tried for being social parasites and being sent to remote prison camps or into foreign exile. The decline of Krushchev in the 1960s after the brief 'thaw' from Stalinism led to period of a kind of stalemate in Russian political leadership. A succession of conservative leaders: Leonid Brezhnev until he died in 1982, followed by Yuri Andropov until 1984 and then Konstantin Chernenko until 1985, seemed determined to do all they could to preserve the creaking Soviet system exactly as it was. The Soviet government was not interested in Leningrad and its fate seemed to be that it would become more and more a provincial city that just happened to have had an imperial past and a heritage of culture that the intelligentsia still valued. The great writers like Alexander Solzhenitsyn and Joseph Brodsky were seen by the stagnant regime as enemies of Communism and forced to leave. Russian political thinking had frozen into an inward-looking bureaucratic mould – the opposite of the intellectual climate that had created St Petersburg as an open window to the outside world. It took the arrival of Mikhail Gorbachev in 1985 to change everything.

On his appointment he stated his aims to attempt to reform the Soviet system from within. He had two complimentary policies: '*glasnost*', meaning openness, and '*perestroika*', meaning reconstruction in the sense of encouraging new political structures. Interestingly, Gorbachev decided in May of 1985 to announce his new progressive policies to the Russian people while on a visit to Leningrad. It was no accident that he chose the one Russian city with a reputation for understanding and encouraging change. It was, however, something of a shock for the average citizen to see the General Secretary drive down Nevsky Prospekt and stop his limousine to go up to people in the street and talk with them. He was to visit the city's major factories and the faculty of the Polytechnic Institute and hold a major political meeting at Smolny. Gorbachev apparently said later that he not only found the city welcoming but that he received good advice from the people there.[1]

One of the almost immediate effects of *glasnost* was the decision taken in 1987 to allow foreign investment in the form of joint

ventures with new co-operatives and the arrival of several thousand foreign businessmen. This factor had a major effect on the nature of discussion and the ending of censorship and on practical matters in the city. Where were all these investors to stay, how quickly could the few hotels be upgraded? These were minor problems compared to the enormous political changes being contemplated and which came to a head at the nineteenth party conference in 1988, which backed Gorbachev's plans for a sweeping reorganization of government and the creation of a Congress of People's Deputies, which would elect the Supreme Soviet.

It was this moment that seemed to release in the city a sense of pride and of freedom – that the history and culture of St Petersburg could be studied again and discussion about its future could be initiated. The great historian of Russian literature Dmitri Likhachev, who had been born in the city in 1906 and lived there through all its tumultuous history, became the unofficial spokesman for its culture and an ambassador for the city. As a young man he had been imprisoned on the gulag island of Solovki and was jailed during the siege of Leningrad. He had trodden an unbelievably delicate path during the Stalin era and miraculously maintained a knowledge and respect for the aristocratic and imperial past of the city and its older values. As a medievalist and scholar of the Old Church he bravely fought for the preservation of church buildings during the

LEFT The Palace Embankment from seen from one of the bastions of the Fortress of St Peter and St Paul.
ABOVE RIGHT Soviet prefabricated construction.

Krushchev years, when the government began renewed attacks on Church property. He was passionate about the architectural history of St Petersburg and especially appreciative and understanding of the meaning of the man-made Arcadian landscapes that were, to him, as important as the palaces that ringed the city. He was prolific writer who, in the Russian tradition, reached the people in the street because he articulated their passion for the city and its history. He also held an official position during *perestroika*, when he was made chairman of the USSR Cultural Fund.

When there was a frightening proposal from the city to join the modern world by building a skyscraper on Vasilievsky Island, to be called The Peter the Great Tower, Likhachev wrote an impassioned article describing the architecture of the city not as a collection of buildings but as a landscape – scaled to an aspirational vision of humanity. He saw the proposed tower not just as a hugely out of scale object in the townscape of the city but as a symbol of the rampant capitalism and materialism that would be so out of tune with his sense of the real values of the city. He was right, and his writing articulates the rare sense of understanding of beauty and

scale and meaning in the city that almost every citizen shares as their birthright. The tower was never built – despite support from leading foreign contracting firms including British ones, rather scandalously supported in the interests of commerce by the British government through its consulate in the city. The protest worked, although there are some who say that it was structural weakness of the wooden pile system that supports St Petersburg that probably made the building of a tower impossible.

Likhachev died in 1999.[3] His values are now probably less widely shared, as advertizing and Western commercialism and the untrammelled profit motive has begun to spread in parts of the city. But Petersburgers are still so proud of the culture of their city that the thinking of writers like Likhachev remains influential. The city still rises above politics to fight for its own spirit.

But it was undoubtedly politics that paralysed thought and drove so many writers and artists underground during the grim Brezhnev years and the new freedoms under Gorbachev brought many of them back to life. The paintings of the Silver Age and other more avant-garde works were brought up from the store rooms of the

ABOVE Central St Petersburg today (left); globalization has again brought western influences to Peter's city, including the ubiquitous McDonald's (centre); Anna Akhmatova's flat is now a museum and place of pilgrimage (right).

Russian Museum and publishers took up the futurists and the symbolists again. The work of Anna Akhmatova, the great poet of the city, was popular again and in 1989 a museum in her memory was opened in her old apartment in Fontanka House – once the old Sheremetev Palace, Her poem 'Requiem', which had last been publicly read at her funeral in 1966, was published, and her 'Poem without a Hero' became an almost immediate cult work.[4] The six rooms of the museum are the rooms where the beautiful poet lived and worked that even today retain a sense of that austere but bohemian life style that is so particular to St Petersburg – a city where artists had to survive surveillance and persecution for so long under autocratic regimes, both Tsarist and Communist.

Exiled writers from St Petersburg began to be published in the city again, among them Nabokov. In 1987 the writers' community felt vindicated and triumphant when their hero Joseph Brodsky was awarded the Nobel Prize for literature. Somehow this level of international recognition demonstrated that Russian writing was still of global importance. It was good for the self-esteem of the city. There was also a spate of apologies and withdrawals of condemnations of writers and artists that had occurred under Communism. Anna Akhmatova and Mikhail Zoshchenko had been condemned by the Central Committee in 1946 and this was rescinded in 1988. Some of the more extreme party leaders like Zhdanov now tasted their own medicine and suffered the same fate as some of the intellectuals, having any reminder of their existence removed – names from buildings and streets and city landmarks.

Celebrations were encouraged for the centenaries of the births of Anna Akhmatova and Osip Mandelstam. The artist Chemiakin was restored to favour, having been both in a mental institution and exiled to Paris. He designed two sphinxes 'To the Victims of Stalinism', which were placed in 1995 outside the headquarters of the KGB on the bank of the Neva.[5]

Freedom of speech grew gradually in the press and the broadcast media and it was Leningrad's Channel Five that led the nation in its programming that encouraged popular political debate and ran intelligent documentaries about the history of the city. Western radio stations were no longer jammed and the BBC and Voice of America were heard for almost the first time in the city. Because of the long history of resident writers and artists in the city, the new media soon flourished creatively and gained a reputation for intelligent comment on art and politics. Popular music also arrived from the West – a mixed blessing – bringing with it a sense of freedom and revolt among the young. There was eagerness in the city for information from all around the world and the sales of books, international magazines and music soared.

LENINGRAD OR ST PETERSBURG?

As a counterpoint to all this, much more serious things were happening in the political world and in the sphere of economic reform. They focussed around a club formed in 1987 by a rising young economist Anatoly Chubais, called Perestroika, which was to work with other groups including the Voters' Association to ensure that the Gorbachev reforms were consolidated and that they continued. This was a completely new kind of activity but those taking part knew that Leningrad, as the second city of Russia, had a chance to influence things at the national level. A democratic alliance was formed called the Leningrad People's Front, which encouraged and organised the election of progressive democratic candidates to the Congress of People's Deputies in the elections of 1989.

Three remarkable candidates were returned to represent the city: Dmitri Likhachev, Alexei – the Metropolitan of Leningrad and Novgorod – and Anatoly Sobchak. Likhachev, the great thinker and protector of the soul of St Petersburg, was eighty years old when he was elected to represent the city in the national congress. He was to play a crucial role in speaking 'as the oldest deputy' to ensure that Gorbachev was elected as President to provide continuity in 1990, because he felt that the old guard's hatred of Gorbachev and his reforms were enough to unseat him and cause a civil war. It is widely acknowledged that it was to Likhachev that Gorbachev owed his Presidency. The two other candidates were soon to play nationally significant roles; Alexei was to become the future Patriarch of Moscow and All Russia and Sobchak became the first democratically elected Lensoviet Chairman in the 1990 election. In 1991 the office of mayor of the city was made an elected post. Anatoly Sobchak was easily the victor and became the first elected mayor of the city. In the same election held in June 1991 the very important question was raised as a matter for city referendum – should the city continue to be called Leningrad or return to the name given to it by its founder, St Petersburg? It was a fascinating debate – and a serious one. The idea of the change seemed to many

to symbolize the final marginalization of reactionary Communism – it would be the outward and visible sign of the end of the party and of Lenin. But there was opposition from the so-called Committee for the Defence of Leningrad, who believed that the city had won the name in the great Bolshevik Revolution and by its incredible endurance during the siege. Gorbachev was pro-Leningrad; Sobchak was for changing to St Petersburg. St Petersburg stood for enlightenment, opening windows on to the world and an acknowledgment of a longer history. Leningrad meant isolationism and the vacuity of Communist atheistic culture. It was Joseph Brodsky who coined the memorable phrase that it was preferable for citizens 'to live in a city named after a saint than one named after a devil'. Only the Supreme Soviet could make the final decision but in the referendum there was a solid majority in favour of changing the name.

The vote to return to the original name of the city coincided with the memorable and dangerous period of the coup against Gorbachev and his recent alliance with Boris Yeltsin. At one point the plotters threatened to send troops into many cities but the real action took place in Moscow with the dramatic siege of the White House. St Petersburg was not immune to the tensions of that time and the presence in the mayor's office of the young Vladimir Putin, former KGB officer and lawyer, certainly helped Sobchak and the city to ride relatively smoothly through the August coup. By the end of 1991 the old Soviet Union had ceased to exist and the old USSR gradually transformed into the Commonwealth of Independent States.

The period of the early 1990s was a strange one for the city. It was described by one resident as 'a time of complete quietness'. There was little money and a lot of idealism, but for several years nothing was built and there were no funds for restoration. It could have been an exhilarating time because St Petersburg seemed ideally placed to build on its reputation for progressive thinking as a place that could attract foreign bankers and financiers. But this was not to be and Moscow's close (and often corrupt) business links to the powerful government, led the capital with its dynamic mayor, Yuri Lushkov, to take the national lead in commercial and financial development.

From the late 1990s building began outside the city centre, bringing some improvements to counter the dull monotony of the endless housing developments of the 1960s and 1970s. But at the same time some of the good ideas of the International Style – light airy spaciously planned neighbourhoods that had been adopted under Communism – were lost and replaced by routine streets and

A new sphinx for St Petersburg, the Monument to the Victims of Stalinism, sculpted by Mikhail Chemiakin.

dull city blocks. In the same period – the awkward 1990s – there were random examples of new buildings, sometimes on important sites, on the Fontanka Canal and close to the Engineers Castle – where there seemed to be no planning control and more than a hint of bribery and corruption in the uncertain world of property ownership and development. Many buildings on the canals that had been in multiple family occupation since the days of Communism gradually returned to more unified ownership and families were happy to move to the newer blocks around the city.

One illustration of the climate of building and restoration comes from the recent work of Sebastian Zinovieff, who returned to the city which his family had left as refugees in 1918 to be a real estate and valuation business in 1991. His business helps buyers to find apartments in the city's nineteenth-century heart – 'One of the few good things to come out of the Communist era was a moratorium on development,' said Zinovieff, 'St Petersburg has more nineteenth-century architecture than any other major European city that, like Atlantis, is just waiting to be unearthed.' After the inevitable brush with the mafia and the tax police, Zinovieff was finally licensed by Vladimir Putin to be one of the first foreign-based companies (Zinovieff came to Russia as an Australian citizen and is now the Honorary Australian Consul in St Petersburg) to be authorized to value and survey property. With his knowledge of the bureaucratic ways of St Petersburg, Zinovieff has also helped the work of the World Monuments Fund in their restoration activities in the city.

Conservation and rehabilitation of the centre of the city and some of the circle of imperial palaces played a key role in the plans to mark the tercentenary of the foundation of the city in 2003. The miracle of the post-war rebuilding of Peterhof, Pavlovsk and other palaces continues, but the tercentenary offered special opportunities to refresh parts of the city that blanket official conservation had failed to touch. And the list is infinite – there were at least three hundred officially recognized smaller projects ranging from stained glass and railings to garden sculpture and mosaics. With the help of private sponsors the city administration tackled the restoration of stained glass in churches such as the English Church of Jesus Christ and the Church of the Holy Apostles Peter and Paul and the glass in the Grand Ducal burial vaults of the Peter and Paul Fortress. Repairs were carried out on the wonderful Art Nouveau glass in the Yeliseyev Brothers store (the Fortnum and Mason of St Petersburg) and on the stained-glass window in the house of E.I. Nabokova.

Throughout the city visitors are conscious of the glorious ironwork everywhere. All the canal bridges and all the parks and parade grounds have railings of extraordinary quality and palace balconies and gates are all of the highest standard. Perhaps the star is the set of railings that enclose the Summer Garden on the Neva side with its fasces, weaponry and armorials – the whole painted in bronze green with gilded panels. This was one of the many sets of railings, fences and gates that were restored under the tercentenary plans. Equally important are the railings of the Mikhailovsky Garden and the magnificent gates to the Palace of the Grand Duke Michael (the Novo-Mikhailovsky) – now restored. Out on the enchanting Yelagin Island, in the Neva on the way to Peterhof, the architect of the palace and the park, Carlo Rossi, designed railings and benches and balconies in the most refined neo-classical style, almost reminiscent of the work of Karl Freidrich Schinkel.

Almost every one of the sixty-eight rivers and canals that criss-cross the city has its distinctive railings and bridges, many of which were repaired and restored for the tercentenary. There are three hundred bridges in St Petersburg and perhaps it is the wonderful Lion Bridge (1825) over the Griboedov Canal, designed by G. Traitteur with sculpture by P. Sokolov, that is the most beautiful pedestrian bridge in the city. The chains that support the bridge are held firmly in the jaws of the four lions while the anchors for the chains are concealed in the lions' bodies. The Krasnogvardeisky Bridge (Red Guards), also over the Griboedov Canal, has been restored with its rows of lion masks looking down over the canal waters. For sculptural strength and masculine power nothing compares to the four horse tamers and their giant horses (sculpted by P. Klodt) on the Anichkov Bridge which crosses the Fontanka Canal on Nevsky Prospect; they have undergone some recent restoration.

Other aspects of the city that were included in the city's list of small restoration projects were parts of the granite landings and embankments of the ever-flooding River Neva and the milestones that are to be seen throughout the city marking the distances from Tsarskoe Selo and other imperial residences. Also, street lamps and lanterns, small fountains and water troughs, which bring richness and dignity to the city, were cleaned and restored along with a remarkable number of clocks and bells that brought back some of the sounds of a lost past. It is the sense of a complete survival of so many elements of a city that makes St Petersburg so rare. For eighty

Peter reinterpreted: this controversial statue of Peter the Great by Mikhail Chemiakin (1991) at the Peter and Paul Fortress is one of St Petersburg's newest monuments.

years the city endured violent political changes, war and siege but it was also, in so many ways, left alone to decay quietly. This it did very slowly. There was no money to demolish and ruin the intact heart of the city and its sheer scale and theatricality made it hard to bring about major changes.

This is not to say that the city has not paid a huge price for neglect and the effects of extreme weather. This was something that the Marquis de Custine observed each winter in the nineteenth century. Writing in 1839 he observed:

The ancients built with indestructible materials under a favourable sky; here, under a climate which destroys everything, they raise palaces of wood, houses of plank, and temples of plaster; and, consequently, the Russian workmen spend their lives in rebuilding, during the summer, what the

winter has demolished. Nothing resists the effects of this climate; even the edifices that appear to be the most ancient have been reconstructed but yesterday; stone lasts here no better than lime and mortar elsewhere. That enormous piece of granite, which forms the shaft of the column of Alexander, is already worn by the frost. In St Petersburg it is necessary to use bronze in order to support granite; yet notwithstanding these warnings they never tire of imitating the taste of southern climes.[6]

Today the climate hasn't changed and the common use of brick and stucco as the principal building materials means that the city is in a permanent cycle of repair and repainting. The maintenance of the megalomaniac vision of Peter the Great and his heirs will remain a major task for local and federal governments and for

ABOVE Restoration and rehabilitation: the newly restored Lion Bridge (left); religious services have returned to St Isaac's Cathedral (centre); conflicting priorities have led to the construction and even reconstruction of lost churches while damaged historic structures are left to deteriorate (right).

owners of historic buildings. The spread of prosperity may also diminish the numbers of people who are likely to want to train as artisans and restorers, thus adding to the problems of permanent maintenance.

In the early 1990s the condition of the façades of the Winter Palace were causing great anxiety in the offices of the Hermitage – especially as the museum's limited funds were already allocated. A special UNESCO project to survey the entire building was carried out by a British architectural firm. They proposed a radical solution that they thought would permanently cure the damage caused by the capillary action of ground water and the severe winters to brick and stone and plaster. The Hermitage declined any such major intervention and decided to continue to do regular 'patch and mend' repairs as and when funds were available. This was probably the right decision to continue to do things as they had always been done since

the palaces were built. There is less risk of things going wrong on a major scale and, as the administration of the museum explained, the elderly get used to things being done in a certain way, and that is just as true for old buildings.

You can do a lot with paint and gilding to make the city look glamorous and for the tercentenary many of the city's domes and spires were handsomely regilded without serious regard for the condition of the roofs beneath. Appearances matter in Russia and the Romanov conviction that there would always be enough money and manpower to maintain the façade of glory still pertains. Rather as the intelligentsia managed to gather and talk philosophy in the Hermitage while the city was brutally besieged, rising above their ghastly conditions, it is the beauty and spirit of the city that will win out over economic shortages and administrative barriers. St Petersburg has a lifeblood of literature, music, political history and thoughtless imperial magnificence that sustains it.

It was that spirit that convinced President Vladimir Putin to seize the opportunity to invite world leaders to St Petersburg – his home city – for the great tercentenary gathering in 2003. To accommodate them and to impress them with traditional Russian hospitality the President did not choose to build new buildings or house the event in Soviet style. Instead he decided to restore the crumbling imperial residence at Strelna on the Gulf of Finland, with its collapsing canals and grottoes in a once spectacular garden and park going down to the sea.

The recent story of Strelna encapsulates the twentieth-century story of many of the imperial palaces, but its chronicle begins long before, when Peter the Great returned from his visit to France in 1716. He was determined to build his own version of Versailles, with great terrace and fountains that would rival the greatest French garden. Peter discussed the idea of his new palace with the architect/sculptor Carlo Rastrelli in Paris, and Rastrelli and his son, Bartolemeo (the future architect of so many major buildings in the city) moved to Russia to make plans and models. In fact Peter then imported the French garden architect Jean-Baptiste Le Blond, who replaced the Rastrelli team. It is the major outline of the gardens by Le Blond that survives today with its three canals and large round island by the sea completed by the time of Le Blond's death in 1719. Another Italian architect took over the project, Nicolo Michetti, and his design introduced the three central arches we see today but his grand colonnades were not built by the time he decided to leave Russia and return to Italy in 1723. A string of architects then took over the project which was by the 1720s really being superseded by Peterhof and not long after Peter the Great's death in 1725 the works were gradually abandoned. Peter's daughter the Empress Elizabeth asked her favourite architect Bartolomeo Rastrelli to prepare plans to finish the palace but he only seems to have completed the façades and some fine entrance gates in the lower park before the Empress lost interest. Life only returned to the project when the Emperor Paul I gave it to his second son Constantine – giving the Palace the name Constantine Palace, by which it is best known. The great architect Andrei Voronikhin was employed to complete the palace as a Grand Ducal home and this was done by 1802. The very next year fire swept through and destroyed the palace which was speedily rebuilt by yet another architect, Luigi Ruska. The Grand Duke Constantine

Pavlovich lived at Strelna until he died in 1831 and for the next ten years the estate gradually fell into disrepair. In 1841 the Emperor Nicholas I gave the palace to his son the Grand Duke Constantine Nicolaevich who used the architects X. Meier and Andrei Stakenschnieder to make some modest improvements for his comfort, and began the restoration of the canals in the Lower Park and the ponds by the palace. The palace had a quiet royal life until the troubled years of the early twentieth century, when it witnessed the First World War, the February and the October Revolutions and the Civil War. The beauty of the place survived all this until the Second World War when it was occupied throughout the siege of Leningrad from 1940 to 1943 by ruthless German Nazis. The palace was set alight, the bridges and weirs in the park were blown up and the trees felled. After the war it was repaired enough for it to be used as a naval college – but the interior of the palace and the gardens were not restored and it was abandoned again in the post-perestroika years. Many developers went to see it and plans were considered for a hotel and country club and a resort by the sea. But only the President of Russia – like any Tsar – had the real powers to save the Constantine Palace.

The fortunate combination of a president who came from and loved St Petersburg and the city's tercentenary energized the project of a full restoration of the palace and the park in the way that made it possible to carry out and complete the project in a miraculous eighteen months. This compares to the demands of the Tsar Nicholas I for the entire Winter Palace to be reconstructed in a year and a half after the fire of 1837.

Although the work at Strelna proceeded every day and night for eighteen months there was no Romanov contempt for the value of human life. In 1837–9 some thirty thousand labourers died from being forced to work on rooms where the temperature was raised to 100°F to accelerate the drying time for the plaster work and then to work outside on the façades where the temperatures went as low as fifty degrees below freezing. The Marquis de Custine in his journal summed up the cruelty and folly of the project: 'Had there been a design to disgust the world with arts, elegance, luxury and all the pomp of courts, could a more efficacious mode have been taken? And yet the sovereign was called father, by the men immolated before his eyes in prosecuting an object of pure imperial vanity.'[7]

But there was a need for an almost imperial chain of command to ensure that the palace was completed in time for the reception of forty-five heads of state for the three-hundredth anniversary of the

Tercentenary celebrations in Palace Square reflect the spectacles of early 1920s Revolutionary Petrograd.

city. The restoration project was organised by the President's office and under the direction of Vladimir Khozin, the head of the Presidential office, a Charitable Trust was established for 'The Constantine Palace and Park Ensemble at Strelna' to secure major sponsorship for the project from business sponsors. It was a success, as Khozin said at the time: 'The hearts and minds of many people were stirred by the idea that the reconstruction and conservation of the Constantine Palace would facilitate the process of reform which is so vital for our country and our people.' The work was carried out by a consortium of specialist firms, which included the Architectural Department of the State Hermitage Museum and the construction arm of the Academy of Sciences (GIPRONI) and a group of building firms that had previously been part of the State Construction office of the Soviet period.

The only two great apartments to have been fully restored rather than just redecorated are the Marble Hall and the Blue Hall, which have been carefully restored with grisaille-painted ceilings after the style of Voronikhin and wall panels and scagliola pilasters and a great deal of gilding. They are used as the two main conference spaces with reproduction eighteenth- and nineteenth-century furniture, textiles and giant new gilt bronze and crystal chandeliers. Throughout he palace the choice was made to refurnish with reproduction styles and some modern furniture and all the technology needed to run a fully fledged international, modern conference centre.

In the east wing are the apartments of the President and in the west wing equivalent apartments for his principal guests. In the grounds are some twenty identical luxurious guesthouses and on

ABOVE AND RIGHT The election of Vladimir Putin, a St Petersburg native, as President of Russia, led to the restoration not only of the city's prominence but also of one of the city's forgotten palaces, Strelna, which is now a world-class conference centre and regional presidential residence.

the island by the sea is a new classical-style pavilion for meetings. Much of the first floor of the palace has been devoted to a special museum including five rooms of patriotic displays from the collections of the Hermitage, based around heraldry, uniforms, medals and decorations, and a display of some historic items connected with the Russian Church. The curators from neighbouring Peterhof have created three special rooms that are decorated and furnished as family rooms would have been before the revolution, using recreations of old flowered wallpapers and original furniture. There is also a reminder of the closeness of the sea and the relatively recent use of Strelna as a naval college in an exhibit by the Maritime Museum.

In the park, which as recently as 2001 was a tragic ruin – its canals empty and its grottoes falling apart – even greater wonders have been achieved than in the palace. Here we can see so clearly the movement from the Versailles style of formal gardening to the more romantic informality of the park of the nineteenth century. From a historical point of view it is the earlier formal gardens of the Lower Park that are the most fascinating as an example of a work of garden design from the Petrine era. This has been preserved for nearly three hundred years and is the original design as laid out by Michetti. Birch trees have now been planted along the east and west canals as shown on the original plans and large copses of lime trees also help to shield from view some of the newer developments in the recreation area. Because of the lack of reliable evidence for the planting of the parterres they follow Michetti's plan and are laid out with red and white gravel and grass. The Upper Park has more of the feel of an English park with its two great ponds – the Great Palace Pond and the Carp Pond – which were landscaped in the nineteenth century. The semi-circular parade ground by the palace now has a new bronze equestrian statue of Peter the Great, which was given by the people of Riga. New railings and gates on the Peterhof Road give the palace a new ceremonial entrance.

Strelna's restoration at the start of the twenty-first century is a revealing glimpse of the official view of the importance of restoration and conservation in St Petersburg. It has its critics – mainly academics and historians who deplore the rapidity of the makeover and the newness of much of the work. But this must be weighed against the new use that has been found for the whole site, which looked beyond hope only a decade ago. There are too many palaces in St Petersburg and it was brave step by the President to insist on the rescue of one of the major ones. There are plenty more

that need help and it must be the case that the right kind of new use is likely to be the key to their rescue and survival.

The Romanovs Return

An earlier president also understood the importance of the history of the city. Boris Yeltsin took the decision to rescue and bury the human remains of the assassinated imperial family in the Romanov, St Catherine chapel of the Peter and Paul Fortress in St Petersburg on 17 July 1998. This was a much more delicate matter than changing the name of the city or finding new flags and symbols for the new Russian Federation. Heraldic scholars settled for the state emblem: a double-headed eagle that is not very different from the symbol of the Romanovs and the shield with St George has returned at the centre of the emblem. Communism is symbolically banished by the adoption of these symbols of the imperial past and of the Christian religion. Similarly the new flag – a tricolour of white, red and blue – had been a state flag in the Tsarist times but it was not the black, yellow and blue tricolour of the Romanovs and it is now accepted as the flag of the Federation. It was because of the need to recreate a lost Russian state that history had to be re-examined and mistakes acknowledged and certain aspects of the past quietly buried.

It would have been difficult to imagine a more anti-Communist scene than the ritual that surrounded the burial of the physical remains of the last tsar, his wife, his son the Tsarevitch and his daughters, who had all been brutally killed by the Bolsheviks in 1918. The long mystery surrounding the execution of the entire imperial family has never been entirely solved. The Soviet authorities denied for years that the Tsar's relations had been killed. The mystery of the authenticity of claimants like Anastasia continued to fascinate the journalistic world and there appeared to be no absolute certainty that all the family were murdered. In more recent years the authenticity of the bones found in the ground near Ykaterinburg has been questioned because of doubts among scientists that DNA testing is not always 100 per cent reliable. The genealogy of some of those tested who were thought to have been biologically related to the Romanovs may not be totally reliable. The Patriarch of All the Russias Alexei II decided that he should not preside at the funeral service because he felt that the bone fragments may not be those of the family. He had already taken the decision to canonize Nicholas II as a martyr of the Church at the hands of the Communist regime. Yeltsin had to find a priest in St Petersburg who was more accommodating to carry out the obsequies.

It was a moving sight as the coffins arrived at St Petersburg's Pulkovo Airport after being transported from their resting place in Ykaterinburg. They were conveyed in a long motorcade through the city and many people bowed as they passed by in the streets. As the motorcade passed by the Winter Place the staff of the State Hermitage stood on balconies and the Director bowed low as the cars passed by the former royal home. In the cathedral at noon there was a full and long Orthodox ceremony of great solemnity attended by politicians and as many members of the Romanov dynasty as could be gathered from all over the world. Many Russians were powerfully moved despite the fact that historically Nicholas II had never been a popular ruler, with autocratic tendencies and inability to adjust to or accept democracy and inevitable political change. The ceremony undoubtedly also attracted the attention of the world – a world that never thought it would see so rapid an end to Soviet Communism or witness such a volte face in the city that had once seen such revolution and rejection of the imperial past. The funeral (whether the bones were genuine or not) closed a guilty chapter in the history of the nation and also marked the absolute end of a dynasty that no longer had any remote significance for the new Russia.

What is the future now for a city of such contradictions and complexities? How will the new Russians determine the fate of the former imperial capital and how much change can the city absorb without losing its beauty and historical character? There was in June 2003 an episode in the city's cultural history that brought out some of the city's ambitions under the international microscope. One of the city's great cultural institutions, the Mariinsky Theatre – home to the Kirov opera and ballet companies – had long wanted to expand and improve its mainly nineteenth-century facilities. The artistic director of the Kirov Opera and principal conductor of the St Petersburg Philharmonic Orchestra, Valery Gergiev, had become in 1996 the Artistic Director and General Director of the entire Mariinsky Theatre (it regained its old name in 1992) and he had huge ambitions for the highly talented companies. He made the company internationally famous by taking it touring around the world. He also expanded its repertoire and initiated a vast recording programme that spread its distinctive reputation globally. It was Gergiev the great maestro that through his relentlessly energetic personality, as well as his talent as a conductor, won international friends and support for the Mariinsky. Naturally, like any great man with cultural ambitions, he wanted to build and make his monument in the great city of St Petersburg.

Gergiev has seized his cultural opportunities since the ending of Communism with both hands and one of his opportunities has been the architectural one of upgrading his theatre and adding to its facilities. The theatre we see today was originally built by the theatre architect Albert Cavos in 1859–60 on the site of the original State Circus. It was named after Maria Alexandrovna the wife of Tsar Alexander II. Over the years it has been altered and modernised and some technical facilities were added along the Kryukov Canal in the 1960s. The feel of the interior of the auditorium and the stage remains strongly nineteenth century with curved rows of boxes and a prominent imperial box.

Valery Gergiev had made several attempts to initiate expansion plans but it was not until 14 January 2003 that the Government and the city authorities announced to the world that they had decided to hold an international competition for a second Mariinsky theatre

ABOVE RIGHT The return to St Petersburg of the remains of Nicholas II and his family, murdered in Ekaterinburg in 1918, marked the controversial Tsar's rehabilitation from tyrant to Christian and political martyr as well as to cultural celebrity.

on a site adjoining the present building. The city architect and the Minister of Culture told the world that the competition was 'an unexampled event both for St Petersburg and for Russia'.[8] The last major international architectural competition held in Russia was for the Palace of the Soviets in Moscow in 1931. That competition acquired international fame because of an entry by Le Corbusier, who attempted to outdo his mentors – the Russian Constructivists – with a design that, he thought, elevated and abstracted Soviet ideals in a futuristic way. How he misread the Communist signs. He was seriously beaten by two Russian architects, B.M. Iofan and I.V. Zholtovsky, who won with a giant wedding cake of a mausoleum with a giant statue of Lenin astride its roof.

The organization of the competition was superbly done by the city and a twenty-person organizing committee was chaired by the Minister of Culture, Mikhail Shvidkoy and the maestro himself Valery Gergiev. Ten experts guided the process, including the world's expert on theatre and concert hall acoustics, Russell Johnson, and the great architectural historian Dmitri Shvidkovsky. An international jury of thirteen members was chaired by the President of the Union of Architects of Russia, Yury Gnedovsky. All this expertise was assembled to judge the work of eleven architectural practices who were invited to compete by the organizing committee who had already reviewed a much longer list of experienced firms. Five of the firms selected were Russian and six were foreign.

There are several reasons why this competition was seen to be so important for the renewal of the city and the most important one was the unspoken and unwritten one – that the city felt it needed a 'signature building' by an outstanding contemporary architect. The competition also gave the city authorities the opportunity to explain what their vision was for the city in the twenty-first century. It also provided a chance for Russian architectural practices to show the world how their talents stood up to serious international competition.

The city appeared to want the new theatre to provide for St Petersburg the kind of international excitement that the Guggenheim Museum (designed by the American architect Frank Gehry) had provided for the Spanish city of Bilbao. But the difference between the two cities is so extreme – Bilbao needed a new monument and some architectural excitement – St Petersburg is quite another architectural context.

The site of the new theatre is a whole city block to the west of the theatre across the canal with a 'technical bridge' linking the old and new buildings across the Kryukov Canal. On the site is one gateway designed by Giacomo Quarenghi in the 1780s for the Litovsky Market which burned in the 1920s. The Quarenghi classical gate has to be retained in any new scheme. A Palace of Culture replaced the market in the 1930s, one of the first named after the Five-Year Plan and it was rebuilt in the 1950s in the Stalinist neo-classical style by three architects – N. Miturich, V. Gorbachev and M. Feinburg. Today it is an active trade union club and leisure centre with a curious atmosphere of an old Communist working men's club, but it will be totally demolished for the new theatre. Close by is the early eighteenth-century area of brick warehouses and docks known as New Holland, which is waiting to be rediscovered as a new cultural centre to be designed by British architect Norman Foster. The brief for the competition demanded a building of some 39,000 square metres and a main auditorium seating 2000 people – thus doubling the size of the present theatre accommodation.

The eventual winner of the competition was French architect Dominique Perrault from Paris – he won by ten votes to two as maestro Gergiev was too busy to come and vote. He let the jury know that he wanted Perrault anyway. Perrault's controversial scheme is an irregular glass geodesic dome like a glass case over a new theatre and foyers, with a telescopic bridge that links the old and the new. The structure is huge and resembles an enlarged model of the eye of an insect. The complicated steel structure supports a double skin of glass. Between the glass is a network of anodised aluminium strips, which are coloured gold. Perrault explained to the jury that in the overall view of the city he saw the golden shape responding to the other gilded domes and spires of the city like St Isaac's Cathedral and the flashing gold of the Admiralty spire and the thin needle on the tower of the cathedral in the Peter and Paul Fortress. The acres of gold reflective glass will somehow have to cope with snow and ice of a St Petersburg winter – according to the architect the surfaces of the glass will be cleaned by robots. The theatre walls will be clad in black marble and in the auditorium the walls are a blank canvas for the projection of different frescoes and wall treatment to suit the mood of the changing productions. The official budget for this hi-tech fantasy of a theatre is 100 million US dollars. The jury, while applauding the dominant idea of the design, expressed quite serious reservations about 'its practicality, maintenance and cost'. They certainly had in mind the controversial Bibliotheque Nationale – one of the Grands Projets in Paris designed by Perrault – which has been described as 'unusable' by scholars and administrators and has had to be substantially modified at considerable cost.

The new Mariinsky – now known as Mariinsky 2 – will no doubt be built as a symbol that St Petersburg is now part of the international cultural world with its own range of 'signature buildings' of the twenty-first century. But it must not be at the expense of the architectural glories of the past where architectural ego was constrained by the shared and cultivated language of classicism.

THE STATE HERMITAGE GROWS

The other great star in the city's cultural firmament is the State Hermitage Museum – one of the greatest art collections in the world and certainly the finest palace museum anywhere. It too has become internationally much better known since the collapse of the Communist regime and, like the Mariinsky, it has been fortunate in having a director who was ready for the changing times and ambitious to improve and enhance the museum. Mikhail Borisovich Piotrovsky became the director of the State Hermitage in 1992, two years after the death of his father Boris Borisovich Piotrovsky, who had been director of the Hermitage since 1964. As Mikhail Piotrovsky often says he had known the Hermitage since he could walk; although he didn't work there until he was made deputy director under Vitaly Suslov in 1990. The museum is in his blood and his charm, intelligence and linguistic skills have ensured that the Hermitage has spread its wings all over the world and now, at the beginning of the twenty-first century, is poised to become the greatest, and the largest, museum of fine and decorative arts in the world as well as being a wonderful palimpsest of the history of Russia.

During the first few years of his directorship Piotrovsky used his diplomatic skills at the highest level both internationally, but almost more importantly, at the highest levels in the government of the Russian Federation in Moscow. He persuaded the government to increase its funding and made all the museum's accounts public. He increased private sector earnings and sponsorship and succeeded in having the museum designated a 'National Treasure'. He also secured the status of the museum as the only cultural institution in Russia under the special protection of the President and the only museum with a special line in the National Budget, which means its funds do not have to filter through the Ministry of Culture. This has not meant that funding has been easy and there have been some anxious moments and the Museum staff are still very underpaid.

None of these difficulties daunt the director and he has continued to pursue impressive plans for expansion. He has opened three international Hermitages – in London, Las Vegas (with the Guggenheim) and a first phase in Amsterdam. All this adds glory and credibility to the city of St Petersburg as well. His real triumph is about to happen as the long nurtured plans to expand the museum into the embracing sweep of the General Staff Building opposite the Winter Palace on Palace Square become reality.

Alongside this he has succeeded in beginning to solve the extraordinary problem – that only five per cent of the museum's three million objects were displayed in buildings that were, often splendid, but not technologically up to date. The grandiose plans of his predecessors in the 1980s to make life easier for visitors and display more objects were approved in 1985 by the city and the national government. These plans proposed building both a new storage facility on the edge of the city at Novaya Derevnya and annexing properties adjoining the museum to provide better services for the museum's offices and conservation studios and free up more exhibition space. It took until 2003 for the storage facility to open free of debt because of the financial difficulties of the late 1990s. It is an important experiment as the first major museum storage to be open to the public. The large seven-storey building is climate controlled to provide perfect conditions for all types of materials and especially advanced fire prevention. A public route through large parts of the building allows special tours to be led through the reserve collections where glass tunnels maintain the special climates and the finest objects are placed closest to the glass walls for visitors to examine. It provides an opportunity to see the imperial carriages and troikas as well as the remarkable collection of Turkish embroidered tents displayed in an adaptable space. The first tent to be put on public view is an embroidered silk tent given to Catherine the Great by Sultan Selim III in the late eighteenth century. Acres of furniture and tapestries as well as Greek and Roman marbles are on view as well as the Russian department's picture collection. The site is not that easy to reach – it is close to the wooded groves of the one of the city's largest Second World War cemeteries and surrounded by Soviet-style high-rise blocks of flats. The Hermitage staff who are used to working in a palace in the city are not overwhelmingly keen on working in the new facility and Mikhail Piotrovsky is trying to ensure that, as a new cultural and exhibition centre, it will serve the communities living in these dormitory suburbs.

More glamorous and exciting are the plans for the General Staff building in the heart of the city. The existing Hermitage occupies 1,170 rooms in the Winter Palace, the New Hermitage and all the ancillary buildings. The General Staff building, built as offices in the early nineteenth century will provide another 806 rooms and five internal courtyards. Originally built by Carlo Rossi as offices for the General Staff on one side of the triumphal arch (Crowned by the Chariot of Victory marking Russia's defeat of Napoleon in 1812) and the offices of the Ministry of Foreign Affairs and Finances on the other, the curved building created the new Palace Square with the Alexander Column at its centre. The Greater Hermitage project will make the museum the largest in the world and Piotrovsky plans to complete it all by 2014 – which is the two hundred and fiftieth anniversary of the Hermitage.

The decision originally was to use much of the space for decorative arts but as plans developed it was decided that there would be more public interest if the nineteenth-century pictures, including the impressionists and post impressionists, were shown in well-lit galleries in the General Staff building, and the courtyards and some other spaces were used for a new twentieth-century art collection to be developed with the help of the Guggenheim Museum in the USA. The World Bank has offered a loan for some of this work and the St Petersburg architectural practice – Studio 44 – run by the Yavein brothers is preparing plans with help from the special advisor, the Dutch architect Rem Koolhaas, who designed the Hermitage space in Las Vegas. The Hermitage Guggenheim Foundation has its first million dollars to initiate work on the grand schemes and Piotrovsky is confident that a mixture of private and public funding can bring about the transformation of the museum. Already the partnership that set up the Hermitage in Las Vegas is producing a good annual income and international giving is generating funds. The future for the great collections is buoyant and the city will benefit enormously from the changes at the Hermitage with its new displays of Fabergé, applied arts, militaria, as well as the great displays of nineteenth- and twentieth-century painting which will cover the whole international scope of the period making it a uniquely powerful display.

The city is, of course, more than its international cultural status and in July 2005 the City Council of St Petersburg approved the long awaited general Development Plan for the city's growth until 2015 and guidelines for its outline development until 2025. This is the first plan drafted since the end of the Soviet Union and it forecasts a considerable expansion of residential areas and development of business zones and further renovation of the historic centre. The Governor of St Petersburg Valentina Matviyenko introduced the plan with a somewhat cryptic statement – 'During the last year and a half all City Hall's responsible committees have participated in drafting the plan which is a strategic document to develop the city. Now we are going to live according to the law, and nobody will be able to make a step to the right or to the left. From now on we're going to live according to the law rather than by prison rules.'[9]

The aim of the plan is to provide for each citizen an average of 300 square feet of living space – up from the present 225 square feet, with an ambition to increase the average to 375 square feet by 2025.

By renovating substantial areas of the city centre some 28 million square feet of residential space can be achieved with the next ten years. The practice of infill and the building of small modern buildings on sites in the centre looks likely to continue, along with the renovation of older buildings that were once in multi-occupancy. The plan wants to encourage environmentally unfriendly industries to move out of the city and make way for more residential accommodation. The most significant changes envisaged in the plan are to cope with the increase in traffic and the growth in private car ownership. As part of the development of the infrastructure the city plans to build two bridges over the Neva and to build a billion-dollar western circular route. New freeways are planned for the embankments of the Obvodny Canal and Bolshaya Nevka as well as parts of the Neva itself. Major changes are proposed for the metro system with some three new lines and the beginning of a new circle line from Vyborgskaya to Vasileostrvskaya within the next decade.

All these strategic plans and ideas are part of the immense changes that the city has to undergo as Russia moves inexorably into the global community. Vladimir Putin has taken his country into the World Trade Organization and joined the G8. He has persisted in methodically initiating reforms that will make the rule of law a reality and control the oligarchs. He has insisted, as Peter the Great did, that Russia is European and that his own city of St Petersburg can show the way by reinventing itself as a place open to all ideas and responsive to its past.

No one can doubt the bravery and inspiration of an urban population that has borne so much – and it is that past that inspires

Carrying the heritage of Russia to the world unshackled from the restrictions of communism, the Hermitage is in the process of catching up to other world-class museums, not only welcoming millions of foreign and Russian visitors but establishing branches in London and even in Las Vegas.

the future. Reading some of the diaries of the people of the city caught up in the 900-day siege show unbelievable courage. Lidyia Ginzburg's *Blockade Diary* tells it well:

> Whoever had energy enough to read, used to read avidly *War and Peace* in besieged Leningrad. Tolstoy had said the last word as regards courage, about people doing their bit in a people's war. He also spoke of how those caught up in this common round continued playing their part involuntarily, while ostensibly busy solving problems affecting their own lives. The people of besieged Leningrad worked (while they could) and saved (if they could) both themselves and their loved ones from dying of hunger. And in the final reckoning, that was also essential to the war effort, because a living city barred the path of an enemy who wanted to kill it.[10]

It is that important, but often ignored, side of the city that still counts and must not be overlooked – the everyday lives of the everyday people of St Petersburg are what sustains it. The sweeping political changes and some terrible errors have left many in desperate poverty. One Russian in three still lives below the poverty line and the state pension is still less than thirty pounds a month. But it is these same Petersburgers who have their wedding photographs taken by the huge bronze statue of Peter the Great that rears up from its rocky base by the Neva. They believe, as Pushkin did when he wrote *The Bronze Horseman* that 'the Bronze Horseman gallops still', but the question remains 'Where will you plant your hooves? And on whom?'[11] It is these people who cut holes in the ice on the river and swim when the world is freezing. It is the underpaid labourers who have done the extraordinary work to restore the palaces and parks and the underpaid curators who so devotedly look after the museums as if they were their own. It is the students at the Academy of Fine Arts who have reopened the chapel in their palatial school and is the descendants of the imperial household who amazingly hid clothes, furniture and photographs of the declining Romanovs to give us today such a poignant picture of the end of a regime. Some of the citizens still have a lingering nostalgia for the days when The Party took care of everything as the price they paid for a lumbering political cruelty and a lack of freedom; but many are hopeful that St Petersburg can again prosper for the majority of its inhabitants.

The city will always have to face its dilemma: that however grand and beautiful, however rich in nostalgia, it is not Moscow. However many times the President flies in the leaders of the world to his palace on the Gulf of Finland – St Petersburg will always have that identity problem. It was the imperial centre of the country but somehow the isolation of the tsars – especially as the twentieth century progressed – made it an unreal place of parks and palaces that had become politically pointless. It took the fierceness of a revolution to change things and then war, siege and long tyranny to enforce it. But the character of the imperial architecture remains at the heart of the city and as a verdant garland of civilization around its outskirts.

In a world of political, ethnic and material uncertainty for so many it is the aesthetic and cultural qualities of St Petersburg that will, alongside the resolute quality of the people, uphold it for a long future. But what must not happen is for the city to become simply a museum. It does today often feel like one, in a fine way, because of the scale of the streets and the public splendour but also, in a less positive way, with incipient decay lingering in courtyards and behind façades. But for any visitor sailing into the city along the Neva (and that is really the only way to arrive) the city on the water triumphs through its gilded and lordly beauty. It is not on the relatively human scale of Amsterdam or Venice – it takes on the big questions of mankind's dominance over nature and climate and it reflects in its classical urbanity the power of order and Western civilization. You feel that St Petersburg has paid the price and borne the pain of the imposition of power. Yet on a June evening when the world is light at midnight it is possible to imagine that darkness itself has been banished and something truly sublime has returned to the earth. May St Petersburg long sustain its transcendent beauty to enrich the world.

A pompous monument to the autocrat Nicholas I in St Isaac's Square seems to bristle uncomfortably at the casual modernity of the new St Petersburg.

'BECAUSE, LOVING OUR CITY AND NOT WINGED FREEDOM, WE PRESERVED FOR OURSELVES ITS PALACES, ITS FIRE AND WATER, THE HOLY CITY OF PETER WILL BE OUR UNINTENDED MONUMENT.'

ANNA AKHMATOVA, 'PETROGRAD' (1919).

NOTES

1. THE FOUNDING OF THE CITY

1. Translation by Oliver Elton.
2. Robert K. Massie, *Peter the Great: His Life and World* (Knopf, New York, 1980), p. 5.
3. Suzanne Massie, *Land of the Firebird: The Beauty of Old Russia* (Simon and Schuster, New York, 1980) p. 63.
4. Robert K. Massie, *op. cit.*, p. 49.
5. *Ibid.*, p. 22.
6. *Ibid.*, p. 36.
7. Virginia Cowles *The Romanovs* (Harper and Row, New York, 1971), p. 29.
8. *Ibid.*, p. 34.
9. *Ibid.*, p. 33.
10. *Ibid.*, p. 37.
11. Robert K. Massie, *op. cit.*, p. 259.
12. Kyril Zinovieff and Karen Hughes, *The Companion Guide to St Petersburg* (Woodbridge Companion Guides, 2003), p. 3.
13. Robert K. Massie, *op. cit.*, pp. 351–2.
14. Zinovieff, *op. cit.*, p. 8.
15. *Ibid.*, p. 16.
16. Arthur and Elena George, *St Petersburg: Russia's Window to the Future, The First Three Centuries* (Taylor Trade Publishing, New York, 2003) p. 30.
17. *Ibid.*
18. Robert K. Massie, *op. cit.*, p. 357.
19. *Ibid.*
20. *Ibid.*, p. 365
21. K. Waliszewski, 'The foundation of the city in 1703' in *Peter the Great* (Haskell House Pub Ltd, June 1968), reprinted in *St Petersburg: A Travellers' Companion*, Lawrence Kelly edit., (Constable, London, 1981) p. 43.
22. William Brumfield, *A History of Russian Architecture* (Cambridge University Press, 1993), p. 204.
23. *Ibid.*
24. Robert K. Massie, *op. cit.*, p. 361.
25. *Ibid.*
26. George, *op. cit.*, p. 39.
27. *Ibid.*
28. *Ibid.*
29. *Ibid.*
30. Christopher Marsden, 'The progress of the city 1704–1712' in *Palmyra of the North* (London, Faber, 1943) reprinted in *St Petersburg: A Travellers' Companion*, p. 47.
31. C.F. Weber, 'The cost of human lives of building the city and the need for autocracy' in *Memoires pour Sevir a l'Histoire de L'Empire Russien sous le Regime de Pierre le Grande* (1725) reprinted in *St Petersburg: A Travellers' Companion*, p. 47.
32. Cowles, *op. cit.*, p. 58.
33. Robert K. Massie, *op. cit.*, p. 364.
34. *Ibid.*
35. George, *op. cit.*, p. 90.
36. Brumfield, *op. cit.*, p. 209.
37. *Ibid.*
38. *Ibid.*
39. Brumfield, *op. cit.*, p. 214.
40. George, *op. cit.*, p. 37.
41. *Ibid.*, p. 41.
42. Dmitri Shvidkovsky, 'The Architecture of the Russian State: between East and West 1600–1700' in *The Triumph of the Baroque: Architecture in Europe 1600–1750*, Henry A. Millon edit., (Yale University Press, London, 1999), p. 152.
43. *Ibid.*
44. Robert K. Massie, *op. cit.*, p. 367.
45. Quoted in *St Petersburg: A travellers' companion*, *op. cit.*, page 52.
46. Suzanne Massie, *op. cit.*, p. 102.
47. Robert K. Massie, *op. cit.*, p. 608.
48. Zinovieff, *op. cit.*, p. 316.
49. Robert K. Massie, *op. cit.*, p. 608.
50. George, *op. cit.*, p. 61.
51. *Ibid.* pp. 62–3.
52. Victor and Audrey Kennett. *The Palaces of Leningrad* (Thames and Hudson, London, 1973), p. 202.
53. Christopher Marsden, in *St Petersburg: A Travellers' Companion*, *op. cit.*, p. 209.
54. George, p. 65.

2. AUGUST AMBITION: THE RISE OF IMPERIAL ST PETERSBURG

1. Mrs William Vigor, *Letters from a Lady who Resided Some Years in Russia to Her Friend in England* (1775) (New York, 1970).
2. P. Stolpianski, *St Petersburg: Kak Voznik, osnovalsia I ros Sankt-Peterburg* (1918, reprint, St Petersburg 1991) quoted in George, *op. cit.*
3. Astolphe de Custine, *Journey for Our Time: The journals of the Marquis de Custine in Russia 1839*, Phyllis Penn Kohler edit., (London, Pheonix Press, 2001).
4. Quoted in George, *op. cit.*
5. *The Triumph of the Baroque: Architecture in Europe 1600–1750*, *op. cit.* Exhibition held in Turin, 1999.
6. Sacheverell Sitwell, *Valse des Fleurs: A Day in St Petersburg in 1868* (Faber, London, 1941).
7. *The Memoirs of Catherine the Great*, Markus Cruse and Hilde Hoogenboom trans., (Random House Modern Library, 2005)
8. A. Kaganovich, *Mednyi Vsadnik: isoria sazdania monumenta* (Leningrad, 1942), p.42.
9. Alexander Pushkin, *The Bronze Horseman, a St Petersburg Tale* (1833, uncensored version not published until 1917), from *Selected Poems*, translated by D. M. Thomas (Secker and Warburg, 1982).
10. Marquis de Custine, *op. cit.*
11. *The Genius of Wedgwood*, exhibition catalogue edited by Hilary Young (V&A Museum, London, 1995), p.134
12. Catherine the Great's correspondence with Voltaire is kept in the Imperial Russian Historical Society: Collected papers, St Petersburg. This quote is from Vol XXIII, 1878, p.157, quoted in Shvidkovsky *The Empress and the Architect: British Architecture and Gardens at the Court of Catherine the Great* (Yale University Press, 1996).
13. Christopher Morgan and Irina Orlova, *Saving the Tsars' Palaces* (Polperro Heritage Press, 2005).
14. Quoted in George, *op. cit.*
15. Henri Troyat, *Alexander of Russia: Napoleon's Conqueror* (New York, 1990).

3. THE BABYLON OF THE SNOWS

1. W. Bruce Lincoln, *Nicholas I: Autocrat of All of the Russias* (Northern Illinois University Press, Dekalb, 1989), p. 39.
2. George, *op. cit.*, p. 270.
3. Lincoln, *op. cit.*, p. 40.
4. *Ibid.*, p. 44.
5. *Ibid.*, p. 45.
6. George, p. 275.
7. *Ibid.*
8. Lincoln, *op. cit.*, p. 45.
9. Charlotte Disbrowe, *Old Days in Diplomacy* (London, 1903) reprinted in *St Petersburg: A travellers' companion*, p. 121.
10. George, *op. cit.*, 276.
11. *Ibid.*, p. 277.
12. Cowles, *op. cit.*, p. 159.
13. T.J. Binyon, *Pushkin: A Biography* (Knopf, New York), p. 79.
14. *Ibid.*, p. 26.
15. *Ibid.*, p. 35.
16. *Ibid.*, pp. 35–6.
17. Alexander Pushkin, *Eugene Onegin*, Charles Johnson trans., (Penguin, London, 1979), p. 41.
18. Binyon, *op. cit.*, p. 68.
19. Pushkin, *Eugene Onegin*, *op. cit.*, p. 47.
20. Binyon, *op. cit.*, p.80.
21. George
22. *Ibid.*, p. 286.
23. *Ibid.*

24. Lincoln, p. 240.
25. Marc Raeff, *Understanding Imperial Russia* (Columbia University Press, New York, 1984), p. 147.
26. George, *op. cit.*, p. 288.
27. Lincoln, *op. cit.*, p. 90.
28. Ibid.
29. Solomon Volkov, *St Petersburg: A Cultural History* (The Free Press, New York, 1995), p. 26.
30. Ibid.
31. Binyon, *op. cit.*, pp. 417–18.
32. Suzanne Massie. *op. cit.*, pp. 241–2.
33. Ibid., p. 242.
34. Binyon. *op. cit.*, p. 610.
35. Ibid., pp. 608–9.
36. George, *op. cit.*, p. 308.
37. Volkov. *op. cit.*, p. 26.
38. Bruce W. Lincoln, *Sunlight at Midnight* (Basic Books, New York, 2000), p. 122.
39. Suzanne Massie, *op. cit.*, pp. 258–9.
40. Nicolai Gogol *The Overcoat and Other Tales of Good and Evil*, David Magarshack trans., (W.W. Norton and Co., New York, 1957), pp. 201–2.
41. Orlando Figes, *Natasha's Dance* (Penguin, London, 2002), p. 161.
42. Astolphe de Custine, *op. cit.*, p. 50.
43. Ibid., p. 57.
44. Ibid., pp. 68-69.
45. Ibid., p. 82.
46. Edward Jerrman, *Pictures From St Petersburg* (London, 1852) reprinted in *St Petersburg: A Travellers' Companion*, pp. 77–8.
47. Custine, *op. cit.*, pp. 82–3.
48. Ibid., pp. 101–2.
49. Ibid., p. 65.
50. Figes, *op. cit.*, p. 421.
51. Volkov, *op. cit.*, p. 62.
52. George, *op. cit.*, p. 316.
53. Ibid., p. 296.
54. Andrzej Walicki *A History of Russian Thought: From the Enlightenment to Marxism* (Stanford University Press, 1979), p. 141.
55. Volkov, *op. cit.*, p. 38.
56. George, *op. cit.*, p. 322.

4. THE CRADLE OF REVOLUTION
1. Cowles, *op. cit.*, p. 182.
2. George, *op. cit.*, p. 332.
3. Bruce W. Lincoln, *In War's Dark Shadow: The Russians Before the Great War* (Touchstone, New York, 1983), p. 106.
4. Bruce W. Lincoln, *Sunlight at Midnight, op. cit.*, p. 145.
5. Lincoln, *In War's Dark Shadow, op. cit.*, p. 106.
6. George, *op. cit.*, p. 337.

7. Ibid., 337.
8. Lincoln, *Sunlight at Midnight, op. cit.*, p. 153.
9. Ibid.
10. Ibid., p. 152.
11. Lincoln, *In War's Dark Shadow, op. cit.*, p. 106.
12. Volkov, *op. cit.*, p. 44.
13. Ibid.
14. George, *op. cit.*, p. 338.
15. Ibid.
16. Lincoln, *In War's Dark Shadow, op. cit.*, p. 107
17. Volkov, *op. cit.*, p. 44.
18. George, *op. cit.*, p. 356.
19. Fyodor Dostoyevsky.
20. W.J. Leatherbarrow, 'Introduction' in *Crime and Punishment* by Fyodor Dostoyevsky (New York, Everyman's Library, 1993), p. xv.
21. George.
22. Walicki, *op. cit.*, p. 189.
23. Ibid.
24. Fyodor Dostoyevsky, *Notes From Underground, White Nights, The Dream of a Ridiculous Man and selections form the House of the Dead*, Andrew MacAndrew trans., (New York, Signet Classic, 1980), p. 93.
25. Leatherbarrow, *op. cit.*, p. xv
26. Dostoyevsky, *Crime and Punishment* (New York, Everyman's Library, 1993)
27. George, p. 359.
28. Volkov, *op. cit.*, p. 51.
29. Ibid., p. 52.
30. Ibid., p. 53.
31. George, *op. cit.*, p. 342.
32. Figes, *op. cit.*, p. 132.
33. Lincoln, *Sunlight at Midnight, op. cit.*, p. 143.
34. Volkov, *op. cit.*, p. 92.
35. Cowles, *op. cit.*, pp. 210–11.
36. Ibid., p. 211.
37. George, *op. cit.*, 347.
38. Mikhail Iroshnikov, Liudmila Protsai and Yury Shelayev, *The Sunset of the Romanov Dynasty* (Terra, Moscow, 1992), p. 49.
39. Grand Duke Alexander Mikhailovich Romanov, *Once a Grand Duke* (Cassell, London, 1908), p. 72.
40. Cowles, *op. cit.*, p. 215.
41. Lincoln. *In War's Dark Shadow, op. cit.*, p. 30
42. Iroshnikov *et al.*, *op. cit.*, p. 62.
43. Cowles, *op. cit.*, p. 232.
44. Figes, *op. cit.*, p. 143.
45. Ibid., p. 139.
46. Ibid., pp. 140–1
47. Ibid., p. 147.

5. IMPERIAL TWILIGHT
1. Volkov, *op. cit.*, p. 68.
2. Figes, *op. cit.*, p. 178.
3. George, *op. cit.*, p. 361.
4. Suzanne Massie, *op. cit.*, p. 339.
5. George, *op. cit.*, p. 362.
6. Figes, *op. cit.*, p. 179.
7. George, *op. cit.*, p. 362.
8. Ibid.
9. Ibid.
10. Volkov, *op. cit.*, 79.
11. Walicki, *op. cit.*, p. 192.
12. Volkov, *op. cit.*, 81.
13. Suzanne Massie, *op. cit.*, p. 347.
14. Figes, *op. cit.*, p. 181.
15. Suzanne Massie, *op. cit.*, p. 350.
16. Volkov, *op. cit.*, p. 88.
17. Ibid., p. 117.
18. Ibid.
19. Ibid., p. 97.
20. Ibid., p. 98.
21. George, *op. cit.*, p. 365.
22. Alexander Poznansky, *Tchaikovsky: The Quest for the Inner Man*, (Schirmer Books, New York, 1991), pp. 582–3.
23. George, *op. cit.*, p. 366.
24. Ibid., p. 350.
25. Suzanne Massie, *op. cit.*, pp. 332–3.
26. Figes, *op. cit.*, p. 229.
27. Ibid.
28. George, *op. cit.*, p. 353.
29. Volkov, *op. cit.*, p. 125.
30. Lincoln, *Sunlight at Midnight, op. cit.*, pp. 199–200.
31. Ibid., p. 200.
32. George, *op. cit.*, p. 386.
33. Volkov, *op. cit.*, p. 130.
34. Ibid., p. 133.
35. Ibid.
36. Katerina Clark, *Petersburg: Crucible of Revolution* (Harvard University Press, Cambridge, 1995), p. 60.
37. Ibid.
38. Volkov, *op. cit.*, p. 136.
39. Suzanne Massie, *op. cit.*, p. 427.
40. Clark, *op. cit.*, p. 60.
41. Robert K. Massie, *Nicholas and Alexandra* (Atheneum, New York, 1967), p. 42.
42. Greg King, *The Last Empress: The Life and Times of Alexandra Feodorovna, Tsarina of Russia* (Birch Lane Publishing, New York, 1994), p. 96.
43. Robert K. Massie, *Nicholas and Alexandra, op. cit.*, p. 59.
44. Cowles, *op. cit.*, p. 248.

45. Dominic Lieven, *Nicholas II: Twilight of Empire* (St Martin's Press, New York, 1993), p. 98.
46. Suzanne Massie, *op. cit.*, p. 412.
47. Robert K. Massie, *Nicholas and Alexandra, op. cit.*, p. 235.
48. Tatiana Fabergé et al., *The Faberge Imperial Easter Eggs* (Christie's Books, London, 1997)
49. Figes, *op. cit.*, p. 173.
50. *Ibid.*, pp. 174–5.
51. George, *op. cit.*, p. 397.
52. *Ibid.*, p. 399.
53. Figes, *op. cit.*, pp. 177–8.
54. King, *op. cit.*, pp. 142–3.
55. George, *op. cit.*, p. 402.
56. Figes, *op. cit.*, p. 190.
57. *Ibid.*, 191.
58. George, *op. cit.*, p. 404.
59. Edward Radzinsky, *The Last Tsar: The Life and Death of Nicholas II* (Doubleday, New York, 1992), p. 71.
60. Lieven, *op. cit.*, p. 161.
61. Robert K. Massie, *Nicholas and Alexandra, op. cit.*, p. 196.
62. Walicki, *op. cit.*, p. 392.
63. George, *op. cit.*, p. 378.
64. Lincoln, *In War's Dark Shadow*.
65. *Ibid.*, *op. cit.*, p. 354
66. George, *op. cit.*, p. 381.
67. Lincoln, *In War's Dark Shadow, op. cit.*, p. 372.
68. George, *op. cit.*, p. 417.
69. Untitled poem from *White Flock* (1917), in *The Complete Poems of Anna Akhmatova*, Judith Hemschemeyer trans., Roberta Reeder edit., (Zephyr Press, Brookline, 1997), p. 183.
70. Clark, *op. cit.*, p. 31.
71. Lincoln, *In War's Dark Shadow, op. cit.*, p. 377
72. Tolstoy, Alexei, *The Road to Calvary* (London, 1945), reprinted in *St Petersburg: A Travellers' Companion*, pp. 291–2.

6. LENINGRAD: FROM RED PITER TO HERO CITY

1. 'Petrograd 1919' from *Anno Domini MCMXXI* (1922), in *The Complete Poems of Anna Akhmatova, op. cit.*, pp. 393–4.
1. Lincoln, *Sunlight at Midnight, op. cit.*, p. 222.
2. Figes, *op. cit.*, p. 252.
3. George, *op. cit.*, p. 252.
4. Volkov, *op. cit.*, p. 199.
5. *Ibid.*, p. 198.
6. Figes, *op. cit.*, p. 258.
7. George, *op. cit.*, pp. 428–9.
8. Volkov, *op. cit.*, p. 217.
9. Figes, *op. cit.*, p. 287.
10. *Ibid.*, p. 289.
11. Robert K. Massie, *Nicholas and Alexandra, op. cit.*, p. 355.
12. Figes, *op. cit.*, pp. 308–9.
13. Richard Pipes, *The Russian Revolution* (Vintage Books, New York, 1990), p. 275.
14. Figes, *op. cit.*, p. 310.
15. Volkov, *op. cit.*, p. 201.
16. Pipes, *op. cit.*, p. 277.
17. Robert K. Massie, *Nicholas and Alexandra, op. cit.*, p. 383.
18. Pipes, *op. cit.*, p. 276.
19. Figes, *op. cit.*, p. 328.
20. Robert K. Massie, *Nicholas and Alexandra, op. cit.*, p. 287.
21. *Ibid.*, p. 385.
22. *Ibid.*, p. 397.
23. *Ibid.*, p. 392.
24. George, *op. cit.*, p. 443.
25. *Ibid.*, p. 442.
26. Figes, *op. cit.*, p. 386.
27. Pipes, *op. cit.*, p. 352.
28. Figes, *op. cit.*, p. 400.
29. *Ibid.*, p. 401.
30. George, *op. cit.*, p. 445.
31.
32. George, *op. cit.*, p. 448.
33. Lincoln, *Sunlight at Midnight, op. cit.*, p. 240.
34. Pipes, *op. cit.*, p. 802.
35. George, *op. cit.*, p. 451.
36. Lincoln, *Sunlight at Midnight, op. cit.*, p. 243.
37. Anna Akhamatova, *The Complete Poems of Anna Akhmatova, op. cit.*, p. 332.
38. George, *op. cit.*, p. 452.
39. *Ibid.*
40. *Ibid.*, p. 453.
41. George.
42. 'Monuments and Society' by Vladimir Ivanov, Rapporteur General of the Leningrad Collquium of ICOMOS (2 November, 1969).
43. Irina Rodimzeva et al., *The Kremlin and Its Treasures* (Rizzoli, New York, 1986), p. 60.
44. Geraldine Norman, *The Hermitage: The Biography of a Great Museum* (Jonathan Cape, London, 1997), p. 150.
45. Brian Moynahan, *The Russian Century* (Random House, New York, 1994), p. 134.
46. George, *op. cit.*, p. 468.
47. 'Petrograd 1919' from *Anno Domini MCMXXI* (1922), in *The Complete Poems of Anna Akhmatova, op. cit.*, p 259.
48. Clark, *op. cit.*, pp. 132–3.
49. *Ibid.*, p. 142.
50. Volkov, *op. cit.*, p. 357.
51. *Ibid.*, p. 337.
52. Brumfield, *op. cit.*, p. 480.
53. Harrison E. Salisbury, *The 900 Days: The Siege of Leningrad* (Da Capo, New York, 1985), p.119.
54. 'Requiem', in *The Complete Poems of Anna Akhmatova, op. cit.*, pp. 393–4.
54. George, *op. cit.*, p. 503.
55. Suzanne Massie, *Pavlovsk: The Life of a Russian Palace* (Hodder and Stoughton, London, 1990), p. 188.
56. *Ibid.*, p. 240.
57. David M. Glantz, *The Seige of Leningrad: 900 Days of Terror* (MBI Publishing, Osceola, 2001), p. 32.
58. George, *op. cit.*, p. 511.
59. David M. Glantz, *The Battle for Leningrad 1941–1944* (University Press of Kansas, Lawrence, 2002), pp. 85–6.
60. Salisbury, *op. cit.*, p. 370.
61. *Ibid.*, p. 377.
62. *Ibid.*, p. 438.
63. *Ibid.*, p. 508.
64. George, *op. cit.*, p. 524.
65. *Ibid.*, p. 524.
66. Nicholas, *op. cit.*, p. 201.
67. Massie, *op. cit.*, p. 281.

7. THE WINDOW OPENS

1. M. Gorbachev, *Memoirs* (Doubleday, New York, 1995).
2. George, *op. cit.*, p. 559.
3. Dmitri Sergeevich Likhachev (1906–99) wrote the eulogy for Tsar Nicholas II and his family's re-burial in St Petersburg.
4. Anna Akhmatova, 'Requiem' (1935–40), 'Poem without a Hero' (1942), in *The Complete Poems of Anna Akhmatova, op. cit.*
5. George, *op. cit.*, p. 559
6. Custine, *op. cit.*
7. *Ibid.*
8. 'Mariinsky 2' (Russian Union of Architects Report, 2003).
9. *St Petersburg Times*, July 2005.
10. Lidyia Ginzburg, *Blockade Diary*, with Alan Myers (London, Harvill Press, 1996).
11. Alexander Pushkin, *The Bronze Horseman, op cit.*

Select Bibliography

Akhamatova, Anna, *The Complete Poems of Anna Akhmatova* (Zephyr Press, Brookline, 1997)

Althaus, Frank, and Sutcliffe, Mark, *Petersburg Perspectives* (Fontanka with Booth Clibborn Editions, 2003)

Belyakova, Zoia, *The Romanovs: The Way It Was* (Ego Publishing, St Petersburg, 2000)

Binyon, T. J., *Pushkin: A Biography* (Knopf, New York)

Black, Will, *The Chinese Palace at Oranienbaum* (Bunker Hill Publishing, 2003)

Brumfield, William, *A History of Russian Architecture* (Cambridge University Press, 1993)

Clark, Katerina, *Petersburg: Crucible of Revolution* (Harvard University Press, 1995)

Cowles, Virginia, *The Romanovs* (Harper and Row, New York, 1971)

Custine, Astolphe de, *Journey for Our Time: The Journals of the Marquis de Custine in Russia 1839*, Phyllis Penn Kohler ed., (Pheonix Press, London, 2001)

De Wassenaer, Cornélie, *A Visit to St Petersburg 1824–1825*, Igor Vinogradoff trans., (Michael Russell, 1994)

Dostoyevsky, Fyodor, *Crime and Punishment*, translated by David McDuff (Penguin, London, 1991)

_____, *Notes From Underground, White Nights, The Dream of a Ridiculous Man and selections form the House of the Dead*, Andrew MacAndrew trans., (Signet Classic, New York, 1980)

Fabergé, Tatiana et al., *The Faberge Imperial Easter Eggs* (Christie's Books, London, 1997)

Feinstein, Elaine, *Pushkin* (Weidenfeld and Nicholson, 1998)

Figes, Orlando, *A People's Tragedy: The Russian Revolution 1891–1924* (Jonathan Cape, London, 1996)

_____, *Natasha's Dance: A Cultural History of Russia* (Penguin, London, 2002).

George, Arthur L., and George, Elena, *St Petersburg: Russia's Window on the Future, The First Three Centuries* (Taylor Trade Publishing, New York, 2003)

Giangrande, Cathy, *St Petersburg Museums, Palaces and Historic Collections* (Bunker Hill Publishing, 2003)

Glantz, David, *The Seige of Leningrad: 900 Days of Terror* (MBI Publishing, Osceola, 2001)

Gogol, Nicolai, *The Overcoat and Other Tales of Good and Evil*, David Magarshack trans., (W.W. Norton and Co, New York, 1957)

Hamilton, George Heard, *The Art and Architecture of Russia* (Pelican, 1990)

Iroshnikov, Mikhail, Protsai, Liudmila, and Shelayev, Yury, *The Sunset of the Romanov Dynasty* (Terra, Moscow, 1992)

Kelly, Lawrence (edit.), *St Petersburg: A Travellers' Companion* (Constable, London, 1981)

Kennet, Victor and Audrey, *The Palaces of Leningrad* (Thames and Hudson, 1973)

Kholer, Phyllis Penn (editor), *Journey for Our Time: Journals of the Marquis de Custine, Russia 1839* (Phoenix Press, 2001)

King, Greg, *The Last Empress: The Life and Times of Alexandra Feodorovna, Tsarina of Russia* (Birch Lane Publishing, New York, 1994)

Lieven, Dominic, *Nicholas II: Twilight of Empire* (St Martin's Press, New York, 1993)

Lincoln, Bruce W., *In War's Dark Shadow: The Russians Before the Great War* (Touchstone, New York, 1983)

_____, *Nicholas I: Autocrat of All of the Russias* (Northern Illinois University Press, Dekalb, 1989)

_____, *Sunlight at Midnight: St Petersburg and the Rise of Modern Russia* (Basic Books, New York, 2000)

Massie, Robert K., *Nicholas and Alexandra* (Atheneum, New York, 1967)

_____, *Peter the Great: His Life and World* (Knopf, New York, 1980)

Massie, Suzanne, *Land of the Firebird: The Beauty of Old Russia* (Simon and Schuster, New York, 1980)

Massie, Suzanne, *Pavlovsk: The Life of a Russian Palace* (Hodder and Stoughton, London, 1990)

Montefiore, Simon Sebag, *Prince of Princes: The Life of Potemkin* (Weidenfeld and Nicholson, 2000)

_____, *Stalin: The Court of the Red Tsar* (Weidenfeld and Nicholson, 2003)

Morgan, Christopher, and Olova, Irina, *Saving the Tsars' Palaces* (Polperro Heritage Press, 2005)

Moynahan, Brian, *The Russian Century* (Random House, New York, 1994)

Norman, Geraldine, *The Hermitage: The Biography of a Great Museum* (Jonathan Cape, London, 1997)

Pipes, Richard, *The Russian Revolution* (Vintage Books, New York, 1990)

Poznansky, Alexander, *Tchaikovsky: The Quest for the Inner Man* (Schirmer Books, New York, 1991)

Radzinsky, Edward, *The Last Tsar: The Life and Death of Nicholas II* (Doubleday, New York, 1993)

Raeff, Marc, *Understanding Imperial Russia* (Columbia University Press, New York, 1984)

Reed, John, *Ten Days That Shook The World* (Penguin, London, 1979)

Rodimzeva, Irina et al., *The Kremlin and its Treasures* (Rizzoli, New York, 1986)

Romanov, Grand Duke Alexander Mikhailovich, *Once a Grand Duke* (Cassell, London, 1908)

Rossica – International Review of Russian Culture, Spring 2003 (Academia Rossica, London)

Salisbury, Harrison E., *The 900 Days: The Siege of Leningrad* (Da Capo, New York, 1985)

Seaman, W.A.L., and Sawell, J.R. (editors), *Russia Journal of Lady Londonderry, 1836–7* (John Murray, 1836–7)

Service, Robert, *Russia Experiment with a People: from 1991 to the present* (Macmillan, 2002)

Shvidkovsky, Dmitri, *St Petersburg: Architecture of the Tsars* (Abbeville Press, New York, London and Paris, 1996)

_____, *The Empress and the Architect: British Architecture and Gardens at the Court of Catherine the Great* (Yale University Press, 1996)

_____. 'The Architecture of the Russian State: Between East and West 1600–1700', in *The Triumph of the Baroque: Architecture in Europe 1600–1750*, Henry A. Millon ed., (Bompiani, Milan, 1999)

Troyat, Henri, *Catherine the Great* (Phoenix Press, London, 2000)

Volkov, Solomon, *St Petersburg: A Cultural History* (The Free Press, New York, 1995)

Walicki, Andrzej, *A History of Russian Thought: From the Enlightenment to Marxism* (Stanford University Press, 1979)

Whittaker, Cynthia Hyla (editor), *Russia Engages the World 1453–1825* (New York Public Library and Harvard University Press)

Zinovieff, Kyril and Hughes, Karen, *The Companion Guide to St Petersburg* (Woodbridge Companion Guides, 2003)

HERMITAGE Magazine
Editor in Chief: Professor Mikhail Piotrovski
Executive Editor: Geraldine Norman
Published quarterly by The State Hermitage Museum, St Petersburg.
www.hermitagemuseum.org

Index

AUTHORS' ACKNOWLEDGMENTS

We would like to acknowledge the help of John Nicoll and his team at Frances Lincoln, who are such great publishers. Special thanks to Michael Brunström, who is the best and most patient and careful of editors, and to Anne Fraser and Sue Gladstone for their kindness and help. The work of Yury Molodkovets our photographer brings the city to life and we are very grateful to Caroline de Souza, who has designed the book so beautifully.

In St Petersburg: Professor Mikhail Piotrovsky, Director of the State Hermitage; Semion Mikhailovsky at the Academy of Fine Arts; Vadim Znamenov the Director of Peterhof and Ivan Sautov at Tsarskoe Selo, and Vladimir Klementiev Senior Curator at the Chinese Palace, Oranienbaum have all been generous with their time and knowledge. Sebastian Zinovieff has always been helpful in the city and St Petersburg wouldn't be the same without the energetic assistance from Tania Tolstoy and her team of guides, especially Elena and Zoia Belyakova.

In London: Our colleagues at the World Monuments Fund in Britain have always supported our enthusiasm for the city of St Petersburg, especially Will Black and Cathy Giangrande, who have been such good company on Russian adventures. Nathalie Brooke has always been generous and hospitable and she brings a special perspective to Russia through her family's own history. Geraldine Norman shares our enthusiasm for the city and her incredible support for The State Hermitage and her exceptional editing of the Hermitage Magazine have been inspiring. Catherine Phillips' passion for the city has always been stimulating and she has never failed to provide helpful assistance. Robin Ballance has been a great support throughout.

In the United States: We would like to thank Kevin Maclellan, Brian and Nancy Curran for their unending patience, enthusiasm and support for this project, without which we would not have written this tribute to our shared passion, St Petersburg.

The city of St Petersburg is a haunting place and this book is dedicated not only to those who made the city but also to the incredible endurance and fortitude of its population over the centuries. The city's beauty has always been sustained by the spirit of its people – often against all the odds.

Colin Amery
Brian Curran

PHOTOGRAPHER'S ACKNOWLEDGMENTS

I would like to thank Ivan Sautov and Iraida Bott, Director and Deputy Director of the Tsarskoe Selo State Museum Reserve; Sergey Nekrasov, Director of the State Pushkin Apartment Museum, St Petersburg; Nina Kukurozova of the Yusupov Palace on the Moika, St Petersburg; Nina Popova, Director of the Anna Akhmatova Memorial Museum; Vladimir Klimentyev, Chief Curator of the Chinese Palace, Oranienbaum; Catherine Phillips.

Yury Molodkovets

PICTURE CREDITS

The Publishers have made every effort to contact holders of copyright works. Any copyright holders we have been unable to reach are invited to contact the Publishers so that a full acknowledgment may be given in subsequent editions. For permission to reproduce the images on the following pages the Publishers thank those listed below.

Akg-images/Erich Lessing: 137
www.bridgeman.co.uk: 10–11 (Tretyakov Gallery, Moscow), 16 (Tretyakov Gallery, Moscow), 24 (Tretyakov Gallery, Moscow), 55 (State Russian Museum, St Petersburg), 109 (Tretyakov Gallery, Moscow), 114 (Tretyakov Gallery, Moscow), 130 (Tretyakov Gallery, Moscow), 135 (State Russian Museum, St Petersburg), 138 (State Russian Museum, St Petersburg), 139, 148, 154 (Bibliothèque de l'Arsenal, Paris), 160 (State Russian Museum, St Petersburg, © DACS 2006), 177 above, 179, 184 (State Russian Museum, St Petersburg), 185
Peter Hayden: 205
Private collection: 13, 28, 48, 92, 107, 116, 140, 150, 202
RIA Novosti: 74, 201